International Political Economy Series

General Editor: **Timothy M. Shaw**, Professor and Director, Institute of International Relations, The University of the West Indies, Trinidad & Tobago

Titles include:

Morten Bøås, Marianne H. Marchand and Timothy Shaw (*editors*)
THE POLITICAL ECONOMY OF REGIONS AND REGIONALISM

Paul Bowles and John Harriss (*editors*)
GLOBALIZATION AND LABOUR IN CHINA AND INDIA
Impacts and Responses

James Busumtwi-Sam and Laurent Dobuzinskis
TURBULENCE AND NEW DIRECTION IN GLOBAL POLITICAL ECONOMY

Bill Dunn
GLOBAL RESTRUCTURING AND THE POWER OF LABOUR

Myron J. Frankman
WORLD DEMOCRATIC FEDERALISM
Peace and Justice Indivisible

Richard Grant and John Rennie Short (*editors*)
GLOBALIZATION AND THE MARGINS

Graham Harrison (*editor*)
GLOBAL ENCOUNTERS
International Political Economy, Development and Globalization

Adrian Kay and Owain David Williams (*editors*)
GLOBAL HEALTH GOVERNANCE
Crisis, Institutions and Political Economy

Dominic Kelly and Wyn Grant (*editors*)
THE POLITICS OF INTERNATIONAL TRADE IN THE TWENTY-FIRST CENTURY
Actors, Issues and Regional Dynamics

Sandra J. MacLean, Sherri A. Brown and Pieter Fourie (*editors*)
HEALTH FOR SOME
The Political Economy of Global Health Governance

Craig N. Murphy (*editor*)
EGALITARIAN POLITICS IN THE AGE OF GLOBALIZATION

Morten Ougaard
THE GLOBALIZATION OF POLITICS
Power, Social Forces and Governance

Jørgen Dige Pedersen
GLOBALIZATION, DEVELOPMENT AND THE STATE
The Performance of India and Brazil Since 1990

K Ravi Raman and Ronnie D. Lipschutz (*editors*)
CORPORATE SOCIAL RESPONSIBILITY
Comparative Critiques

Ben Richardson
SUGAR: REFINED POWER IN A GLOBAL REGIME

Marc Schelhase
GLOBALIZATION, REGIONALIZATION AND BUSINESS
Conflict, Convergence and Influence

Herman M. Schwartz and Leonard Seabrooke (*editors*)
THE POLITICS OF HOUSING BOOMS AND BUSTS

Leonard Seabrooke
US POWER IN INTERNATIONAL FINANCE
The Victory of Dividends

Timothy J. Sinclair and Kenneth P. Thomas (*editors*)
STRUCTURE AND AGENCY IN INTERNATIONAL CAPITAL MOBILITY

J. P. Singh (*editor*)
INTERNATIONAL CULTURAL POLICIES AND POWER

Susanne Soederberg, Georg Menz and Philip G. Cerny (*editors*)
INTERNALIZING GLOBALIZATION
The Rise of Neoliberalism and the Decline of National Varieties of Capitalism

Kenneth P. Thomas
INVESTMENT INCENTIVES AND THE GLOBAL COMPETITION FOR CAPITAL

Helen Thompson
CHINA AND THE MORTGAGING OF AMERICA
Economic Interdependence and Domestic Politics

Ritu Vij (*editor*)
GLOBALIZATION AND WELFARE
A Critical Reader

Matthew Watson
THE POLITICAL ECONOMY OF INTERNATIONAL CAPITAL MOBILITY

Owen Worth and Phoebe Moore
GLOBALIZATION AND THE 'NEW' SEMI-PERIPHERIES

Xu Yi-chong and Gawdat Bahgat (*editors*)
THE POLITICAL ECONOMY OF SOVEREIGN WEALTH FUNDS

International Political Economy Series
Series Standing Order ISBN 978–0–333–71708–0 hardcover
Series Standing Order ISBN 978–0–333–71110–1 paperback

You can receive future titles in this series as they are published by placing a standing order. Please contact your bookseller or, in case of difficulty, write to us at the address below with your name and address, the title of the series and one of the ISBNs quoted above.

Customer Services Department, Macmillan Distribution Ltd, Houndmills, Basingstoke, Hampshire RG21 6XS, England

---

Investment Incentives and the Global Competition for Capital

Kenneth P. Thomas
Associate Professor of Political Science
Fellow, Center for International Studies
University of Missouri-St. Louis, USA

palgrave
macmillan

First published 2011 by
PALGRAVE MACMILLAN

Palgrave Macmillan in the UK is an imprint of Macmillan Publishers Limited, registered in England, company number 785998, of Houndmills, Basingstoke, Hampshire RG21 6XS.

Palgrave Macmillan in the US is a division of St Martin's Press LLC, 175 Fifth Avenue, New York, NY 10010.

Palgrave Macmillan is the global academic imprint of the above companies and has companies and representatives throughout the world.

Palgrave® and Macmillan® are registered trademarks in the United States, the United Kingdom, Europe and other countries.

ISBN: 978–0–230–22905–1 hardback

This book is printed on paper suitable for recycling and made from fully managed and sustained forest sources. Logging, pulping and manufacturing processes are expected to conform to the environmental regulations of the country of origin.

A catalogue record for this book is available from the British Library.

A catalog record for this book is available from the Library of Congress.

10 9 8 7 6 5 4 3 2 1
20 19 18 17 16 15 14 13 12 11

Printed and bound in Great Britain by
CPI Antony Rowe, Chippenham and Eastbourne

To my wife, Mary, as we go forward in life together

Contents

Tables

Preface

The battle by national, state and local governments to attract investment has been in high gear for decades. Indeed, by all indications, in most of the world it has been intensifying, even before the onset of the world economic crisis. It reflects the twin facts that the state is structurally dependent on capital, and that capital is mobile. In my book, *Competing for Capital*, I first examined the feasibility of controlling some of the effects of capital mobility by placing limits on the use of location subsidies. There, the problem was modeled as one of international cooperation (an n-person Prisoners' Dilemma in which n was increasing), and the European Union's state aid rules were examined in depth as the most far-reaching effort in the world to control subsidies. The EU's rules affect all subsidies, but it was only in 1997 that it adopted the Multi Sectoral Framework, which directly targeted incentives to mobile investment.

Ten years after *Competing for Capital*, I expand the analysis to encompass literatures from multiple disciplines and include examples from developing as well as industrialized countries. I now have ten years' more experience of the Multi Sectoral Framework (now incorporated into the Regional Aid Guidelines) to draw upon, and an equal expansion of experience with the workings of less ambitious controls on competition for investment in (restricting only the use of subsidies to induce the relocation of existing facilities) Canada and Australia. The results are similar, but somewhat depressing.

Using a variety of analytical frameworks, the theoretical case for regulation of investment incentives is more robust than ever. Moreover, the experience of the EU demonstrates the feasibility of such regulation even more convincingly, as the Multi Sectoral Framework rules have been highly successful at controlling incentives, and the European Commission has made huge strides in its control of non-notified subsidies since *Competing for Capital* was published. In the United States, however, bidding wars for investment set new records and a legal challenge to state incentives under the Commerce Clause of the US Constitution was dismissed by the US Supreme Court. Meanwhile, developing countries are finding that their industrialization comes at a tremendous price in subsidies that frequently exceeds levels given in the United States. Wherever you look outside of the European Union, transparency is improving slowly at best.

Canada and particularly Australia may provide hopeful signs. Banning relocation incentives could serve as a stepping-stone to control of incentives generally. As we will see in Chapter 8, while cases of job poaching have not disappeared in Canada, they are smaller than in the 1990s when the Code of Conduct on Incentives was adopted. In Australia, outside of Queensland (which has not signed the Interstate Investment Cooperation Agreement), poaching is close to non-existent and states do cooperate to avoid bidding wars over investments that appear to have decided to locate in Australia. What seems to separate their success from failures in the US is not small numbers, but the fact that policy-makers in the signatory states and territories have internalized the view that poaching and bidding wars are wasteful. In other words, to act on a Prisoners' Dilemma, it is necessary to recognize that as one's strategic environment. This means that ideas have a role to play in the regulation of investment incentives.

That is where this book comes in. Progressive social change requires winning a battle of ideas. Persuading citizens and politicians of the inefficiency and inequity of investment incentives can free up money for more socially desirable purposes. While technical discussions are a necessary part of life for those of us privileged to be in academia, we need to remember why we came to study politics in the first place.

Acknowledgements

'It takes a village' to write a book. This one had its genesis as a research report, 'Investment Incentives: Growing Use, Uncertain Benefits, Uneven Controls,' for the Global Subsidies Initiative (GSI) of the International Institute for Sustainable Development (IISD) in 2007. My debts, therefore, begin there: with Ron Steenblik, then Research Director, who commissioned the project, and with Greg LeRoy of Good Jobs First, who recommended me to Ron. At GSI, I received advice and comments from Ron Steenblik, Chris Charles, Luke Peterson, Charles Tsai, Donna Bush-Huffam, Michelle French, Tara Laan and Damon Vis-Dunbar. I also want to thank the peer reviewers of that project in both the academic and policy communities: Howard Mann, Sébastian Miroudot, Ted Moran, John Mutti, Bill Schweke, Fiona Wishlade and several individuals who wish to remain anonymous. All helped to make it a much improved work.

Growing that report into a book has added many more debts. Umut Aydin generously shared her dissertation with me, invited me to a panel at the 2009 European Union Studies Association where part of this work was presented, and commented on numerous parts of the new material. Fiona Wishlade co-authored that EUSA paper, and has commented on that and other parts of the work as I have developed it further. Glauco Arbix hosted me when I was in São Paulo and gave me a lot of food for thought with his insights into Brazilian politics and beyond. Isaias Coelho provided valuable suggestions, particularly on my chapter on developing countries. Jack Jacobsen set me on the right path for my chapter on Ireland, providing numerous contacts and insights as well as commenting on the final product. Peadar Kirby and James Wrynn met with me while I was in Dublin, and both provided helpful feedback and suggestions. Séan Ó Riain corresponded with me and generously shared some of his unpublished work, 'Addicted to Growth.'

The section on Vietnam in Chapter 7 was initially presented at the 2009 American Political Science Association conference in Toronto. I would like to thank everyone at the panel for their feedback, especially Eddy Malesky. Thomas Jandl commented on a revised version of the paper, for which I am very grateful. My interest in Vietnam was sparked by work I did for IISD's Trade Knowledge Network (TKN) on investment incentives and sustainable development. This was kicked off at a 2008 meeting in Phnom Penh, organized by Flavia Thomé and Heike Baumüller, where I met with a research team from Vietnam, led by Vu Xuan Nguyet Hong, as well as with teams from Indonesia and Singapore. My thanks go out to everyone involved in the project.

I had the privilege of representing IISD at a November 2009 workshop of the World Association of Investment Promotion Agencies in Ljubljana, thanks to Mark Halle and Oshani Pereira. Carlos Bronzatto of WAIPA and Kaja Kastner at the Slovenian Agency for Entrepreneurship and Foreign Investment (JAPTI) organized the workshop, and I would like to thank them and all the participants for two days of valuable discussions. There I met Henry Loewendahl of the *Financial Times'* fdi Markets, and we have continued the discussions based on our panel.

In Beijing, I was hosted by the Chinese Academy of Social Sciences in June 2009 through an exchange program with the Center for International Studies Association at the University of Missouri-St. Louis. At the Center I want to thank Joel Glassman and Hung-gay Fung, and at CASS Li Bin and Xi Yanbin. While I was there, I spoke on the subject of investment incentives at Nankai University in Tianjin, thanks to Jiang Dianchun and his then-student (now Ph.D.) Ma Yongliang. Hongbin Cai and Daniel Treisman offered helpful suggestions on the work, and I met with Changhui Zhou in Beijing.

Table 5.1 is reproduced from J. J. Lee, *Ireland, 1912–1985: Politics and Society* with the kind permission of Cambridge University Press.

A number of people helped with my estimate of US state and local incentives and subsidies. Among them are Greg LeRoy and Caitlin Lacy at Good Jobs First, Mike LaFaive and James Hohman at the Mackinac Institute, Kate Brewster at the Poverty Institute, Bill Schweke of the Corporation for Enterprise Development, Barry Boardman at the North Carolina General Assembly, Vermont economic development consultant Doug Hoffer, John Hickey and Shannon Wobbe (formerly) with the Missouri Citizen Education Fund, Dick Lavine of the Center for Public Policy Priorities, Frank Mauro of the Fiscal Policy Institute, Sara Beth Gehl of the Georgia Budget and Policy Institute and Zach Schiller of Policy Matters Ohio. Unfortunately, the data for some of their states was not complete enough to be used in the estimate, but I thank all of them for their help.

Of course, I could not have completed this projected without the help of my graduate research assistants, Richard Ehui, Sterling Recker, Anna Martirosyan and Todd Combs, who did great work on this and related projects.

I am sure I am leaving people out; please accept my apologies. Despite all the help I've received from so many quarters, there are no doubt errors which remain, which are my responsibility.

The work of the Global Subsidies Initiative was supported at that time by the governments of Sweden, the Netherlands, and New Zealand, and by the William and Flora Hewlett Foundation. My research in Canada was supported by the Canada-US Fulbright Foundation, for research at the Center for North American Politics and Society at Carleton University. I want to especially thank Laura Macdonald of Carleton for inviting me there. The Center for International Studies at the University of Missouri-St. Louis supported my research in Ireland. I want to thank everyone for their help. Needless to say, my views should not be construed as representing those of any of my funders.

While this book started with the GSI report, Chapters 1, 5, 6, 7 and 9 are entirely new, and the other chapters are substantially updated, including a new industry case study in Chapter 4. I want to thank GSI for use of the material which I have carried over from that report. Chapter 1 was presented at the International Studies Association/Brazilian Association of International Relations conference in Rio de Janeiro, July 2009. As mentioned above, the first part of Chapter 6 was presented at the 2009 European Union Studies Association conference, and the Vietnam section of Chapter 7 at the 2009 American Political Science Association annual meeting.

I want to thank Alexandra Webster and Renée Takken at Palgrave for all their help on this project, and Tim Shaw, the IPE series editor. It has made writing a fairly painless process – on my end at least!

My wife, Mary Hildebrand, has seen me through this entire project which, in its earliest incarnation, goes back almost as long as we have been married. Her moral and intellectual support has helped me out in ways big and small.

Finally, I want to thank my dad and my late mother, without whom none of this would have been possible.

Abbreviations

A$	Australian dollar
ACOA	Atlantic Canada Opportunities Agency
ACORN	Association of Community Organizations for Reform Now
ACT	Australian Capital Territory
AIT	Agreement on Internal Trade (Canada)
AMD	Advanced Micro Devices
ANFAVEA	Associação Nacional dos Fabricantes de Veículos Automotores (Brazil)
ASEAN	Association of South East Asian Nations
ATM	automatic teller machine
BIT	bilateral investment treaty
BMW	Border, Midlands, West (Ireland)
BNDES	Banco Nacional de Desenvolvimento Economico e Social (Brazil)
C$	Canadian dollar
CAP	Common Agricultural Policy (EU)
CBA	community benefits agreement
CDBG	Community Development Block Grant (US)
CEE	Central and Eastern European
CEO	chief executive officer
CIA	Central Intelligence Agency (US)
CIT	corporate income tax
DG	Directorate-General (European Union)
DRAM	dynamic random access memory
EC	European Communities
ECJ	European Court of Justice
ECSC	European Coal and Steel Community
EI	Enterprise Ireland
EMEA	Europe-Middle East-Africa
EPTR	Export Profit Tax Relief (Ireland)
ETDZ	economic and technological development zone
EU	European Union
FDI	foreign direct investment
FTA	free trade agreement
FTZ	free trade zone or foreign trade zone

GAO	Government Accountability Office (US)
GATT	General Agreement on Tariffs and Trade
GATS	General Agreement on Trade in Services
GDP	gross domestic product
GDT	General Department of Taxation (Vietnam)
GGE	gross grant equivalent
GM	General Motors
GNP	gross national product
HPI	human poverty index (UNDP)
IBGE	Instituto Brasileiro de Geografia e Estatística
IBM	International Business Machines
ICMS	Imposto Sobre Circulação de Mercadorias e Serviços (Brazilian value-added tax)
ICT	information and communications technology
IDA	Industrial Development Authority (Ireland)
IIA	investment incentive agreement
IICA	Interstate Investment Cooperation Agreement (Australia)
IMF	International Monetary Fund
IPA	investment promotion agency
IR£	Irish punt
LLC	limited liability corporation
M&A	mergers and acquisitions
MEP	Member of the European Parliament
MIOL	Microsoft Ireland Operations Limited
MNC	multinational corporation
MSF	Multi-Sectoral Framework
MSME	micro, small, and medium-sized enterprises
NAFTA	North American Free Trade Agreement
NESC	National Economic and Social Council (Ireland)
NGA	National Governors' Association (US)
NGO	non-governmental organization
NOL	net operating loss
NSW	New South Wales
OECD	Organization for Economic Cooperation and Development
OPIC	Overseas Private Investment Corporation
PD	Prisoners' Dilemma
PPP	purchasing power parity
PPS	purchasing power standards
PT	Partido dos Trabalhadores (Workers Party, Brazil)
PTI	Press Trust of India
R$	Brazilian real

R&D	research and development
RAG	regional aid guidelines
RIM	Research in Motion
(A)SCM	(Agreement on) Subsidies and Countervailing Measures
SEZ	Special Economic Zone
SFI	Science Foundation Ireland
SME	small and medium-sized enterprises
SMIC	Semiconductor Manufacturing International Corporation
TDD	transportation development district
TIF	tax increment financing
TILMA	Trade, Investment, and Labour Mobility Agreement (Canada: British Columbia and Alberta)
TRIMS	(Agreement on) Trade-Related Investment Measures
TWA	Trans World Airlines
UK	United Kingdom
UNCTAD	United Nations Conference on Trade and Development
UNDP	United Nations Development Programme
UPS	United Parcel Service
US	United States
VAT	value-added tax
WTO	World Trade Organization

1
Competing for Capital Revisited

Over the course of the 1980s, Japanese and US automakers built six new assembly plants in the United States, each receiving subsidies from the state and local governments that were chosen as the winners of very public auctions. The cost per job rose steadily from $11,000 for Nissan in 1980 to $50,588 per job for Subaru and Isuzu in 1986 (Milward and Newman, 1990, pp. 34–7). This pattern spread to developing countries in the 1990s, with three auto assembly facilities receiving from $54,000 to $340,000 per job in Brazil, and a Ford factory in India from $200,000 to $420,000 per job, depending on the discount rate used in the calculation (Oman, 2000, p. 80). By contrast, in Europe, while assembly plants in the poorest areas of the EU received similarly large amounts in the 1990s (Oman, 2000, p. 80), in 2006 Hyundai received only about $70,000 per job for a $1.1 billion facility in the Czech Republic (Czech News Agency, 2006; EU, 2007a), a much poorer jurisdiction than Alabama, which in 2002 gave Hyundai about $117,000 per job on a present value basis comparable to EU calculations.[1]

Governments around the world compete for investment, on every continent and at every level of administration from the local to the supranational. They do so because governments need investment to generate tax revenue and favorable macroeconomic outcomes (Thomas, 2000, pp. 24–5). At the same time, capital is increasingly mobile, transforming what might otherwise be national negotiations over the conditions of investment into a series of bidding wars for particular investments, or 'locational tournaments' (David, 1984; Mytelka, 1999). To attract investment, governments use investment incentives, that is, subsidies designed to affect the location of investment. These incentives can take many forms, including grants, tax preferences or holidays, free land or other inputs.[2] They can also take the form of regulatory policy concessions (Oman, 2000), but that is not the focus of this book. The bargaining over location subsidies and other investment conditions are characterized by substantial information asymmetries between potential investor and potential host, and the increasing understanding by firms of how to exploit this situation, abetted by the rise of the site location consulting industry.

The policy responses of governments to this situation have varied substantially, as illustrated by the mini-history above. In the developed countries, location subsidies have been strongly part of the landscape for 40 years and more. In the nineteenth century, US cities used subsidies to attract railways (Sbragia, 1996). The use of incentives in developing nations is a more recent phenomenon, a result of their being 'drawn into this competition for FDI' (Moran et al. 2005, p. 382; for a Thailand vs. New Zealand example, see O'Sullivan, 2007) and subnational competition in large developing countries like Brazil, China, India and Vietnam (see Chapter 7). Finally, the EU has pioneered multilateral control of investment incentives through its Regional Aid Guidelines as they apply to large investments (Thomas, 2007c, p. 41). As we will see later, there are other approaches to dealing with the collective action problem of controlling competition for investment, but the EU's is the most comprehensive and the most successful.

Why study investment incentives? One reason is the sheer size of the monies given to investors. From $26.4 billion in 1996 (Thomas, 2003) to $46.8 billion in 2005 (see Chapter 6 below), state and local governments in the US have given substantial sums year in and year out. In the EU, the figure is likely lower, as only €9.9 billion[3] was given in 2007 by the EU-27 in the form of regional aid, the type most likely to be used for investment incentives (EU, 2009a). For other economies, data are sparser, but International Monetary Fund (IMF) economist Kevin Fletcher (2002, p. 13) estimated that Vietnam gave tax incentives equal to 0.7 percent of its GDP, while Botman et al. (2008) estimate the Philippines has spent 1.0 percent of GDP on 'redundant' incentives,[4] both of which would substantially exceed the figure spent by state and local governments in the US as a share of GDP. Jauch (2002, p. 102) reports that Kenya has given approximately $514 million in export processing zone incentives, but has created a mere 2000 jobs, an astonishing $257,000 per job.

Second, incentives are important because their use is so widespread and growing. They are used on every continent (except, of course, Antarctica), by every size of government,[5] and are given to firms large and small.[6] It is virtually impossible to find governments that ceased using incentives, while the number of governments that have adopted them after long resisting their use is much larger. Alberta ceased using incentives in 1995 in favor of a low-tax regime fueled, in part, by oil revenues (Thomas, 2000, p. 181).[7] Many of the Central European transition countries abolished incentives in the mid-1990s (Cass, 2007, p. 95), but most now have at least modest incentive programs, including all of the CEE countries that joined the EU (Cass, 2007, pp. 119–20). In particular, the Czech Republic started offering incentives in 1998 after losing repeatedly to Hungary and Poland in its attempts to attract investment (Bjorvaten and Eckel, 2006, p. 1892). Previously resistant jurisdictions that have begun using incentives include Indiana (Aydin, 2007, p. 113) and North Carolina (Aydin, 2007, p. 159) in the US; Ontario, Canada, in the auto industry (Arnold, 2004, p. A01; *Site Selection*, 12 June 2006); and South Africa for call centers (*Business Day*, 2006; Thornton, 2006, p. 46).

Third, there are numerous policy issues involved with incentives. As I have argued elsewhere (Thomas, 2000, pp. 4–5), location subsidies have efficiency, equity and potentially even environmental consequences that must be taken into account when considering their use, what I have come to call 'the three E's'. To summarize them briefly, incentives raise efficiency concerns partly because they can lead to overproduction of the good produced, a characteristic of subsidies generally, but more specifically because they can induce companies to choose suboptimal locations for their facilities. The equity problem is that the post-tax, post-subsidy distribution of income becomes more unequal because incentives transfer income from average taxpayers to owners of capital. The existence of these two critiques explains the frequency of 'strange bedfellows' coalitions against specific incentive projects: conservative critics motivated by efficiency concerns (a well-known statement is Rolnick and Burstein, 1994) and liberals motivated by equity issues. As *Competing for Capital* showed, there has been substantial cooperation between liberals and conservatives (especially libertarians) at the national level on 'corporate welfare', as they often call it; North Carolina is a state with substantial activism on the issue from both ends of the ideological spectrum. In addition, we will see in Chapters 6 and 7 that there is an international equity issue as well: in many cases, developing countries pay more for investment incentives than industrialized countries do, which constitutes a drain on development and a bar to worldwide income convergence. Finally, some investment incentives carry environmental problems as well, for instance by building in floodplains, creating sprawl or overproducing a polluting product. As David Pearce (2002, p. 5) has written, '...there is a *prima facie* case for supposing that subsidies which encourage more production will be environmentally harmful'. As a result, we can ask whether investment incentives are effective in promoting sustainable economic and social development.

At the same time, location incentives present policy issues because they are widely thought to produce economic growth and affect the location of investment (Blomström and Kokko, 2003). As a result, investment promotion agencies have proliferated worldwide.

Fourth, studying investment incentives can give us important insights into the phenomenon of globalization. Since the increasing mobility of capital is one of the key elements of globalization, the analysis of competition for investment relates directly to the question of whether globalization forces states to 'race to the bottom' in terms of taxes, wages, labor and environmental regulations, or continually provide more subsidies to business. The perspective of *Competing for Capital*, that controlling this competition is a collective action problem (an n-person Prisoners' Dilemma), suggests that races to the bottom are not inevitable, precisely because we know that it is sometimes possible to achieve cooperation in a Prisoners' Dilemma situation.

There are two other perspectives in which races to the bottom are not inevitable. As Rogowski (2000) has argued, one conclusion that can be drawn from Charles Tiebout's (1956) analysis is that competition among governments can lead to the continuing co-existence of high-tax, high-service and low-tax, low-service jurisdictions.[8] Similarly, the 'varieties of capitalism' literature (Hall and Soskice, eds, 2001) argues for the persistence of both 'liberal market economies' and 'coordinated market economies' despite the rise of globalization (Hall and Soskice, 2001, pp. 56–60), though it could be suggested that their argument does predict a race to the bottom in liberal market economies. Interestingly, however, within the paradigmatic liberal market economy, the United States, one can see evidence of a similar bifurcation, between what are usually referred to as 'high road' and 'low road' approaches to economic development, where the former is characterized by high taxes, heavy expenditures on health and education, and high wages, while the latter is made up of low-wage, low tax jurisdictions that use investment incentives heavily (Minnesota vs. Mississippi, perhaps). To the subsidy reform campaigners at the NGO Good Jobs First, 'high road' essentially means attaching job quality standards to agreements with firms receiving investment incentives (Mattera, 2009).

Despite widespread use of the term 'FDI incentives', investment incentives need not be directed solely or even primarily at foreign investors. This is easiest to see in industrialized countries that are both sources and destinations for FDI (GM's Saturn plant in 1985 touched off a 30-state bidding war [LeRoy, 2005, p. 23] featuring seven state governors appearing on the 'Donahue' television show to pitch their states' attractiveness for the project [Neal, 1985, Business p. 1]), but with the increase in FDI coming from developing countries such as India, China and Brazil, it is clear that they could equally try to obtain incentives in their home country (Coffin, 2008, notes the wooing of the Indian multinational Tata for the production of its Nano car by Indian states).

The importance of locational tournaments

Bidding wars are referred to as 'tournaments' because payoffs are not awarded to all participants, but only to the winner (David, 1999, p. 115). Even though many jurisdictions expend substantial administrative and promotional costs over the course of the tournament, only one of them can have a potentially positive outcome from it (and that is not guaranteed: the winner may pay too much, a phenomenon usually characterized as the 'winner's curse').[9]

The totality of locational tournaments can be thought of as comprising what Guisinger (1985) called the 'market for investment'. Governments seek investment and investors seek locations, and overall outcomes can be affected by the competitiveness of various segments of this market, and by the ability or necessity of the players (governments and investors) to cooperate with each other to restrict competition among themselves. As Thomas (2000, pp. 27–33) has argued, there are multiple reasons to think that in most cases the dominant trend is that governments will compete for investment rather than investors compete for locations. One basic factor is that the number of really large investments made per year is far smaller than the number of governments competing for them, and governments do not generally know when the next large appropriate project will become available. The number of governments in the market for investment in North America alone numbers in the thousands, because both state governments and local governments in the US have substantial amounts of fiscal autonomy (by contrast, in Canada, most provinces prohibit their municipalities from offering investment incentives; while in Mexico, subsidy negotiation is centralized at the federal level and relatively opaque). According to fdi Intelligence, the number of greenfield FDI projects totaled about 10,000–14,000 annually before the financial crisis (Loewendahl, 2009).

These bidding wars are characterized by substantial asymmetry of information between governments seeking investment and the firms making location decisions (Thomas, 2000, pp. 32–3). Governments have little information on the exact intentions of a potential investor, what its operating costs at various locations might be, what competitive offers it might be entertaining, and so forth. On the other hand, companies seeking to invest can take advantage of the fact that much information is published by and about multiple jurisdictions (especially in democracies). In some instances, firms will use the services of site location consultants to exacerbate this information asymmetry, at times going so far as to have the consultant negotiate for them without even disclosing their identity. As Joseph Stiglitz (2002, p. 11) has shown, even small asymmetries in information can lead to large differences of outcomes in bargaining situations.

As they are generally portrayed, an important outcome of locational tournaments is that the locational rents of various jurisdictions are transferred to the investors (David, 1999, p. 116). As I have put it elsewhere (Thomas, 2007c, p. 52), companies have discovered that the site selection process is itself a rent-generating activity and acted to take advantage of this.

To summarize, locational tournaments help determine the actual patterns of direct investment (which may or may not be foreign), transfer locational rents from governments to investors, and impose costs on losing jurisdictions. Indeed, they may impose economic costs on regions by interfering with the process of forming agglomerations or clusters that produce more efficiently than more geographically dispersed production (David, 1999, p. 116). Since their frequency and geographic spread have tended to grow over the last 30 years, their importance for real economic activity has become increasingly significant.

Overview of *Competing for Capital*

Competing for Capital (Thomas, 2000) marked my first comprehensive treatment of the phenomenon of competition for investment. It argued that investment competition represents a collective action problem among governments, and emphasized the centrality of cooperation theory to understanding the issues. While this book focuses more specifically on investment incentives, it is useful to review some of the key points of *Competing for Capital* to help situate the current work.

First, I argued that competition for investment is rooted ultimately in the combination of the structural dependence of the state on capital, and the increasing mobility of capital. The theory of structural dependence implies that because governments need investment to produce the tax revenues needed for any goal they might have, and to obtain favorable macroeconomic results to bolster citizen support, they are constrained to act in ways that do not threaten the basic interests of the owners of capital (Przeworski and Wallerstein, 1988).[10] Capital mobility transforms what might be a national negotiation over the conditions of investment into a series of bidding wars among governments seeking to attract investment. I adopted (and slightly adapted) Stephen Guisinger's (1985, pp. 11–14) concept of a 'market for investment', in which governments and firms compete among themselves and against each other. However, I argued, three major factors reduce this market to a one-sided competition of governments to secure investment: the increasing mobility of capital, the greater ease of cooperative (or at least convergent) activities by firms compared with states, and major information asymmetries in the process of bargaining over investment (Thomas, 2000, pp. 27–32). Second, I suggested there that the EU's state aid rules might be a feasible real-world response to the collective action problem implied by competition for capital. Thus, three of the book's seven chapters were devoted to explaining the EU's rules, tracing their development over time, and evaluating their effectiveness, respectively. Chapter 8 of this book will review EU policy, emphasizing what in 2000 were recent rules specifically focusing on investment incentives. My evaluation of EU state aid policy at that time was generally positive, in the sense that state aid as a whole was falling, as were those types of aid most likely to be used for investment incentives (then, as now, the EU did not specifically aggregate investment incentives as a category of its own, which is why I analyze incentives to specific firms in Chapter 6). However, I concluded that it was less certain that state aid policy was contributing to the EU's cohesion goals, in view of the fact that aid was actually falling faster in the Cohesion Countries (Greece, Ireland, Portugal and Spain) than in the wealthier Member States, and that wealthier states devoted a larger proportion of their state aid to research and development than did the Cohesion states. Third, I compared the EU with the unregulated competition for investment in the United States, and the barely regulated competition in Canada. I estimated state and local subsidies to business circa 1996 (for my new estimate, see Chapter 6), recounted regulation of state and local government use of federal subsidy programs, and discussed the 'strange bedfellows' nature of subsidy reform politics in the US. In

Canada, I reported on a promising element of its 1994 Agreement on Internal Trade, the Code of Conduct on Incentives. Now 15 years old, I evaluate it in Chapter 8. Finally, I examined EU and OECD efforts to control tax competition and tax havens, and WTO subsidy rules and notification requirements.

In this book, I expand my focus geographically from Europe and North America to the entire world, including a number of developing countries. At the same time, the focus narrows from subsidies generally to investment incentives more specifically. The wider focus was necessary in *Competing for Capital* because the EU's state aid regulations, covering all types of subsidies, were not well-known in US academic circles at the time. Now that they are better known, I devote little time to the general state aid rules and refer the reader to *Competing for Capital* for a broader overview. The theme of controlling investment incentives, which for me is motivated by the desire to control the effects of increasing capital mobility, remains prominent in this book, as the length of Chapter 8 attests. The overall argument of this book is that investment incentives are generally an undesirable policy, but because all jurisdictions face the same strategic imperative to compete for capital, cooperative regulations are necessary to control the use of incentives.

Reactions to *Competing for Capital*

Competing for Capital was the first book to consider EU state aid rules as a model for controlling competition for investment. It sparked increasing interest among academics and policy analysts in the EU's subsidy regime. The most tangible expression of this was the 2004 University of Minnesota conference, 'Reining in the Competition for Capital' organized by Ann Markusen (Markusen, ed., 2007). This conference brought together prominent academics, researchers and policy-makers from the United States along with officials from the EU and the Organization for Economic Cooperation and Development.

The book was also the first to offer an estimate of state and local government subsidies in the US. While obviously subject to imprecision, the figure of $48.8 billion for 1996, of which $26.4 billion would be considered investment incentives, gave analysts and activists alike an idea of the scale of the problem. This factoid is the single most frequently cited aspect of the book, testifying to the widespread need for such a figure. This estimate was later confirmed by Alan Peters and Peter Fisher (Peters and Fisher, 2004, p. 28).

One theoretical innovation of the book was the use of 2×2 games that went beyond Prisoners' Dilemma. The basic result, endorsed by Basinger and Hallerberg (2004), was that as the cost of incentives rose relative to the value of a job, the strategic situation ceased to be a Prisoners' Dilemma, being transformed first into Assurance and then into Harmony, with it being easier and easier to agree to refrain from using location incentives. This suggests the possibility that incentive use might top out even without cooperation among jurisdictions, though I was skeptical of that in *Competing for Capital.* The evidence in the United States is mixed. In 1999, Alabama gave Honda $144 million on a present value basis,[11] an aid intensity of 36 percent of the investment or $96,148 per job. Three years later, it gave Hyundai about $234 million, 23 percent of the investment or $116,968 per job. Considering that the state had given Mercedes 58 percent of its investment and $116,000 per job in 1993 (Blum with Ginsberg, 1995, p. 1), it does not appear that there has been any real acceleration in Alabama. By contrast, when Mississippi landed its first assembly plant in 1999, it gave Nissan $290 million, equivalent to 30 percent of the investment and $72,417 per job. Yet, seven years later, Toyota received $292 million for a smaller investment, yielding an aid intensity of 36 percent and $145,817 per job, hardly evidence of topping out.

One point the book helped advance was the importance of site location consultants. While I had flagged how multinational corporations were learning how to take advantage of their mobility in my dissertation/first book (Thomas, 1992, 1997), Buchholz (1998) gave the first extended analysis of consultants' influence, noting how they increase the information asymmetry between governments and firms. In *Competing for Capital,* I pointed out that location consultants helped coordinate direct investors' actions (analogous to Sinclair's [1994] pathbreaking work on credit rating agencies), and reported on one European location consultant who recommended that his clients tell governments they had competing sites whether it was true or not. Since then, LeRoy (2005, pp. 68–91, 192–3) gave what is probably the best account of the history of the site location industry and offered concrete proposals to reform it. Markusen and Nesse (2007) went as far as to argue that the rise of location consultants is the main explanation for increasing incentives, privileging it above even increasing capital mobility. Certainly, the spiraling of incentives for automobile manufacturing firms in the US in the 1980s was far more rapid than could be accounted for by increasing capital mobility; at the same time, it preceded the widespread use of consultants. More likely, in my view, the rapid increase was due to bidding dynamics and firms' benchmarking their goals for incentives based on the results of recent locational tournaments. Nonetheless, I believe that the rise of location consultants has opened the way for smaller firms to benefit from stronger information asymmetries than they otherwise would have been able to.

Another important reaction has been an attempt to determine the impact of capital mobility on the subsidies granted by governments. Aydin (2007) argues that polities with higher ratios of mobile (manufacturing, financial services) to immobile (extractive industry, retail, etc.) assets will have higher levels of subsidies. While she finds this to be true for both the EU and the United States, the result for the US is undermined because her measure of state subsidies is simply the number of *types* of incentive programs offered by a state (not even the number of actual programs), which I believe is too many steps removed from the amount of actual subsidies to be a valid measure. Zahariadis (2008) also addresses this issue, though he focuses solely on the EU due to the poor quality of data for the US. Both of these major works address other determinants of the use of subsidies (and not simply investment incentives).

Beyond *Competing for Capital*

In this book, two important, intertwined themes make up the theoretical advance beyond *Competing for Capital*. First, in what is ultimately a return to Stephen Hymer's (1960) early analysis of the multinational corporation, I stress the importance of corporate rent-seeking to understand MNC behavior in general and location decisions in particular. As Hymer argued, the purpose of a multinational is to create and exploit monopoly rents (1960, p. 24). While authors such as Blomström and Kokko (2003, p. 17) have emphasized the danger of rent-seeking behavior in the location process, I would go further and argue that companies have realized that the site selection process itself is a rent-generating activity as governments bid to attract their investments. Rent-seeking is the norm, not the exception.

Second, the centrality of rent-seeking means that investment incentives almost always matter in the location decision. Why make a profitable investment in a location that does not give incentives when there is always another jurisdiction that will offer an incentive making your investment even more profitable? Firms therefore generally will screen out locations where incentives are not available. Ontario found this out the hard way. The Conservative governments of 1995–2003 refused on principle to give investment incentives to the automobile industry. As a result, no new assembly plants were built in the province during that time, even as existing facilities closed or reduced production. Instead, investments went to the United States, particularly to southern states. When a new Liberal government took office in 2003, it set up a C$500 million fund to provide investment incentives, and the flow of investment resumed (Arnold, 2004, p. A01; *Site Selection*, 12 June 2006).[12] This screening-out may be negated when agglomeration effects are important, but even here incentive regulation is critical. Fashion design agglomerates in Paris and financial services in New York, but in the latter there is a long list of firms that have threatened to move across the river to New Jersey, either receiving retention incentives from New York City (Good Jobs New York, 2010) or relocation incentives from New Jersey. By contrast, Paris cannot offer such incentives due to EU state aid rules (see Chapter 8).

The fact that investment incentives matter has important theoretical and practical implications. Prominent critics of location incentives, such as LeRoy (2005, p. 52) and Peters and Fisher (2004, p. 31), claim that the effect of state and local taxes and incentives are too small to affect location; therefore, it is a bad policy to use incentives and low taxes (see further below). I argue that it is precisely because incentives do affect location that their use is bad policy. It is only because incentives matter that there can arise strategic interaction among governments making the use of game theory relevant to incentive analysis. To put it differently, to have a game, it is necessary that one actor's behavior affects the payoffs of another. If location incentives do not affect location, this prerequisite is not met. Therefore, LeRoy is incorrect in describing competition for investment as a Prisoner's Dilemma (2005, p. 55) because his theoretical premises preclude it.

Do investment incentives really affect the firm's location decision?

The purpose of investment incentives is clear: to influence the location decisions of firms. Yet whether they in fact do affect corporate decision-making is still controversial. In particular, many American critics argue that incentives (and even tax differences) are of too small a magnitude to affect location decisions. LeRoy (2005, p. 52) is a typical example:

> Internal Revenue Service statistics show that all state and local taxes make up only 1.2 percent of the typical company's cost of doing

> business, far less than labor, materials, marketing, overhead, transportation – the business basics. And then companies get to deduct those state and local taxes when they file their federal tax returns, so Uncle Sam actually foots up to 35 percent of the bill. The bottom line: after federal deductibility, state and local taxes make up only 0.8 percent of the average company's costs.

Empirical studies show mixed results.

1. Surveys of investors, for many years, tended to show that incentives had little or no effect on investment decisions. These surveys tended to take one of two forms: ranking a list of location determinants, or asking directly whether incentives affect the investor's choice in general, or affected particular location decisions. With the first type of survey, the basic determinants of economic feasibility (market size, labor cost and availability, infrastructure and so on) unsurprisingly dominated the top spots. With the second type of survey, few respondents identified incentives (or even taxes) as significant. Guisinger (1985, p. 38) writes:

> On the one hand, if incentives of various countries offset one another, or even only nearly offset one another, investors will state, quite correctly, that the presence of incentives in a country does not seriously influence location decision or that it does not influence them at all. This statement does not mean, however, that the absence of incentives would not affect investment location decisions.

Based on this Prisoners' Dilemma analysis of how the market for investment works, Guisinger and his team posed the question differently (1985, p. 39): 'Would a foreign investment project have located in a particular country if that country had eliminated its incentives and disincentives while other countries maintained incentive policies at existing levels?' They interviewed corporate officials regarding 74 investment projects by over 30 multinationals in four industries (automobiles, petrochemicals, food processing and computers) and found that in two-thirds of them, incentives 'were the decisive factor – that is, in the absence of incentives, a foreign investment would not have been made, or it would have been located in another country' (1985, p. 48). Moreover, even if we eliminate investments oriented toward the domestic market of the host country, where the incentives tended to be tariff protection, we find that of the remaining 38 projects, 15 (39 percent) were driven by location subsidies, 1 (3 percent) by tariff protection, 6 (16 percent) by what Guisinger called implicit incentives driven by government or strategic considerations and 16 (42 percent) by factors unrelated to incentives (Guisinger, 1985, pp. 48–9).

While more recent surveys unfortunately have not posed the questions in this way,[13] respondents have nonetheless been increasingly more likely to accord a significant role to incentives in their investment decisions (Markusen and Nesse, 2007, p. 10).[14] Blomström and Kokko (2003, pp. 4–5) also note that opinions have recently shifted on the importance of incentives on the location of investment, that more studies are finding them significant, and more business executives are willing to say they matter.

2. Quantitative studies of investment tend to show that incentives do affect the location of investment. As Moran (1999, p. 100) writes, 'Grants, tax holidays, and reduced tax rates do, in short, play a role in multinational corporate choice among locations for investment.' Pre-2000 literature reviews (summarized in Thomas, 2000, p. 24) generally reach this conclusion as well, with some arguing that more recent studies in their reviews are more likely to reach this result. One recent review (Dembour, 2008, p. 91) considers that more recent studies have made a persuasive case that taxes affect location. For further discussion of these studies, see Chapter 2.

The author's view is that incentives do affect investment location. LeRoy (2005, p. 57) is correct that a site location decision-maker will, in the final stages, only be talking to locations that are inherently profitable. However, all the other finalists are inherently profitable locations as well. Something needs to differentiate them. Not only this, but the processes of globalization mean that over time, there is an increasing number of locations that are inherently profitable for any given investment (Thomas, 2000, pp. 28–9). While 1.2 percent or 0.8 percent of costs may not sound like much, this is money that is directly going to the bottom line and, therefore, represents a much greater percentage of profits. For example, Advanced Micro Devices (AMD), which received a $1.2 billion subsidy from New York State in 2006, finished 2006 with $5.6 billion in sales and a net loss of $166 million. From 2002 through 2006, the most it made was the $165 million of 2005 (AMD, 2007, p. 51), and it did not make a profit again until 2009, with net income attributable to AMD common stockholders of $304 million (AMD, 2010, p. 40). While this is an extreme case, it is not an unprecedented level of subsidization for microchip fabrication (see Chapter 4). Moreover, this example is supported by the methodology used by site location consultants for determining the effect of an incentive on the profitability of an investment project. Loewendahl (2009, slide 45) shows how different types of incentives affect what location consulting firm PriceWaterhouseCoopers calls the 'profitability index' of a project, with the heaviest impact from incentives that reduce a company's capital expenditure, such as a cash grants. Therefore, the effect of an incentive is far bigger than its share of operating costs would suggest.

Plan of the book

Chapter 2, 'Models, Models and More Models', investigates the main approaches used to analyze competition for investment, including Prisoners' Dilemma, Tiebout, spillovers and the global vs. local efficiency matrix. First, the question of whether incentives achieve their stated goal of affecting the location of investment is considered. The chapter then goes on to assess the strong and weak points of each model. Game-theoretic models more complicated than Prisoners' Dilemma (Barros and Cabral, 2000, and subsequent literature) will be considered here. Both Prisoners' Dilemma and the more complex game-theoretic analyses considered imply that optimal regulation of investment incentives enhances efficiency. The best exposition of the general spillover justification (Dreyhaupt, 2006) is shown to be unproven in real-world conditions due to the pervasiveness of rent-seeking in the site selection process. Moreover, metaanalysis of empirical studies of spillover effects shows some evidence of publication bias in the direction of finding that such effects exist (Görg and Strobl, 2001). Analysis in the Tiebout tradition is cast in doubt because of its assumption of perfect information, whereas negotiation over investment incentives is characterized by major information asymmetries. In any event, none of the models directly considers the equity effects of incentives.

Chapter 3, 'Policy Studies', considers general policy studies covering a wide variety of issues, including effectiveness, cost, transparency, monitoring, rent-seeking and targeting. Transparency is perhaps the most important issue, because too much of incentive policy is conducted behind closed doors. Monitoring of incentive agreements is frequently lacking, and many companies have received subsidies only to close their doors soon thereafter, or were granted incentives and never fulfilled their job creation promises. Because of the frequent lack of transparency, we often have no idea what a jurisdiction's overall spending is (this is true for most US states, for example). Many studies cast doubt on whether using incentives really increases investment, a finding that has been replicated in a number of countries (Fletcher, 2002, and the literature cited there). The chapter highlights the difficulties in evaluating the costs and benefits of incentives, the common lack of *ex post* auditing of incentive programs, clawbacks, the problem of rent-seeking, spillovers and incentives for research and development, the role of site location consultants in obtaining incentives, the design of incentive programs, the politics of investment incentives, and how best to promote benefits from an investment receiving incentives.

Chapter 4, 'Industry Case Studies: Steel, Biofuel Production, Semiconductors, Automobiles, Call Centers', considers a number of sectors based on their societal impact and the lessons they show about incentives in general. As I will show, some industries (autos and semiconductors in particular) simply will not invest without incentives. However, the chapter also examines non-marquee projects to show that they very frequently receive incentives as well. Indeed, in some cases, it appears that the subsidy intensity continues to increase in various jurisdictions. Another important lesson is that locations without a history in a particular industry tend to pay the most, putting pressure on existing locations to offer more. Finally, the chapter notes that places with the most economic need are not always able to give the biggest subsidies, undermining an important argument by Bartik (1991) that this would make subsidy wars efficient.

Chapter 5, 'The Celtic Tiger: Incentives, Infrastructure, Tax Rates, Luck?' examines a case many economic development officials take as the proof that low taxes and/or high investment incentives pave the road to economic success. Among policy-makers in Ireland itself, the importance of low corporate income taxes to the country's economic boom of the 1990s and early 2000s is largely unquestioned. Nevertheless, the story is more complicated because Ireland followed the very same economic development policy from 1959 to 1989 with little success, especially in terms of converging with average EU living standards. In fact, the Irish case strongly shows that giving investment incentives in the absence of having achieved more basic economic fundamentals is a poor policy choice. The chapter shows how Ireland did gain some of those fundamentals, from sources as disparate as EU Structural Funds and the administrative discipline they required; a 'social partnership' (albeit an unequal one) between labor, capital and the state; and investment in education, particularly post-secondary education. But Ireland's low taxes and large investment grants certainly played their role in the country's rapid economic growth, though both are controversial within the country (especially because of increased inequality) and within the EU (due to conflicts over state aid rules and tax competition, with Ireland's tax sovereignty even playing a role in the country's rejection of the Lisbon Treaty in the first referendum in June 2008). With economic success, however, new policy challenges have arisen, notably sharp cuts in Ireland's Structural Funds and a much reduced ability to give incentives to investors, as well as growing political pressure against the country's low corporate income tax.

Chapter 6, 'Who Provides the Most Investment Incentives: EU vs. US', revisits *Competing for Capital*'s conclusion that the EU's state aid policy was largely successful in its goals of controlling subsidies in general, and subsidies likely to go to mobile investment in particular. There, it was necessary to rely on aggregate data on total subsidies, regional aid, general aid, and aid for R&D, the latter three then the most common types of aid used for mobile projects. Now that the EU has adopted rules specifically addressing investment incentives (beginning with 1997's Multi Sectoral Framework, whose rules are now incorporated in the regional aid guidelines), I am now able to approach the question through a direct comparison of incentives in the EU and the United States. What the chapter shows is that, comparing the 25 largest recent incentives in both areas, it is clear that US state and local governments put together larger subsidy packages for investors than do EU Member States. Moreover, the US locations giving larger incentives are more prosperous than the highest subsidizing EU locations, which are largely in the former Communist states of Eastern Europe. The chapter then moves to an estimate of US state and local governments' aggregate level of investment incentives and subsidies to business.

Chapter 7, 'The Spread of Investment Incentives to Developing Countries', documents the more recent adoption of incentives in developing countries around the world. Some see this as largely a defensive reaction to their use in the North (Oman, 2000; Moran et al., 2005, p. 382), while another important driver is fiscal decentralization in countries such as Brazil, China, India (Markusen and Nesse, 2007), and Vietnam (Hong et al., 2009). In all these countries, we see numerous cases of subnational competition for investment comparable to those in the US. As in the United States, there is very little regulation of this competition, even though in the Brazilian case the main incentive used by the states was technically illegal. Vietnam actually has made the greatest efforts to regulate subnational incentives, with differentiated aid maxima à la the European Union, but in 2005 newspaper reports revealed widespread violation of these maxima by provincial governments (Hong et al., 2009; Malesky, 2008).

Chapter 8, 'Controlling Incentives and Maximizing the Value of Inward Investment', analyzes the ways that policymakers around the world have tried to control investment subsidies and evaluate their success. While a number of studies, such as Head et al. (1999) and Albornoz and Corcos (2007), offer theoretical justification for multilateral control of incentives, this chapter considers real-life attempts in that direction. First, I will analyze the rules and effectiveness of the most comprehensive disciplinary effort, that of the European Union. The general outline of rules as well as the most important framework applying to investment incentives *per se*, the regional aid guidelines, are considered. The various rules in the GATT Uruguay Round agreements that affect subsidies, including the Agreement on Subsidies and Countervailing Measures, the General Agreement on Trade in Services (GATS), and the Agreement on Trade-Related Investment Measures, are then explained. Third will be two sub-national agreements on incentives among Canadian provinces and territories, and among Australian states. Both now have enough of a track record to assess whether they have been successful or not. Fourth, I will examine the history of voluntary agreements in the United States. The chapter finishes with an analysis of the disciplines that exist in a small number of the many bilateral investment treaties (BITs) and investment incentive agreements (IIAs) in force around the world, as well as in bilateral or regional free trade agreements. I argue that these agreements, designed to protect investors rather than regulate incentives, should be largely avoided by developing countries if they want to maximize the value derived from inward investment.

Chapter 9, 'A Policy Agenda for the 21st Century: Transparency and Beyond', recognizes that different countries around the world have sharply divergent needs for reform of investment incentive policy. In most places, transparency remains the critical first reform goal. However, the analysis in this concluding chapter lays out a number of national and regional agendas for the reform of incentives.

2
Models, Models and More Models

This chapter investigates the main approaches used to analyze competition for investment through investment incentives. We begin with general approaches to assessing the use of incentives, including Prisoners' Dilemma, models in the Tiebout (1956) tradition, incentives as necessary to generate spillovers and the global vs. local efficiency matrix. Next, we move to a consideration of game theoretic models more complex than Prisoners' Dilemma, either relaxing its assumptions or using a more general 'subsidy game'. After that, the spotlight turns to statistical analyses of the effects of tax and incentives on investment. Finally, we survey significant case studies from both developed and developing countries.

Perspectives on incentives

This section groups competing perspectives on investment incentives based on their overall evaluations. First, some analysts come to positive evaluations using a variety of general arguments. For example, some studies argue that incentive competition enhances economic efficiency by leading to an optimal sorting of firms to localities with their preferred package of taxes and services, a line of thinking that can be traced to Charles Tiebout (1956). Another approach sees incentives as a way of ensuring that all socially valuable investments are made within an economy; in particular, investments that provide positive spillovers to actors beyond the investor, whose private returns are therefore lower than the social returns (and may therefore refrain from investing under certain circumstances). Dreyhaupt (2006) is a good recent illustration of this argument. Bartik (1991) argued that incentive competition could generate efficiency if it allocated investment from areas of low unemployment to those of higher unemployment; we can see an echo of this in European Commission decisions on state aid according a higher value to investments in lower income areas of the EU (a recent example is the approval of Polish regional aid for Dell; see European Union, 2009f, p. 39). Finally, strategic trade theory recommends the use of subsidies at times in industries with increasing returns to scale and imperfect competition. Second, negative interpretations see incentives competition as leading to insufficient investment in public goods due to loss of revenue (Oates, 1972). An alternative, though complementary view is based on seeing incentives competition as a Prisoner's Dilemma in which governments are individually better off but collectively worse off when they give location subsidies, a view that can be traced back to Stephen Guisinger (1985). Third, a mixed or contingent evaluation of incentives comes from the local vs. global efficiency matrix approach adapted from Cheshire and Gordon (1998) by Rodriguez-Pose and Arbix (2001), and subsequently used in several OECD reports.

The market for investment

Stephen Guisinger (1985) proposed the notion of a 'market for investment', and divided this market into three types based on the location to be served. Investment incentives differ according to market type. Domestic-market-oriented investment tends to garner the fewest incentives as the location choice is constrained to that market. Food processing is an industry that tends to fall into this category. By contrast, common-market-oriented investment requires the existence of a free trade area among jurisdictions, such that the entire common market can be served from a single location. Guisinger states that such investments tend to create intense bidding wars due to the company's ability to locate in any of the jurisdictions. While his main focus was on the European Union, it can be argued that these dynamics also hold within large federal states such as the United States and Brazil. The automobile industry is an example of one where production and consumption tend to be located within the same regional market. Finally, some investment is oriented to the entire world market, as for example many branches of the computer industry. Certain types of computer investments may find competition coming from countries as geographically diverse as Ireland, Germany, Israel, Singapore and the United States. Again, we find that the competition among governments to obtain these investments is often intense.

Positive interpretations of incentives

Here we address in turn the four main ways in which it can be argued that investment incentives are beneficial: Tiebout-style analyses; spillovers/positive externalities; reallocation of investment from low- to high-unemployment areas and strategic trade theory.

1. Charles Tiebout (1956) argued that the fragmentation of local governments made it possible to achieve market-style outcomes for individuals in terms of their preferred package of public goods and taxes. The key to this was household mobility: with many local governments offering varying patterns of municipal services and taxation, families would move to the suburb (or central city) that most closely approximated their preferred mix. Instead of needing a political mechanism to determine voters' preferences for public goods and taxes, mobility would make it possible for people to reveal their preferences directly through their decisions on where to live. When transposed into debates on investment incentives (or even globalization; see Rogowski, 2000), Tiebout's theory has served as a basis for arguing that the presence of competition does not necessarily imply a 'race to the bottom'. Moreover, this competition assures efficiency.

Translated into the issue of location incentives, firms replace households, but governments (not just local, but also national) still compete to attract them to their location. In this vision, governments use incentives and tax competition to offer companies a particular tax price for the services they provide. With subsidies, this price could even be negative (Fisher, 2002, p. 772). In Tiebout-inspired models, companies migrate to locations that give them their preferred combination of services and taxes.

Black and Hoyt (1989) follow this logic to conclude that competition for investment can be efficient when it moves governments to provide public services at marginal cost rather than average cost. However, this depends on the assumption that firms and governments know the relevant investment costs at all locations – information that firms guard jealously (Thomas, 2000, p. 5). Moreover, in cases where the tax price is negative, it has obviously been reduced below the marginal cost of providing the services it receives. Finally, Tiebout-style models only address efficiency issues arising from the use of incentives, not equity questions.[1]

2. Dreyhaupt (2006) provides a recent example of an analysis suggesting that investment incentives can increase efficiency. The key to his analysis is that many investments have positive externalities or

spillovers, making the social rate of return on the investment higher than the private rate of return on investment. There is a subset of these potential investments where the private rate of return is negative but the social rate of return is positive.[2] In this situation, giving incentives will increase the country's welfare by ensuring that all socially valuable investment projects take place. However, with open competition among countries, it is possible that incentives may equal or exceed the difference between the social and private rate of return, meaning that companies appropriate the entire extra benefit and none accrues to government (2006, p. 146). Thus, capping incentives at the level needed to make the investment a break-even one is the ideal solution, something he considers approximates what European Union state aid policy does (see Chapter 8 on disciplines for discussion of this policy). However, he admits that it is difficult in practice to determine the social value of a private investment, making overbidding more of a risk than it would be in a perfect information situation (2006, p. 149).

However, this is not the only problem with the practical applicability of the model. For the incentive-granting situation to be efficient, there needs to be 'a sufficiently high number of investment projects with positive externalities that take place regardless of subsidies' (2006, p. 146, n. 456). In other words, projects that have positive private returns need to be undertaken without subsidies. Otherwise, such subsidies are eating into the externalities presumably available. In reality, there are countless investments occurring where the project would have been profitable without incentives (LeRoy, 2005, has numerous examples). Investment incentives are marked by pervasive rent-seeking, and Dreyhaupt essentially assumes it away. As Blomström and Kokko (2003, p. 17) point out, discretionary benefits make rent-seeking a risk. This does not negate Dreyhaupt's point that restrictions on incentives can limit the scope for rent-seeking, but it means that his overall claim that incentives can be efficiency-enhancing is unproven in anything like real-world conditions.[3] Moreover, like most Tiebout-inspired models, this approach only addresses efficiency, not equity.

3. Bartik (1991) introduces a different sense of efficiency, that the transfer of investment from low unemployment to high unemployment areas is a more efficient use of capital. He further contends that in the market for investment, the jurisdictions with the greatest need (such as high unemployment) will offer the largest location subsidies. Thomas (2000) (for the European Union) and Fisher and Peters (1998) (for the United States) both find that there are many instances when poorer areas are outbid for investment by richer locations. Fisher and

Peters (1998, p. 26) concluded, '...the antecedent conditions for Bartik's argument that incentives may have net national benefits is not true: The spatial patterns of taxes and incentives in America is not likely to promote the redistribution of jobs from places of low unemployment to places of high unemployment'. As Fisher puts it (2007, p. 70), 'Incentive programs...are viewed as essential policy in good times and bad, in poor states and rich states.' As long as prosperous jurisdictions stay in the incentive game, less affluent areas will not catch up. The greater financial resources in the former mean they are able to offer higher incentives, and can bid on more projects, than poorer areas can. Nevertheless, this assumption continues to crop up in models of subsidy games, as Dembour (2008, p. 96) shows in her review of a number of these studies.

4. Strategic trade theory counsels policy-makers facing a specific set of circumstances: increasing returns to scale and imperfect competition (Krugman, 1994, p. 2). In particular, this theory has been used to justify subsidies in the international airliner field, that is, Boeing vs. Airbus. Most of the adherents of this theory admit that there may be very few industries where these dynamics hold and that it is very difficult in practice to identify cases where they are relevant. As Krugman (1996, p. 110) writes, 'In general, however, we can say that most economists working on international trade have agreed that strategic trade policy can work in principle but have been highly skeptical about its importance and usefulness in practice.' In any event, strategic trade theory is not oriented toward achieving global efficiency, but to the advantages available to particular nations, so it is not a sort of universal justification for incentives comparable to Tiebout or to externalities-oriented arguments.

Negative views of location subsidies

Many scholars are critical of the use of investment incentives. There are three main arguments adduced against them: they force governments to provide undesirably low levels of public services; local governments provide subsidies to companies that would invest *somewhere* in the larger jurisdiction anyway (for instance, US states subsidizing automobile plants that would have located somewhere in the country, regardless of incentives); governments could cooperate with each other to reduce the use of incentives, but find it difficult to do so because of their competition for investment (a Prisoners' Dilemma-based argument).[4]

1. One possible consequence of the high and growing use of investment incentives, spending money on grants in the current period or mortgaging future tax revenues through abatements and other tax-based incentives, is that a government will have insufficient funds for important programs, including ones that contribute to economic development such as education or infrastructure.[5] Oates (1972, p. 143) argues, 'The result of tax competition may well be a tendency toward less than efficient levels of output of local public services. In an attempt to keep taxes low to attract business investment, local officials may hold spending below those levels for which marginal benefits equal marginal costs, particularly for those programs that do not offer direct benefits to local businesses.' As Robert Lynch puts it (2004, p. vii): '...there is little evidence that state and local tax cuts – when paid for by reducing public services – can promote economic development and employment growth.' From this perspective, then, not only can the revenue reductions mean a declining quality of life as governments cut programs, but incentives may not even have their desired effect since they require offsetting service reductions.

2. Thomas (2000) argues that from a national point of view, state or local incentives are often irrational in the sense that the investment will be made somewhere in the country. The case of Japanese and German auto factories in the United States, beginning in the 1980s, is one example. For the Japanese especially, investment in the United States was an important strategy to head off protectionist pressures there. Had the United States been able to negotiate directly with foreign multinational corporations, it could have leveraged the advantage of a large domestic market (see Thomas, 1997, pp. 9–18, for a review of the extensive literature on bargaining between states and MNCs, and further analysis of the Japanese investments in the United States). However, due to the fact that foreign firms could negotiate with 50 state governments, it was possible for them to extract investment incentives they would not have received from the federal government. Such irrationality is only compounded when the investment concerns not new jobs,[6] but simply a shift in existing ones. As he writes of proposed incentives for Trans World Airlines (TWA) to relocate its corporate headquarters while it was in bankruptcy (2000, p. 33), 'Thus, subnational governments prepared three sets of investment incentives to reward TWA for creating *no* new jobs in the United States.' This view of national-level irrationality leads directly to Prisoners' Dilemma approaches, which are considered next.

3. Prisoners' Dilemma analyses of incentives posit that there is a conflict between the individual incentives of local governments and what is collectively best for governments as a whole. One consequence, as Oman (2000, p. 78) argues, is that this logic makes bidding wars a 'permanent danger'. Guisinger (1985, pp. 38–9) was the first to analyze location subsidies as a Prisoners' Dilemma, although there is at least one precursor in Cooper's analysis of economic interdependence (1972, pp. 168–71). Guisinger wrote (1985, p. 38):

> In the market for foreign investment, a prisoner's dilemma arises among countries when one country's increase in incentives is matched by increased incentives by a competitor. A point will be reached when the incentive levels stabilize and no country will be better off: unchanged relative incentives will produce the same market share as before. Indeed, both countries may be worse off because income is transferred to firms with no gain in market share. Only if incentives stimulate an increase in the total supply of investment to compensate for the loss of revenue can incentive matching increase the welfare of host countries.

Harding and Javorcik (2007, p. 21) provide empirical support for the key point that not using incentives leads to lost investment: if other countries in a region use investment incentives, your country's FDI falls. Head et al. (1999) have similar findings. Their results show that US states competing for Japanese investment tended to match each other's incentives, leading to little aggregate effect on the location of investment. Moreover, they found (1999, p. 213) that unilateral removal of foreign trade zones (FTZs) would cost 50–75 percent of a state's investment, whereas multilateral removal would have little effect. Note that while this result shows a Prisoners' Dilemma dynamic among firms that had already decided to locate in the United States, it does not tell us whether or not the use of FTZs brings more investment to the country overall.

Du et al. (2008, p. 423) find that in Chinese provinces, the presence of national special economic zones or economic and technological development zones increased the amount of FDI a province received. This would be evidence of incentives affecting the amount of FDI obtained. Finally, we noted in Chapter 1 how Ontario lost automobile industry investment when it ceased to provide incentives from 1995 to 2003. These findings are critical to grounding the Prisoners' Dilemma interpretation of incentive competition because to have true strategic interaction, it is necessary for one party's actions to affect another party's payoffs. Actually losing investment by not giving incentives is what gets us beyond actors' ideas and perceptions (numerous studies show that jurisdictions do react competitively, e.g., Li, 2006; Mason and Thomas, 2010) to genuine strategic interaction.

Thomas (1997, 2000) extends this framework by arguing that rising capital mobility increases the number of locations that are capable of competing for a given project; following well-known analyses of collective action (Hardin, 1982; Olson, 1965), this implies that it will be ever-more difficult to achieve cooperation among competitors. With large numbers of governments involved, the most likely way to achieve cooperation among them is through enforcement of an agreement by a higher body. This is his interpretation (2000) of the European Union's state aid regime (see Chapter 8 below).

Guisinger's quote alerts us to two possible limitations to Prisoners' Dilemma analysis. First, the 'no subsidies' and 'all subsidize' distributions of investment may be different, a point taken up below. Second, it is possible that investors take into account the fact that subsidies will be available for their projects, and increase their investments accordingly. Guisinger states that it depends on the elasticity of investment in response to incentives. Research within the United States suggests that it is relatively low, in the range of –0.2 to –0.3 (Fisher, 2007, p. 66), although these estimates may not hold outside the United States. Further bearing on this question, Oman (2000, pp. 77–8, 115) argues that increased FDI flows led to increased use of incentives, rather than the other way around, which implies that the use of incentives does not increase the total value of investment.

A third problem with Prisoners' Dilemma approaches is that they may be too coarse to encompass the complexity of the political process (Markusen and Nesse, 2007, pp. 19–20). Markusen and Nesse argue that the model 'cannot easily encompass institutional changes in interests, power and actors, including the rise and behavior of site consultants' (19). Basinger and Hallerberg (2004), in their analysis of tax competition, suggest that institutional and electoral factors mitigate the pressure to reduce corporate income tax rates. Note that the Prisoners' Dilemma does not disappear: tax cuts abroad still create pressure for a country to cut its own taxes, but whether a country does reduce taxes will be mediated by a host of other factors.[7]

The local vs. global efficiency matrix

Andrés Rodríguez-Pose and Glauco Arbix (2001) suggest an innovative model for understanding the impact of investment incentives, based on the effect of subsidized investment on local and global (meaning 'national' in the context of their analysis of the Brazilian auto industry) efficiency. Following the analysis of 'territorial competition' by Cheshire and Gordon (1998), they suggest that the results of competition among local governments can have combinations of effects that they fit into the following 2×2 matrix:

	Global Level	
	Inefficient	**Efficient**
Locally Efficient	Zero Sum	Growth Enhancing
Locally Inefficient	Pure Waste	

They leave the fourth quadrant empty, an issue to which we will return shortly. A competitive policy that is both locally and globally efficient they term 'growth enhancing'. In other words, increased economic welfare at the local level is not offset by negative externalities (such as exporting unemployment) in other parts of the country. By contrast, if the improvements in efficiency at the local level cause losses elsewhere in the country, they would be considered zero-sum (for Cheshire and Gordon, investment incentives all fall into this category [1998, p. 325]). Worse still, it is possible that competitive policies such as incentives could be so expensive as to offset all the local gains, *and* in addition would have negative impacts elsewhere in the country. This outcome of 'pure waste' (an outcome Rodríguez-Pose and Arbix emphasize much more than Cheshire and Gordon do) is how they characterize the so-called 'fiscal wars' among Brazilian states over automobile production in the late 1990s (2001, p. 137). Rodríguez-Pose and Arbix argue that the legacy of authoritarianism in Brazil has left its states with little experience in bargaining with foreign companies (2001, p. 150). This inexperience, combined with the mobility of the car firms themselves, led to excessive incentives that created local inefficiency manifested in the bankruptcy of seven of Brazil's states, and a global inefficiency in the form of tremendous job losses in the São Paulo heartland of the industry (2001, p. 151). Brazil's fiscal war is considered further in Chapter 7.

Two studies by the OECD (Charlton, 2003; Christiansen, Oman, and Charlton, 2003) have extended this approach. In particular, they fill in the fourth quadrant, terming it the 'winners' curse' (Charlton, 2003, p. 12).[8] How can a scenario of local inefficiency but global efficiency occur? Charlton (2003, p. 13) argues that it can occur when a local jurisdiction overbids for an investment (local inefficiency) but it happens to be the location at which the facility will operate most efficiently (global efficiency). Another, perhaps more plausible, way to envision it is in terms of an incentive that shifts an existing facility from a low-unemployment area to a high-unemployment area, a situation Charlton explicitly accepts (2003, pp. 13–14) as an efficiency gain à la Bartik. (Recall that Rodríguez-Pose and Arbix treat the global gain as a mixture of gains locally with possible offsetting losses elsewhere in the global jurisdiction.)

In either case, however, it is difficult to see how there could be an inefficiency for the local jurisdiction and efficiency for the larger jurisdiction. It is easy to show this for the case of a relocation: Let N represent the social value of the investment at the new location, O its value at the old location, with both N and O strictly positive, and G, the difference between the two, is the gain in national efficiency, such that N-O=G. Under Bartik's formulation, G will be positive when unemployment is higher at new than it is at old. For incentives under these circumstances to be *locally* inefficient at the new location, they would have to exceed the social value, N. But since O is positive and is subtracted from N, this implies that subsidies are globally (N-O) inefficient as well. To put it another way, let's look at the four quadrants in terms of these N and G, plus I representing the incentive.

N>G>I is the growth enhancing situation, that is, global and local efficiency.

N>I>G is the zero-sum situation, local efficiency but global inefficiency.

I>N>G is pure waste, local and global inefficiency.

G>I>N would be winner's curse, local inefficiency and global efficiency, but this is impossible since by assumption N>G.

We can immediately see that in the case of a new investment, it could only be locally inefficient and globally efficient if G>N. This would mean that there are some positive spillovers of the investment from N to the rest of the country. Not only that, these spillovers would need to exceed the administrative costs incurred by unsuccessful subnational bidders for the investment. In theory this may be conceivable, but in practice it is a high bar to reach. Moreover, for the incentives to have a systematic, rather than random, tendency to increase national efficiency, it is necessary to rely on the empirically dubious (and whose uncertainty Charlton acknowledges) assumption that 'the country bidding the highest will *ceteris paribus* be the one where the potential efficiency gains are the largest' (Charlton, 2003, p. 12).

In Christiansen et al. (2003), more care is taken to weigh the benefits of incentives against their costs. Reanalyzing the case of Brazil, they suggest that while the relocation of some automotive production from São Paulo to poorer areas of the country[9] increased national efficiency, the high costs in state subsidies (up to $340,000 per job) 'could be taken to indicate that subsidies have been paid in excess of the additional efficiency gains from reallocating plants within Brazil (hence a case can be made for inefficiency at the national level)' (2003, p. 18). They leave open the possibility, however, that in some of the recipient states the efficiency gains outweighed the incentive costs. Indeed, this would be necessary to have national efficiency gains, since there were clearly losses in the São Paulo region, with manufacturing employment falling by half over 10 years (Rodríguez-Pose and Arbix, 2001, p. 151). Puzzlingly, they do not even consider the possibility that the huge influx of automotive investment may not have been efficiency-enhancing at the world level, but more a result of the high protective tariffs of the New Automotive Regime, a factor they do take note of (Christiansen et al. 2003, p. 17). Adding weight to the view that there was indeed national inefficiency, Farrell et al. (2004) report that, by 2002, Brazil had 80 percent overcapacity in the auto industry and that costs were inflated by 20 percent due to the low capacity utilization. Similarly, but not quite as astonishingly, ANFAVEA reports that the Brazilian auto industry produced 3.2 million cars in 2008, but had a capacity of 4 million (2009, pp. 10, 56), or 25 percent overcapacity.

More recent work in the 'territorial competition' tradition sheds further light on the use of investment incentives in a wide variety of countries. Chien and Gordon (2008, p. 32) note that the language of 'territorial competition' was coined in Europe, where the intended contrast the term draws is with regional policies controlled by the national government. In the United States, competition among subnational governments arose without a pre-history of centralized regional policy, and at a much earlier date than in Western Europe. They see important differences due to the importance of the frontier in the US West, as well as the contrasting views on the appropriate level of government intervention in the economy manifested in the two areas. At the same time, they stress two important similarities, democratic elections and private property, factors that exist as well in Brazil's case, where they cite Rodríguez-Pose and Arbix. The puzzle that interests them is the case of China, which is neither democratic nor based on private property, yet which nevertheless seems to exhibit substantial territorial competition (Chien and Gordon, 2008, pp. 32–3). On top of those major structural differences, they find that the Chinese economy is not integrated internally, making it difficult for Chinese firms to use the large national market to achieve internationally competitive economies of scale (2008, p. 42). These factors combine to make subnational competition for investment particularly pernicious in China, they argue, reporting that at the same time that many firms are below minimum efficient scale, there is also widespread overproduction in some industries such as textiles and electronics (2008, p. 43), a situation reminiscent of that described in Brazil above. They conclude that in some ways Chinese territorial competition is worse than that in the US: 'This lack of regulation is even more radical than in the American case, because it involves the absence of effective control over regional protectionism, as well as over financial bidding wars' (2008, p. 44).

Conclusions

All of these perspectives contribute to our understanding of investment incentives. While strict Tiebout models may be vitiated by the realities of bargaining with asymmetric information, theories based on the possibility of externalities highlight an important potential gain from using location aid. Prisoners' Dilemma approaches provide an important focus on the possibility of cooperation between governments in reducing the cost of achieving potential efficiency gains. Finally, the local/global matrix explicitly balances the gains at one location versus losses elsewhere and has opened the door to a broadly comparative research agenda under the rubric of 'territorial competition'.

Game-theoretic analyses

One strength of game-theoretic analyses of incentives is that they can model subsidies directly, rather than simply measure taxes. While subsidies can in principle be thought of as negative taxes, in practice a statistical analysis will always show taxes as positive, though different among different countries or regions. While it can highlight some important regularities, statistical analysis cannot capture the specificity inherent in incentives.

Prisoners' Dilemma analysis has been considered earlier in this chapter. Although not strictly required, PD tends to assume that the players are undifferentiated, their payoffs are symmetric, or both. Thus, a number of analysts have worked to modify these assumptions.

Several factors should be kept in mind when analyzing these studies. First, most of them consider only efficiency, not the equity or environmental aspects of investment attraction. Second, many of them lump together incentive competition with tax competition. To some extent this can be justified by the idea that a subsidy is simply a negative tax, but the identity can break down in the sense that many of the studies treat all investors as facing the same tax rate (even if it is negative), when the whole point of an incentive is to treat different potential investors differently. As is apparent from studying the European Union, using automatic location subsidies is more expensive than taking a discretionary approach to incentives, and the tendency for two decades or more in the EU has been to move toward increasing discretion (Thomas, 2000, p. 11). More recent work on the greater cost of automatic incentives can be found in Fisher (2007, p. 67) and Bartik (2007, pp. 107–8).

Barros and Cabral (2000) consider a subsidy game between two unequal countries seeking the same investment. Country A is larger, while Country B has higher unemployment. One implication of the latter assumption is consistent with Bartik (1991) in terms of meaning that total efficiency is higher if the firm locates in Country B rather than Country A. On the other hand, locating in Country A means there are lower transportation costs due to its assumed geographic centrality. Without subsidies, the firm will locate in Country A for this reason. However, if location incentives are allowed, the company's choice is determined by the relative importance of the employment gains in Country B compared with the difference in size of the two countries. In equilibrium, two outcomes are possible. If the employment gains are large relative to the difference in size, Country B gives a subsidy and receives the investment. If the employment gains are relatively small, Country A gives an incentive and the firm invests there. Country A must give an incentive in this case because Country B is offering incentives as well. Country B is better off with subsidies allowed even if it does not get the investment, because the subsidy means higher production by the company and lower prices for consumers. Country A, by contrast, is always worse when subsidies are allowed, because it either has to give subsidies or lose the investment. This conflict in interest implies that a first-best solution exists: it would correspond to a small subsidy by B when employment gains are relatively high, or a zero subsidy by A when employment gains are relatively low. However, the first-best solution is worse for the losing country (because a subsidy would have lowered the prices it had to pay for the good produced), so it is probably not attainable without side payments.

The lessons of this analysis are several. First, with asymmetric countries, the possibility of offering incentives increases welfare. Second, the use of incentives does affect the location of investment (Blomström and Kokko, 2003, p. 9). Third, cooperation between the two countries can lead to higher welfare than unbridled competition, but is difficult to achieve in the absence of side payments. Interestingly, the first-best solution corresponds well to the European Union's policy on regional aid: low incentives in poorer regions and zero incentives in richer regions.[10] Finally, the difficulty in achieving the first-best outcome highlights why subsidy competition is so entrenched in the real world, reinforcing the lesson we take from Prisoners' Dilemma (Thomas, 2000, pp. 36–7).

At the same time, there are limitations to this analysis. First, Barros and Cabral assume that the firm being attracted will be a monopolist, but this is hardly ever the case.[11] Thus, they assume away the problem of FDI possibly displacing existing investment (the US–Canadian auto industry is a good case in point).[12] Second, Barros and Cabral implicitly assume that Country B will be able to offer a higher subsidy than Country A, but there are good empirical reasons to believe this is not always, and maybe not even usually, the case (Fisher and Peters, 1998, p. 26; Thomas, 2000, p. 6).

Bjorvaten and Eckel (2006) study a more complicated version of this model. Their paper includes a competitor to the multinational, which is located in the larger Country A. In this model, the multinational is subject to two conflicting forces: In Country A, the market size is larger, but in Country B, it has no competitor. When these two factors are in close balance, both countries offer location subsidies. When the two factors dictate that one country or the other has a big inherent advantage, there will be less competition and, indeed, the winning country will be able to tax the multinational rather than subsidize it. As they point out (2006, p. 1902, n. 12), '...strong location advantages increase the bargaining power of potential host countries and may lead to taxation rather than subsidies...' This is consistent with the findings of the literature on bargaining between multinationals and host countries in international relations (Thomas, 1997). What is important is their finding that this remains true even with a competing location. Whether the two countries together are better off with or without policy competition depends crucially on trade costs between the two, where low levels of trade costs (which should, of course, be interpreted as greater capital mobility) means intense competition, and they are worse off in the absence of side payments. With high trade costs and hence lower capital mobility, Country B has a big advantage (and can tax the multinational rather than subsidize it) and total welfare can be higher without side payments.

Albornoz and Corcos (2007) consider the interesting situation of incentives to an existing firm considering relocation within a regional trade area, a situation that has arisen within NAFTA, the European Union and Mercosur, among others. In this case, a total ban on subsidies may be more efficient than allowing subsidy competition, in contrast to the above two studies. However, coordinated incentives may have higher regional welfare still. This is particularly the case with a MNC from outside the region, and they suggest this implies that in such instances, a ban on subsidies will be a better policy than allowing them, if it is not possible to coordinate them optimally.

Dembour (2008) provides a recent overview of the game-theoretic literature. She reports important findings that location decisions are affected by tax rates (see also the discussion of statistical studies below) and substantial evidence of tax competition among governments (2008, p. 91). Note, however, that this is not the same thing as showing that firms respond to incentives, although at one level we can think of incentives as negative taxes (incentives are intended to discriminate among individual firms, unlike taxes). Nor does the presence of competitive responses by governments to others' use of incentives show that they have understood their strategic situation correctly; instead, what we need to show is that not offering incentives leads to the loss of investment, because this is the necessary antecedent to make governments' payoffs in subsidy games truly interdependent (and hence a game at all).

One important study she cites is that of Haufler and Wooton (2006), which considers the timely case of three countries competing for a monopolist MNC's investment, with two of the countries both members of a union (read: EU). In their analysis, and contrary to several previous studies, it is not always the case that the two union members can increase welfare by cooperating to raise taxes or lower investment incentives given. If the firm's preference for the union is weak, the union members should cooperate to lower taxes or increase subsidies (2006, p. 289). This finding should hearten the Irish, who have fought against EU state aid rules on the grounds that they are harming the competitiveness of EU countries relative to nonmembers (Wishlade, 2008a, pp. 61–3).

Haufler and Wooton (2008b) consider a model where two unequal countries compete for a variable number of firms. They note falling corporate tax revenues and high levels of investment incentives in some EU countries and question whether firms are paying any tax net of incentives (Ibid., 2008a, p. 3). They reach the interesting finding that economic integration reduces tax rates initially, but that as trade costs continue to fall, they rise again (2008b, p. 21). They suggest this gives them an explanation on why corporate income tax rates in the EU have moderated their fall and why investment incentives have begun falling on the biggest projects (see also the discussion of this fall in Chapter 6).

What lessons can we draw from these studies? Many of the results are sensitive to the assumptions built into the models. In particular, the assumption that the poorer region can outbid the richer region is questionable, although in the European Union, the availability of Structural Funds that can co-finance investment incentives in the poorer regions (such as the Dell plant in Poland) makes this assumption more realistic. Another questionable assumption is that there will be productivity spillovers that justify the incentives. According to Havránek (2009, p. 132), 'As all available meta-analyses (Görg & Strobl 2001; Meyer & Sinani 2005; Wooster & Diebel 2006; Havránek & Iršová 2008) illustrate, there is no persuasive empirical evidence of technological and knowledge diffusion…' Ironically, he nevertheless goes on to build his own model in which spillovers are a critical explanation for incentives!

As noted above, the EU may be reasonably close to Barros and Cabral's 'first-best' situation. As a whole, the results of these studies do argue for using regional policy rather than allowing uncoordinated bidding by rich areas as well as poor areas, but not necessarily for a total ban on incentives. They also reinforce the view that moving away from the status quo of subsidy competition is difficult to achieve.

Statistical analysis of the effects of incentives and taxes on investment

This literature is so vast that it is difficult to summarize it all. Fortunately, a recent paper (De Mooij and Ederveen, 2005) provides not only a literature review, but a meta-analysis, of 31 widely known studies on the issue of how taxes affect investment (more precisely, the responsiveness of investment to changes in taxation, i.e., the elasticity). Since these studies made 427 estimates of this elasticity under a variety of circumstances, the authors were able to analyze the results in terms of major characteristics of the articles, such as the type of investment, how taxes were measured, and so forth.

De Mooij and Ederveen, following Devereux and Griffith (2002), classify empirical studies into four broad categories: time series, cross-sectional, discrete choice and panel. They perform a regression in which the dependent variable is the semi-elasticity of investment to taxation (i.e., the response to a 1 percentage point change in the taxation variable, rather than a 1 percent change as is the basis for calculating elasticities), for which in some cases they had to calculate from the data of various studies, and the independent variables are various characteristics of the articles analyzed. The semi-elasticities vary widely, and de Mooij and Ederveen start out by excluding extreme values (over two standard deviations from the mean for each of the four categories; 2005, p. 19). Not all of the studies analyzed found statistically significant semi-elasticities; by category, 44 of 105 time series (42 percent), 48 of 77 cross-sectional (62 percent), 55 of 136 discrete choice (40 percent) and 71 of 109 (65 percent) panel semi-elasticities were statistically significant for the dataset with extreme values removed. Overall, 51 percent of the semi-elasticities were significant. The median semi-elasticities were –2.75 for time series, –4.24 for cross-section, –2.80 for discrete choice and –2.41 for panel, with an overall median value of –2.91 (2005, p. 19, table 4.1). In other words, for a 1 percentage point increase in the tax rate, FDI fell by 2.91 percent.

Besides looking at the type of study, de Mooij and Ederveen consider a number of other variables: whether the FDI data controls for investment in plant and equipment and investments related to mergers and acquisitions (M&A) separately; how the studies measure their tax variable;[13] whether the home country uses an income tax system based on exemptions for overseas income, or taxes total worldwide income with credits for taxes paid abroad; whether certain variables such as agglomeration were controlled for; the median year for the study's data, to determine if higher levels of capital mobility characterize the later studies; and whether the study focused solely on intra-EU FDI flows. These were analyzed via dummy variables compared with a benchmark of (a) time series analysis using (b) all types of FDI with (c) national statutory tax rates and (d) no controls.

What does the meta-analysis show? The results (2005, p. 25, table 4.2) show that the type of study done has a substantial impact on the results of the study (adjusted R-squared of 0.48 – all reported statistics are for the full specification unless otherwise noted). The most striking finding is that, compared with time series studies, cross-sectional studies of asset allocation by US multinationals show semi-elasticities that are an absolute value of 11.21 points higher (in the negative direction).

Considering that the median semi-elasticity of cross-sectional studies is –4.24, and the mean –7.16, this is a very large effect. By contrast, and despite having the second-largest median semi-elasticity, discrete choice studies actually showed lower effects than the baseline, by 3.08 points. The effects of panel data were not statistically different.

Studies which focus on plant and equipment FDI rather than total FDI, which is often dominated by mergers and acquisitions (M&A),[14] show systematically greater effects of tax differences, with semi-elasticities 3.60 points higher. By contrast, studies focusing solely on mergers and acquisitions were 5.92 points lower than the benchmark; indeed, these studies often showed that higher taxes in the host country led to more FDI via M&A. It appears clear that lumping these two types of FDI into aggregate data is misleading. This finding is especially relevant for the study of investment incentives, since location subsidies are given for such physical investment, not for mergers.[15] If we think of incentives as negative taxes, this metaanalysis gives some support to the view that they do affect the location of investment.[16]

The type of tax data used also has a significant effect on the results in the studies analyzed. As compared with using country statutory tax rates, the use of state statutory rates, or marginal or average effective tax rates, increased the estimated semi-elasticities from between 1 and 2.5 points, while using either micro or macro average tax rates had no effect.

Studies that controlled for tax exemption vs. tax credit source countries were not significantly different, but studies with more recent data had a significant but tiny (0.13) increase in estimated effect, while studies using intra-EU data had a lower estimate by 1.60 points (the opposite of that expected by the authors; 2005, p. 24), while studies with controls for openness or agglomeration had estimated semi-elasticities that were 2.43 and 1.11 points lower, respectively (2005, p. 25, table 4.2).

These results are rather bewildering for the making of policy. De Mooij and Ederveen find that only half of the estimated semi-elasticities were statistically significant, and the various results are heavily dependent on the methodology used (cross-sectional studies having hugely higher estimates). For their part, Devereux and Griffith (2002, p. 98) conclude their survey of this literature quite tentatively, saying '...there is some evidence that taxes affect firms' location and investment decisions, although we do not have a very good idea about the size of this effect'. For her part, Dembour (2008, p. 91) finds the evidence for an effect of taxes on investment to be persuasive.

Case studies

Numerous case studies of incentives have been conducted. This section gives just a small sampling of them. Two lessons that stand out are that it is difficult to maintain the geographic focus of aid programs with specific economic criteria due to political special pleading and that countries with 'weak fundamentals' cannot make up for it via incentives alone.

Greenbaum and Bondonio (2004) conducted a comparative study of US Empowerment Zones and EU Objective 2 regions.[17] They examined three successive rounds of area designation in both programs to determine if they maintained a focus on the poorest areas they were designed to serve. In both cases, regression analyses predicting area designation performed much better in the first round than in subsequent rounds, from which they concluded that the programs lost some of their focus on the poorest areas (2004, pp. 328–9).

Bondonio and Greenbaum (2006) examine the incentives given to small and medium enterprises in the Objective 2 regions of northern Italy. Using a difference-in-difference methodology, they find a positive and significant effect of the incentives on employment in the relevant areas, at a cost between €15,900 and €29,400 per job. While higher than the per-job estimates reached with different methodologies, they were lower than the cost of enterprise zones in the UK or the US (2006, pp. 29–30). However, the biggest gains came in the areas that had seen the least decline, suggesting that these programs might not be as successful in promoting development in poorer areas (2006, p. 30).

Ayele (2006) examines the effect of incentives on small business start-ups in Ethiopia. In common with many other places, the government's location subsidies were ineffective in inducing firms to locate in the areas most needing investment, and the benefits were concentrated in just a few industries. The author argued that the incentives were relatively ineffective and he cautions other developing countries in their use.

International Monetary Fund economist Kevin Fletcher (2002) has analyzed tax incentives in Southeast Asia, specifically Cambodia, the Lao People's Democratic Republic and Vietnam. He found that they were frequently expensive (0.7 percent of GDP in Vietnam; 2002, p. 13), with no evidence that they increased investment, especially compared with 'simple, uniform regimes with low to moderate rates of taxation', and he recommended accelerated depreciation over tax holidays (2002, p. 16). Moreover, he cites similar results in related studies for Mexico, Pakistan, Indonesia, Brazil and Malaysia (2002, pp. 11–12).

Aldaba (2005) notes the creation in the Philippines of ever more generous incentive programs, primarily in export processing zones. She argues that despite having programs similar to those of Thailand, Indonesia and Malaysia, the Philippines lagged behind in attracting foreign investment. She concludes that countries with 'weak fundamentals' cannot make up for that with investment incentives (2005, pp. 24–5).

By contrast, IMF economists analyzing the case of the Philippines, while recommending replacement of tax incentives, came down against adding accelerated depreciation to a general tax rate reduction (Botman et al. 2008, pp. 25–6). They report that the cost of 'redundant' incentives, that is, those given to investments that would have been made even in the absence of the tax holiday, was about 1 percent of GDP (Botman et al. 2008, p. 6), even higher than Vietnam. They argue that tax holidays are particularly prone to the redundancy problem, because highly profitable investments certainly would have been undertaken anyway. Further, the problem they see for the Philippines is tax rates that are higher than its neighbors', and this is true with and without incentives as its neighbors also give generous incentives (2008, pp. 11–12).

Further considerations for developing countries

Moran et al. (2005, p. 382) report the disturbing trend that there has been increasing competition between developing and industrialized countries for particular investments. They cite findings that MNCs' responsiveness to taxes and incentives has increased the most for manufacturing investment in developing countries. In their view, developed nations led the increase in incentives and 'Developing countries [were] drawn into this competition for FDI' (p. 382). They argue for an agreement that would limit incentives in the North and permit greater investment subsidies in developing countries. A recent example is the competition between cities in Brazil, Mexico and the US states of Tennessee, South Carolina, North Carolina and Georgia for an ATM manufacturing plant built by NCR Corp. Columbus, Georgia, won the facility with a $10 million incentive package (Williams, 2009).

Whether incentives promote growth in developing countries is a difficult question. If FDI increases growth, and incentives increase FDI, the answer must be yes. While some analysis (e.g., Carkovic and Levine, 2005) finds that FDI *per se* does not promote growth, Blonigen and Wang (2005), studying developed and developing countries separately, show that FDI increases growth in developing nations but not industrialized countries. Recent IMF research (Klemm and Van Parys, 2009) challenges even this finding. Their analysis in a panel of developing countries found that while incentives increased FDI in these host countries, they did not increase either overall investment or economic growth, a result they attribute to possible crowding out of domestic investment by foreign investment (Klemm and Van Parys, 2009, pp. 19–20). While Moran (2005) found that FDI only increases growth in developing countries when coupled with open trade policies,[18] Klemm and Van Parys controlled for openness, contradicting Moran's finding. Mutti (2003, p. 68) shows that US MNCs are particularly sensitive to taxes in developing countries when considering export-oriented projects, adding to the discussion above suggesting that incentives do matter. However, it is unclear if locational tournaments will drive up incentives enough to dissipate the gains, a problem Moran (2005, p. 309) acknowledges.

Conclusion

The literature on investment incentives is rich and deep. Some of the most important themes that emerge from it are the potential for enhancing efficiency if investment is channeled to areas of greater poverty or higher unemployment, the possibility that optimal incentive regulation can promote greater welfare, and the difficulty in achieving cooperation for such regulatory goals. Moreover, overbidding for investment is a constant danger, perhaps particularly so in developing countries. Even in industrialized countries, uncontrolled auctions can break out when there are many jurisdictions with similar characteristics competing for an individual investment. Part of the reason for this is the tendency for geographically targeted programs to become less focused over time. Finally, while incentives do appear to have some effect on the location of investment, they may not be very useful if a jurisdiction does not already have supportive political and economic fundamentals in place. Furthermore, the Prisoners' Dilemma-style interactions of bidding for projects may reduce or even eliminate any gains that come from attracting investment.

3
Policy Studies

This chapter will consider general policy studies covering a wide variety of issues, including effectiveness, cost, transparency, monitoring, rent-seeking and the specific concerns of developing countries. Transparency is perhaps the most important issue, because too much of incentive policy is conducted behind closed doors. Monitoring of incentive agreements is frequently lacking, and many companies have received subsidies only to close their doors soon thereafter, or never fulfill their job creation promises. Because of the frequent lack of transparency, we often have no idea what a jurisdiction's overall spending is (this is true for most US states, for example). Many studies cast doubt on whether using incentives really increases investment, a finding that has been replicated in a number of countries.

This chapter highlights some of the main policy issues that arise in connection with investment incentives, except for disciplines, which are considered in Chapter 8. In particular, we focus on the need for transparency, the difficulties in evaluating the costs and benefits of incentives, the common lack of ex post auditing of incentive programs, clawbacks, the problem of rent-seeking, spillovers and incentives for research and development, the role of site location consultants in obtaining incentives, the design of incentive programs, the politics of investment incentives and how best to promote benefits from an investment receiving incentives.

Transparency

Transparency is both a political and a research issue. The ability to know what has been given to a particular company cannot be taken for granted. Negotiations over incentives are often conducted in secret; indeed, a government may not know the identity of the company, dealing only with a site location consultant instead. Governments that are competing for a specific investment, whether they obtained the investment or not, frequently wish to obscure from their competitors what they offered or were willing to offer. Moreover, as LeRoy (2005) points out, secret negotiations make democratic accountability close to impossible. For the researcher dealing with incentives globally, the amount of information varies widely, and is close to non-existent for non-democratic governments. Even in the European Union, which ranks tops in transparency due to Treaty requirements that all state aid must be notified in advance to the European Commission, not all aid is classified in a way that it can be identified as an investment incentive. While most regional aid is used for incentives, not all is; similarly, some but not all subsidies for research and development may be functioning as an investment aid, and a small amount of aid for energy and the environment also consists of investment incentives, such as for biofuel production facilities.

In Australia and Canada, annual reports on state and provincial incentives are made pursuant to their respective anti-poaching agreements (see Chapter 8). However, in both countries these documents are not public records, significantly reducing transparency.

In November 2007, the NGO Good Jobs First evaluated all 50 US states and the District of Columbia for their online disclosure of subsidies, procurement and lobbying. It considered ease of use, completeness of data and how far back it went and how soon data were made available. Subsidy disclosure was by far the worst of the three, with an average score of 28 out of 100. Twenty-seven states and the District of Columbia scored 0, while 23 had some level of subsidy disclosure. However, only two, Illinois and Iowa, scored above 80 (Mattera et al., 2007, pp. 3–5). There is a clear trend for more states and better disclosure, but it is happening slowly.

With the situation in many developed countries as bad as it is, it will be no surprise to the reader that the number one policy recommendation remains the same as in *Competing for Capital*: improve transparency.

Evaluating the costs and benefits of incentives

Evaluating incentives in terms of costs and benefits is fraught with difficulties. The costs of incentives, especially in the aggregate, are often hidden from outside observers. Even where the terms of an incentive are not hidden, it can still be problematic to evaluate costs. One has to decide whether to count the cost to government or the benefit to the recipient. Fisher and Peters (1998, p. 3) point out that this important distinction is sometimes even ignored in economic development literature.

For example, suppose that a state government expands an airport as part of an incentive package for a manufacturing operation. Clearly the firm is not the only beneficiary from the incentive, so the benefit to the recipient is some fraction of the cost. On the other hand, the government would not have undertaken the airport expansion at that time, absent the intended private investment, and had to pay the full cost of the expansion. A second difficulty is that the costs often extend many years into the future, for example, in the case of tax abatement. In this case, the costs need to be measured in terms of present value, a point rarely appreciated by the press and occasionally absent even in academic discussion. The OECD (1995) has published a list of the interest rates it uses as discount rates for each of its member countries.

A special point to note is what might be called the illusion of costlessness. Many economic development and elected officials believe that offering incentives is costless because incentives are only awarded if you receive the investment. This is not correct for a number of reasons (UNCTAD, 2003, p. 124). First, if the investment would have been made without receiving incentives, the government will have directly given away grants or mortgaged future tax revenues. Second, there are opportunity costs to be considered: there might have been a better use of government money than attracting a business. Obvious examples are education, infrastructure and healthcare (LeRoy, 2005, pp. 197–200). Third, there are administrative costs. Fourth, if the incentive creates inefficiency (e.g., by inducing a firm to operate in an inefficient location), there is an economic cost to be paid even if there is not a visible financial cost to government. Fifth, discriminating among different firms or types of firms may introduce distortive effects. Sixth, tax breaks may lead to abusive transfer pricing.[1]

In addition to the problems adduced by UNCTAD, and contra the claim (2003, p. 141, n. 84) that tax incentives to firms that really would not otherwise have located *are* costless, this is not correct. As Klemm (2009, p. 11) points out, a subsidized investment indirectly creates losses in tax revenue when it crowds out unsubsidized ('more highly taxable') investment. Moreover, even if the investment would not have come absent the incentive, the incentive contributes to a strategic structure that creates losses for all parties as other jurisdictions offer incentives to offset those given in your jurisdiction (the 'arms race' metaphor). Your jurisdiction's subsidies create competition for existing firms in other jurisdictions (or even one's own), which will reduce their production or sales, or force them out of business as a consequence. Other jurisdictions will give subsidies, and this will harm existing firms in your jurisdiction or even their own. Retail facilities and North American auto assembly plants have both experienced this dynamic. For example, the East-West Gateway Council of Governments (2009, pp. 23–8) found that despite approximately $2 billion in subsidies to retail in the St. Louis region from 1990 to 2007, actual retail employment in the 2.5 million metropolitan area grew by only 5400 jobs (or $370,370 per job!), local retail sales per capita were flat, and local retail sales as a percentage of personal income actually fell. Thus, the $2 billion in subsidies essentially created repeated reshuffling of the location of retail sales without any significant increase in retail sales or employment.

Assessing the benefits of incentives is even more of an art form. Many governments compare an expected future increase in tax revenues with the taxes foregone, a methodology which again raises the issue of calculating their present value.[2] The biggest difficulties are determining what would likely have happened in the absence of the incentive and how much of the economic activity was really due to the incentive. While site location consultants and many government economic development officials will attribute all employment connected with a new investment to the incentive (as well as a multiplier effect, itself subject to controversy), recent studies suggest this leads to exaggerated claims.

Gabe and Kraybill (2002) find in a sample of 366 companies making expansions in Ohio from 1993 to 1995 that firms receiving incentives substantially overestimated the number of jobs they would create, while firms not given incentives made more accurate estimates. Indeed, they find that companies receiving subsidies created 10.5 *fewer* jobs than they would have otherwise (2002, pp. 717–19). They speculate (2002, p. 719) that this worsened outcome may be due to the effect of rent-seeking by the incentive recipients. Luger and Bae (2005), analyzing North Carolina's regionally differentiated Lee Act find that only one out of every 30 jobs claimed by subsidy recipients as being due to the incentives were actually induced by the incentives; that is, only 3.6 percent of the announced jobs 'otherwise would not have been created' (2005, p. 339). This changed the program's cost per job induced from about $5000 to $147,463! (2005, pp. 337–8). Similarly, Peter Fisher argues that for a fairly typical incentive package creating a 30 percent tax cut, only 9 percent of the claimed jobs will actually be induced by the incentive (2007, p. 67).

A recent study (Mejia et al., 2007) compared the economic models used in North Carolina and Virginia to determine how much to offer in incentives to a prospective investor. While this might seem like an arcane technical subject, the authors showed that they led to such divergent estimates of the value of a Dell computer-manufacturing facility that Virginia offered $37 million for it – while North Carolina received the investment with an offer of $242 million! Moreover, North Carolina estimated that 8086 jobs would be created or induced by the Dell investment, while Virginia's estimate was 4113 (Mejia et al., 2007, p. 1). They argued that North Carolina's model was flawed by using projected sales instead of job creation for estimating the economic impact, and in the case of Dell the state Department of Commerce made things worse by accepting Dell's sales estimate rather than deriving its own.

Beyond the technical problems that may be present in cost-benefit analysis, it may be argued that any such analysis that stops at the jurisdictional border is beside the point (Thomas, 2000, p. 10): it does not consider the effects on neighboring jurisdictions and it does not consider the counterfactual of obtaining an investment without incentives.

The need for evaluation of incentives and incentive programs

LeRoy (1994) was one of the most comprehensive early works on the administrative oversight of incentive programs. It is a litany of broken promises, subsidized job piracy (often using federal funds), and documented rent-seeking without any post hoc evaluation of the results of incentive programs. Did companies hire as many people as they said? What were the wages paid? If legislation requires that this information be reported for all company-specific deals, it is possible in principle to carry out such evaluation. In the case of automatic incentives, such as tax-credit programs, there are no individual agreements to enforce on companies, as can be done with clawbacks of granted subsidies.[3] However, as LeRoy points out, if firms are required to disclose the tax credits they receive, it becomes possible to determine the overall job performance of firms awarded these subsidies (2005, p. 189). Again, this dovetails with the importance of transparency, which is necessary to make evaluation possible.

Rent-seeking by firms

The possibility of firm-specific benefits creates the possibility of rent-seeking behavior by firms (Blomström and Kokko, 2003, p. 17), which is exacerbated by the secrecy with which most subsidies are negotiated.[4] Markusen and Nesse (2007, p. 11) note that many firms did not initially see the potential for extracting rents in their site selection and relocation processes. While they attribute the rise of site selection consultants as key to this process, and location consultants are now a key factor exacerbating it, Bartik (2007) makes a convincing argument that the underlying declines in transportation in communications costs (i.e., an increase in the mobility of capital) were more critical. Moreover, some companies were learning to take advantage of their increasing mobility without using consultants (Thomas, 1997, p. 140).

LeRoy (2005) documents numerous cases of corporate rent-seeking. Indeed, any time an investment is made that would have been profitable without incentives, we should presume that the receipt of an incentive indicates the presence of rent-seeking. One way to control rent-seeking is to reduce the information asymmetries in the bargaining process by regulating site location consultants as lobbyists (LeRoy, 2005, pp. 192–3). See below for discussion of ways to minimize rent-seeking through incentive design.

The significance of spillovers

Blomström and Kokko (2003) review the evidence on spillovers which, as we saw in Chapter 2, is an important potential reason for using incentives. They conclude that spillovers do exist but are not automatic, and probably require a minimum level of technological and workforce sophistication among domestic firms for spillovers to occur (2003, p. 16). They note, however, that it is difficult to calibrate subsidies to the spillovers that will result from any given investment, creating the danger that governments may pay too much and actually reduce national welfare, a situation that is more likely when there is a multitude of governments bidding for FDI (2003, p. 17). Thus, in their view incentives should form part of a comprehensive industrial policy that may include incentives to domestic companies to make them better able to absorb spillovers (2003, p. 21).

Turning to an area in which the spillover argument is especially apropos, research and development subsidies (some of which takes the form of investment incentives) seem to be increasing. In the European

Union, it was the third largest horizontal aid in 2005 at €5.7 billion (European Union, 2006b, Table k5_4). Many Canadian provincial officials have come to favor R&D support as a relatively nonspecific subsidy that is less likely than other types of aid to attract countervailing duty complaints from the United States (interviews, spring 2007). Numerous US states have tax incentives for R&D. Its popularity notwithstanding, it is likely that R&D aid exacerbates regional inequality, as Thomas (2000) reported. Richer countries within the EU devoted more of their state aid to R&D than did the Cohesion Countries in the 1990s (2000, pp. 220–3); today, however, both Spain and Ireland have converged on the EU-27 average, as have a number of the new Member States (European Union, 2010b). On the other hand, if we compare industrialized and developing countries' use of R&D subsidies, the disparity is likely wider than that which prevailed in the EU in the 1990s.

The emergence of incentive reform politics

In many democratic countries, a politics of investment incentives has emerged. Large numbers of critics have entered the political process to end or limit subsidies. Thomas (2000) documents some early examples in the United States and Canada. He points out also that the existence of multiple critiques of incentives means that there has been scope for unusual alliances bridging the usual Left/Right divides. In Israel, a large subsidy given to Intel Corporation led lawmakers to cut the maximum subsidy from 38 percent to 20 percent of the cost of the investment (24 percent for small investments). That first $600 million incentive was to have been cut as well, but Intel threatened to leave if the original agreement was not honored, which successfully obtained the subsidy but left a bad taste in a lot of people's mouths (Sher, 1999, p. 40; Toronto Star, 2000). Israel refused to provide even 20 percent in 2000 (Lyons, 2000, p. 16), and lost a bidding war to Ireland over a subsequent chip plant (O'Connor, 2000, p. 55).

The politics of investment incentives has spread to democratic developing countries as well. In Brazil, the 1998 elections in the state of Rio Grande do Sul brought the Workers' Party (PT) into office for the first time. The new administration immediately challenged incentives its predecessor had agreed to provide to Ford and General Motors for assembly facilities there and reopened the negotiations on these projects. While a new agreement was reached with GM, Ford rejected the government's demands and relocated the project to Bahia after a new six-week bidding war (Cavalcante and Uderman, 2004).

In India, the seizure of farmland for industrial development (analogous to eminent domain in the United States) has provoked sometimes violent responses from farmers. The Tata Nano project, originally slated for the state of West Bengal, was met with two years of resistance by farmers claiming they were underpaid for their land, including physical blockades of the property and violence (Coffin, 2008, p. 14; Kinetz, 2008). Ironically, in this case it was a left-wing government defending the Tata facility, which was ultimately abandoned and moved to Gujarat when the company gave up on West Bengal (Leishemba, 2008). At the same time, the leading party in the West Bengal Left Front, the Communist Party of India (Marxist), was a major opponent of the national Special Economic Zone (SEZ) legislation, particularly in the area of transferring land to private developers, land speculation and loss of state government revenue (Communist Party of India [Marxist], 2006).

One question that arises when incentives are politicized is whether it makes economic sense for an individual government to unilaterally cease offering investment subsidies. If there is a strategic element to incentive competition, the answer is probably 'no'. The most desirable locations with the most bargaining power might be able to avoid providing incentives, but other jurisdictions would find it more difficult to do so.

Practical questions of incentive design and maximizing benefits from investments

An important question in designing incentive policies is whether subsidies should be given up front or over a period of time. Bartik (2007, p. 118) points out that incentives have more effect on business decision-making if they are paid sooner rather than later, in part because firms use large discount rates when factoring in future benefits. By contrast, Blomström and Kokko (2003, p. 19) argue against up-front incentives, suggesting that governments would be better off paying subsidies for R&D, education and training as they actually occur. Weber and Santacroce (2007) contend that paying for performance reduces rent-seeking and obviates the need to use clawbacks when commitments by investors are not fulfilled.

How can a government that has already decided to give incentives gain the most benefit from them? Weber and Santacroce (2007) suggest that the first key point is that a government must draw up an explicit contract with a company receiving subsidies (2007, pp. 3–4). While this recommendation is based on the history of US court cases in which unclear agreements were not held to bind companies to their commitments, this would appear to be good advice in any legal environment. Second, governments must be able to draw up reliable estimates of the costs and benefits of the incentives (Ibid., pp. 6–7) which, as noted above, is a difficult exercise to say the least. Third, the contracts must specify explicit goals and performance requirements that the investor must satisfy (Ibid., pp. 11–15). This includes such factors as the number of employees that must be hired to receive the subsidy, the wages and benefits that must be paid and so on. Note that these particular requirements do not violate the WTO's Agreement on Trade-Related Investment Measures (TRIMs), as it only bans export and domestic content requirements (see Chapter 8).

The contract should also ban relocation of a facility for a specified period of time as well as specify the date by which the company should have fulfilled its performance requirements (Ibid., pp. 18–20). Fourth, monitoring and disclosure requirements must be built into the subsidy agreement. Fifth, penalties for breach of contract should be substantial, including clawbacks of incentives awarded. Even better is for incentives to be back-loaded whenever possible – that is, subsidies should only be paid when a firm reaches its performance goals.

The European Union's Regional Aid Guidelines lay down broadly comparable rules. In the *Guidelines for National Regional Aid 2007–2013* (EU, 2006f), it is required that companies maintain the jobs supported by regional aid for a minimum of five years (three years for SMEs) and that the investor contribute 25 percent of the investment cost from its own funds or private financing (EU, 2006f, p. 8). As discussed further in Chapter 8, every region of the EU has a maximum aid intensity (subsidy divided by investment), and these maxima are progressively reduced for projects larger than € 50 million.

Conclusion

The policy challenges of using investment incentives are many. They are frequently not transparent, hindering democratic participation and accountability. Determining either the costs or benefits of incentives is difficult at best. But elected officials and economic developers should not fall victim to the illusion that incentives are costless. The possibility of rent-seeking behavior by firms is very real. Transparency, post-hoc evaluation and incentive design can all help reduce this danger. Up-front subsidies may have more of an incentive effect, but are more vulnerable to rent-seeking by investors. Spillovers are a potential justification for the use of incentives, but it is important to realize that not all investments have spillovers, and not all countries can take advantage of them even when they do exist. Bidding wars can offset or negate any spillover that is captured. Finally, it is worth noting that in many countries, the use of location subsidies has become subject to more open debate. Demands for greater transparency and accountability of subsidy use have occurred across the political spectrum.

4

Industry Case Studies: Steel, Biofuel Production, Semiconductors, Automobiles, Call Centers

This chapter will present case studies of incentives in five industries. The first concerns the steel industry. Classic locational tournaments have characterized the announcement of new plants, while during the current recession, companies have been asking for subsidies to avert shutdowns. The second case examines the use of incentives to biofuel production facilities (note: *not* general subsidies to biofuels) in a number of countries throughout the world. The third case is microchip fabrication, which pits several locations in the US and Europe against developing countries like Singapore, China and soon, India. Fourth, there will be a brief recounting of selected bidding wars for auto facilities in both the industrialized and developing world. Finally, we analyze a much less capital intensive sector, the call center industry. It will focus in particular on the use of incentives in the spread of this industry to India, South Africa, the Philippines, parts of the Caribbean and Canada, as well as some cases in the US where the use of incentives have been credited with a decision in their favor over competing jurisdictions in India. In all of these cases, there is no way to be exhaustive; instead, limitations of space and information availability play a role.

Steel

The steel industry is one of the pillars of industrial production, but one which has seen substantial global overcapacity for many years (Szladek, 2008). The European Union has had several sectoral frameworks on state aid to the steel industry stretching back to the 1980s until the expiration of the European Coal and Steel Community (ECSC) Treaty in 2002. These were aimed at promoting viable restructuring of steel firms in the context of capacity reductions (Thomas, 2000, p. 107). After the ECSC's expiration, the steel industry was covered by the Multi-Sectoral Framework or MSF (see Chapter 8), which simply banned regional aid to the industry (Szladek, 2008).[1] Hungary did propose an investment subsidy of €37.4 million to Dunaferr, the country's largest steelmaker in 2006, for what it said were non-steel projects in a less-developed region of the country (Hartley, 2008; European Union, 2008a). The European Commission launched an investigation under the MSF because of the ban on aid to the industry in April 2008, forcing the cancellation of the proposed support (European Union, 2008a). Because of this ban, there have been no bidding wars for new steel plants in the EU, in sharp contrast to the situation in the rest of the world, to which we now turn.

1. United States

The biggest recent incentive package in the US, and the country's third biggest ever, went to ThyssenKrupp's first US facility in Mt. Vernon, Alabama, just north of Mobile. This $3.7 billion plant created 2700 jobs and received an $811 million incentive package (*Site Selection*, 2007). This is worth $734.3 million in present value terms (see Chapter 6), 19.8 percent of the investment or $271,963 per job. The site selection process was a classic location tournament, with site location consultant Cushman & Wakefield Global Consulting visiting 33 sites out of 67 initially considered, winnowed it down to 12 sites that were visited by ThyssenKrupp staff, considered three sites in Arkansas, Louisiana and Alabama, then conducted a public auction between Louisiana and Alabama beginning in January 2007 (*Site Selection*, 2007). The governors of both states made trips to Germany in February to make pleas to the company (Rawls, 2007a). The incentive was so large that it required the Alabama legislature to call a referendum for voters to approve a constitutional amendment raising the state debt limit from $350 million to $750 million, a measure that was overwhelmingly approved (Lyman, 2007, p. B01). The Alabama legislative action came in response to the Louisiana legislature approving a $300 million package for ThyssenKrupp in December 2006 (Rawls, 2007b). Alabama turned down pleas from US Steel that the incentives for its German competitor would harm the company, saying the investment was going to be made anyway (*Site Selection*, 2007). In the end, Louisiana officials said they could not provide as much as the company wanted, and 'We felt it was too rich for us to compete on that level' (Deslatte, 2007). In May, ThyssenKrupp announced it had chosen Alabama, and voters approved the debt limit increase on 5 June (*Site Selection*, 2007).

Alabama triumphed again when Swedish steelmaker SSAB held an auction between the locations of two of its existing facilities, in Apex, Alabama and Montpelier, Iowa, in 2008. At stake was a $460 million expansion to add a heat-treating line expected to create 180 jobs at wages of approximately $65,000 per year. Although Iowa offered $81 million in incentives, Alabama offered $45 million (not present value) in tax breaks plus a hard-to-value investment tax credit over 20 years (Amy, 2008, p.1). This equals $250,000 per job, though only 9.8 percent of the investment, based on the part of the incentive that can be calculated. According to a company representative, Alabama's incentives were 'superior' (Amy, 2008, p. 1).

A number of other localities won locational tournaments for steel plants in the US in the last two years, only to see the projects cancelled because of the recession. Among them was Scioto County, Ohio, which beat out locations in Québec, Arkansas and Kentucky for a $1 billion project by Russia's OAO Magnitogorsk Iron & Steel Works (Petry, 2008). At the same time, the recession saw companies demanding incentives from local governments if they wanted to avert a shutdown. Brazilian steelmaker Gerdau Ameristeel sought support from state and local officials for its Sand Springs, Oklahoma, facility in July 2009, but closed it in October (Arnold, 2009, p. E1; Hollingshead, 2009, p. E6). Gerdau also sought subsidies from Jacksonville, Florida, in January 2010, but the outcome was not known at the time of this writing (Harding, 2010, p. D-1).

2. Russia, Vietnam and Thailand

The use of incentives for new steel projects is occurring in developing countries as well, though detailed information is less available than it is in industrialized nations. For example, Russian steelmaker OMK-Steel was slated to receive a $117.6 million tax incentive package from the Nizhny Novgorod regional government for a $1 billion casting plant, including a reduced corporate income tax rate (SKRIN Market & Corporate News, 2008). Meanwhile, in 2008 Vietnam gave a special 10 percent corporate income tax (the usual rate is 32 percent) for a gigantic steel mill/port complex to Son Duong Formosa, a Taiwanese firm. The project is located in the Vung Ang Economic Zone in Ha Tinh province, one of the poorest in the country, with a planned first phase costing $7.9 billion (Vietnam News Briefs, 24 December 2008).

Vietnam was also competing for a mega-project from Thailand's Sahaviriya Steel Industries Plc, a planned 500 billion baht (approx. $15 billion) smelter that would be the first of its kind if located in Thailand. Originally planned for Bang Saphan in central Thailand (to supply its steel plant there), the company claimed it would cost 90 billion baht less to build it in China or Vietnam (Thai Press Reports, 2008). Moreover, the company ran into strong local opposition concerned about the environmental and health impacts of the facility. As a result, at the time of this writing the company was considering all options, working on a 'health impact assessment' at the Bang Saphan location, while also seeking to either acquire or build a smelter elsewhere within ASEAN (Thai Press Reports, 2010).

3. Conclusion

Like the other capital intensive industries studied in this chapter, the steel industry routinely seeks and receives investment incentives, even in the face of global overcapacity. The lure of thousands of high-wage jobs continually draws economic development officials like a moth to a flame, enabling companies like ThyssenKrupp to conduct massive 20-state locational tournaments capped off with an auction between two finalists. Reinforcing the truth of Peter Fisher's comment that governments use incentives 'in good times and bad, in poor states and rich states' (Fisher, 2007, p. 70), steel firms demand incentives when they invest during expansionary periods, and demand them again by threatening to shut down during recessions. The case of Sahaviriya Steel Industries in Thailand is a fascinating one as an example of state-firm bargaining: negotiations have gone on seven years already (Thai Press Reports, 2010), suggesting that the company strongly prefers the domestic site near its steel mill, but the government so far has called its bluff. In this high-stakes battle, a deciding factor may be the ASEAN Free Trade Agreement, which increases Sahaviriya's ability to import from lower cost countries like Vietnam, representing an increase in the company's mobility in production: 'Reducing tariffs ... makes countries more substitutable for each other' (Thomas, 1997, p. 56).

The situation in the European Union stands in sharp contrast to that elsewhere. The seemingly inexorable progress the EU has made on controlling investment incentives, first under the Multi Sectoral Framework and now through the Regional Aid Guidelines into which the MSF has been incorporated, has meant an end to the use of investment subsidies in the steel sector of the EU. Hungary's Dunaferr learned first-hand that the European Commission meant what it said when it banned state aid to the industry. In Chapter 8, we will review EU state aid policy at length.

Biofuels production facilities

Koplow (2006) has examined the subsidies to biofuels in the United States, which include mandates to use biofuels as well as direct subsidies at the federal and state level for fuels such as ethanol and biodiesel. Here we consider only support for individual biofuel production facilities. As Koplow (2006, pp. 32–4) notes, state and local governments in the United States have rushed to provide new incentives for these plants, as well as providing location subsidies under existing economic development laws. The same is true in countries around the world.

Biofuels plants do not generate large numbers of jobs. An $80 million plant might only have 80 employees. Nevertheless, there have been a number of instances where bidding wars broke out among competing jurisdictions, in part because they also increase demand for local agricultural products such as corn or canola. This shift has a dark side: it drives up the prices of food for consumers in poorer countries.

In January 2006, Bangor, Michigan and Fremont, Indiana, competed for a $7.5 million facility from Michigan Biodiesel LLC. Bangor got the plant with a package of tax abatements and the creation of a Renaissance Zone. Zone status allowed it to exempt the plant from virtually all state and local taxes (Smith, 2006, p. B2).

In March 2006, the town of Claypool and the state of Indiana gave $7 million to Louis Dreyfus Agricultural Industries LLC to build the world's largest biodiesel plant at a cost of $135 million. When completed, the facility was expected to employ 85 people (Smith and Glenn, 2006, p. B7). One Louis Dreyfus official 'said the company looked for a long time and picked Indiana for several reasons, including the abundance of soybeans, competitive truck and rail access to feed markets, and support from state officials' (Groppe, 2006), suggesting a competitive dynamic was at work in this site selection process.

In July 2006, a bidding war broke out across the 49th parallel as five local governments in North Dakota, Manitoba and Saskatchewan were named as finalists for a James Richardson, Inc., canola crusher (Lyons, 2006, p. C5). In September, the company announced that the $100 million plant would be built in Yorkton, Saskatchewan. According to Saskatchewan's regional economic development minister, the company received training grants and road upgrades (Broadcast News, 2006). The significance of this facility is that canola oil can be used for biodiesel.

In the Czech Republic, the government awarded 'significant' subsidies to PLP for a $57.6 million biofuel plant in Trmice in 2006. Not revealed, however, was either the exact amount of the award, or the possible existence of competitor locations (*Central Europe Energy Weekly*, 18 August 2006).

Also in 2006, the Swedish firm Sekab announced that it would build four ethanol plants in Hungary at a cost of €343 million. According to *Central Europe Energy Weekly* (8 July 2006), 'Sekab plans to apply for state subsidies for its project, dubbed EnviroParks, but declined to specify a forint amount, noting only that EU rules allow subsidies of up to 40 per cent of project costs.'[2]

In Germany, Ethanex announced that it was teaming up with a group of governments (the city of Berlin, five *Länder* and the federal government) to build ethanol plants in the country. Based on European Union mandates to use biofuels, the company planned to build a series of plans in Germany, accessing investment incentives of up to 50 percent for the facilities (*Kansas City Business Journal*, 2006).

In Egypt, Sokhna Biodiesel Company planned a $17.5 million biodiesel facility in the North West Suez Economic Zone. This plant was also oriented to the European market based on the EU fuel mandates (*The Middle East*, 2006). Foreign trade zones in Egypt are exempt from corporate income tax and enjoy a host of other benefits (Diamond and Diamond, 2006, pp. 2–25).

Brunei's first methanol plant was announced in February 2006. The Brunei Darussalam Methanol Consortium unveiled plans for an 850,000 ton per year facility to be built in the Sungai Liang Industrial Park. Its agreement with the government required the consortium to source 80 percent of its needs from domestic small and medium enterprises (SMEs) and to set up a technology center, in return for unspecified incentives (Othman, 2006). While methanol is not a biofuel, it is a key ingredient of biodiesel.

In Brazil, Goiás state gave tax breaks worth five times the amount of the investment, approximately $209,333 per job to Canadian ethanol producer Usina Canada in April 2009. The R$53 million, 600-jobs facility was to locate in the city of Acreuna, and receive R$273 million, about $125.6 million at the time of the announcement (Latin America News Digest, 2009).

Biofuel production facilities are springing up rapidly throughout the world. Due to the agricultural inputs needed, many of these are located in quite small communities. As a result, incentives are also spreading to small municipalities where they may have never been used before.

Microchip fabrication

Microchip fabrication is a highly capital-intensive process that is essential to the high-tech economy. Facilities are expensive, and governments are willing to grant correspondingly large incentives. Long dominated by US-based Intel, the industry is seeing heavy investment by two Chinese companies, Grace Semiconductor Manufacturing Corporation and Semiconductor Manufacturing International Corporation (SMIC). Boosted with heavy government subsidies, they have ramped up production rapidly (*Site Selection*, 2004).

One common feature in semiconductor site location decisions is a preference for clustering. New plants are often built adjacent to old ones, and when companies do pick a greenfield site, they usually obtain extra land to allow for future clustering. For example, in 1993 Intel examined locations in six US states for a $2 billion fabrication plant, all of which were adjacent to existing facilities (Thomas, 2000, p. 174). In fact, 'Intel, which makes chips in the United States, Ireland and Israel, hasn't built a fab [fabrication plant] at an entirely new site in 15 years' (Clark, 2007, p. B6). (In 2007, this came to an end when it decided to build a fabrication facility in China.)

Though these facilities define the cutting edge of technology, they are not without their drawbacks. In particular, they use enormous amounts of water, and can be quite polluting: Intel has three locations that qualified for so-called Superfund cleanup in California (SouthWest Organizing Project, 1995, pp. 13, 73–8). The use of numerous toxic chemicals in the fabrication process has an environmental impact that is multiplied by the rapid technical obsolescence of chips (Mazurek, 2002, p. 193).

In 2000, International Business Machines (IBM) received substantial incentives from New York, with about $475 million in a variety of tax breaks and $28.75 million in loans and grants from the state for its facility in East Fishkill (*Site Selection*, 2000).

Also in 2000, Intel awarded a new $2 billion fabrication plant to Leixlip, Ireland, which had competed against Israel, New Mexico, Arizona and Oregon. For this facility, it received about $105 million in state aid (Lyons, 2000, p. 16; O'Connor, 2000, p. 55).

In 2003, Advanced Micro Devices (AMD) decided to build a new plant in Dresden, Saxony, in the former East Germany. Dresden is located in an 'A-level' assisted region for state aid purposes and an 'Objective 1' region for EU regional funds, and therefore able to offer large incentives with EU co-funding (Marsh, 2007). This $2.4 billion factory received

$1.5 billion in aid, but as most of it was in the form of a loan guarantee, the gross grant equivalent (GGE) was deemed to be only 22.67 percent of the cost of the investment, or about $544 million (Landler, 2003, p. C1; European Union, 2004a). Both East Fishkill, New York and Austin, Texas, the latter of which had substantial investment from AMD already, bid on this project.

In 2004, Intel and Ireland agreed to a €1.6 billion fabrication plant at Leixlip, again beating out Israel, the United States and unnamed greenfield sites (Smyth, 2004, p. 1). However, the European Commission refused to allow Ireland to award a €170 million aid package. A comparison with the Dresden AMD package is instructive. Both were examined under the Multi Sectoral Framework (see Chapter 8). Even though the aid intensity in Germany was twice as high as in Ireland, it was approved while the Irish support was rejected. Two factors were key: First, Ireland's award was to Intel, the dominant producer in the industry, with 74 percent of the world semiconductor market at the time (O'Brien, 2006, p. C3). By contrast, Germany's award was to the distant #2 producer, AMD. Second, the level of economic need was much greater in Dresden than in Leixlip. Indeed, Leixlip, near Dublin, was already slated for a 2006 end in eligibility for regional aid (Staunton, 2005, p. 18). However, Intel hinted that it would have to reconsider further investment in Ireland in the wake of this decision, despite having sufficient space on its Leixlip site for two additional fabrication plants (Irish Times, 2005, p. 18; Smyth, 2005b, p. Finance 1).

In 2006, AMD announced a new microchip fabrication facility for Malta, New York, about 25 miles north of the state capital, Albany. The $3.2 billion plant received a total of $1.2 billion in incentives from the state and federal government (*Site Selection*, 10 July 2006). AMD also considered sites in Dresden, Germany and in Asia.

Meanwhile, New York was also attempting to land a semiconductor plant from Samsung, the Korean electronics giant. Unverified rumors put the offer at over $500 million (entirely plausible, since it gave more than twice as much to AMD), but in April 2006 Samsung announced it would build the new facility adjacent to its existing one in Austin, Texas. Incentives in Texas were 'only' $233.4 million (*Site Selection*, 4 May 2006).

Also in 2006, AMD announced a $2.5 billion (€2.2 billion) expansion of its two plants in Dresden (O'Brien, 2006, p. C3), expected to create 565 jobs, according to the European Commission's decision to raise no objections. In return, the company received €262.4 million in aid (European Union, 2007d), which equals 11.9 percent of the investment but a massive €464,425 per job.

In late 2005, Intel announced that it would build a $3.5 billion fabrication plant in Kiryat Gat, Israel, in return for $525 million in aid (15 percent of the investment) for the facility from the Israeli government. The facility was slated to employ 2000 (Devi, 2005, p. 23). The company also agreed to invest another $900 million in an adjacent existing fabrication plant. The grant was essential in securing the plant's location in Israel, according to the company:

> Intel Israel general manager Alex Kornhauser told the Finance Committee that work on the plant would begin within a few days and that the promise of state aid had helped Intel decide to build the plant in Israel rather than elsewhere. Alex Kornhauser explained to the committee members that one of the proposals Intel was considering was building a new factory in India, but because the government wouldn't provide a grant the management decided not to build a plant there, the Finance Committee said in a press release (Grayeff, 2005, p. 17).

Singapore has been an attractive destination for chip manufacturing as well. For example, in 2006, Intel and Micron announced a joint venture to build 30mm chips at a price of $3 billion (S$4.7 billion). While the incentives for the plant were not announced, one report pointed out the hot competition for iPods and other products using the chips, and noted, 'An equally competitive race among countries like Singapore to host their factories has also been ignited. Industry sources in the United States said Singapore's attractive tax incentives and the strong base of companies supporting the semi-conductor industry gave it an edge over Europe for the plant' (Ng, 2006b). This was a competitive situation, but it was not clear what other locations were considered (Ng, 2006a). In another case, Singapore beat out Portland, Oregon, when Siltronics declined to expand a facility in Portland in favor of building a new one in Singapore. Industry analysts were quoted as saying that Singapore's tax incentives for the $1 billion project 'far exceeded' Oregon's (Rogoway, 2006, p. C01).

In 2007, Intel announced that it would build a $2.5 billion fabrication facility in Dalian, China. While the company would not release the details of its investment subsidies there, Intel CEO Paul Otellini said it would be the company's 'most cost-effective' plant due to Chinese incentives. 'Intel has argued that it costs Dollars 1bn more to build, equip, and operate a chip fab in the US than in countries with more generous tax and other incentive policies', writes Dickie (2007, p. 27). However, due to US technology restrictions, Intel cannot build its most technologically advanced chips at the Dalian plant.

More countries want to get onto the fabrication bandwagon. India, which still imports all its chips from abroad, offers incentives that could be worth up to 35 percent of an investment (Velloor, 2007), but so far has had no takers and is turning to creating the 'India Microprocessor' from scratch (Singh, 2009).

The semiconductor industry is one where companies demand incentives and will not invest without them. This does not mean there is no room for negotiations, especially beyond the first factory at a given location, but the recent rise of Asian locations is going to strengthen the bargaining power of the companies in the coming years.

Automobiles

Investment incentives are a way of life in the automobile industry. Thomas (1997) examines the increase of location subsidies, first in terms of subsidy as a percentage of investment and later in terms of dollars per job, for the industry in the United States, United Kingdom and Canada over the period 1960–94. The cost of subsidies in North America increased over this period for pairs of companies and host governments (Ford and Canada, Chrysler and Illinois, etc.), while in the United Kingdom an initial increase was followed by a decrease (this finding led to the exploration of EU state aid policy in Thomas, 2000). A trend was also seen toward greater capital intensity, as aid began to fall in terms of incentives as a percentage of investment but continued to rise in terms of dollars per job. The case of the Brazilian automotive 'fiscal war' of the 1990s has been recounted in Rodriguez-Pose and Arbix (2001) and re-analyzed in Christiansen, Oman and Charlton (2003). Venkatesan and Varma (1998) discuss early incentives in the auto industry in India, which is elaborated in Oman (2000).

Central and Eastern Europe saw a series of location tournaments in the first part of the 2000s. Attracted by low labor costs and the prospect of eventual accession to the European Union, many of the multinational automobile manufacturers invested during this period. According to Hájek (2007), automakers locating in the Czech Republic have received investment incentives since 1998, which increased with the 2000 Act on Investment Incentives. For instance, in 2006 Hyundai received a package of grants, reduced-cost land and tax breaks totaling

€194.49 million on a €1.148 billion plant in Moravia-Silesia, Czech Republic (European Union, 2007a). Previously, however, the Czech Republic lost out to Slovakia for a Kia plant, despite 'offering the South Korean company 200 hectares of prime industrial land for 7 euros' (Bilefsky, 2004, p. B14). Also among the finalists was Poland, but no western European sites (Mackintosh, 2004, FT Report 4). Both Poland and Slovakia had offered parent company Hyundai 'tax relief, free land and new infrastructure' for the €1.1 billion facility (Ward, 2004, p. 15). In 2002, Poland had lost to the Czech Republic for a Toyota/Peugeot joint venture worth €1.5 billion (Ward, 2004, p. 15). The Czech Republic offered incentives, while Poland had not. Poland had, however, managed to attract $20 billion worth of foreign investment since 1989, but was in the process of revising its laws to create investment incentive programs (Reed, 2002, p. 13). Among other projects receiving incentives in Slovakia were the Getrag Ford transmission plant in Košice, where the company received €53.5 million for the €345 million facility (European Union, 2006c). This represented a reduction from the €77 million in aid initially agreed to by the Slovak government in December 2004, because it exceeded the region's 15 percent aid limit (Agence France Presse, 2004).

In 2005, Korean tire maker Hankook considered sites in Poland, Slovakia, the Czech Republic and Hungary before finally choosing the latter (Balogova, 2005b; Czech News Agency, 2005). Initially, the company had agreed to build its plant in Slovakia (Balogova, 2005a), but the coalition government's Cabinet decided against the Economy Ministry's 21 percent offer or a later proposed 19 percent offer. Moreover, incentives at that level would have run afoul of the Multi Sectoral Framework (see Chapter 8), which limited the aid it could receive there to 15 percent (Economist Intelligence Unit, 2005). When it became clear that the European Commission would not approve the 21 percent aid Hankook was seeking,[3] the firm reopened discussions with Hungary. Its decision sent the plant to Dunaújváros, where the rules of the Multi Sectoral Framework allowed an aid intensity of 21.82 percent. The Commission approved aid from Hungary of €92.6 million on an investment of €424.9 million, just under the limit (European Union, 2006d).

In 2007, Hyundai and Caoa Montadora S.A. opened a factory in Anápolis, in the Brazilian state of Goiás, with tax breaks from the state government and waived duties on imported Hyundais given by the federal government (Newton, 2007). In 2008, São Paulo state won a bidding war with Rio de Janeiro state for a Toyota plant for an undisclosed incentive package (Newton, 2008; interview, Rio de Janeiro, July 2009).

The year 2008 saw eight states in India vie for the Tata Nano plant after the company withdrew from West Bengal over land disputes with farmers (Mitra, 2008). Gujarat was the winner of this auction (Leishemba, 2008) with an incentive package estimated at £500 million (Blakely, 2008, p. 73). For further details, see Chapter 7.

In a case with multiple lessons, Toyota announced a new assembly facility for its RAV 4 sport utility vehicles in Woodstock, Ontario, in 2005 (Bruns, 2005). First, this only occurred after a long period in which Ontario received no new assembly plants while others had closed or reduced production. Indeed, according to Bruns (2005), it was the first new assembly plant in 20 years. Thus, it was only with the inauguration of Ontario's Auto Investment Strategy Fund in 2004 that the province resumed offering incentives to automakers after a long hiatus. Second, the project was noteworthy because Ontario only provided about a US$100 million incentive (Bruns, 2005), while several US states were offering substantially more for the 1300-job plant (Good Jobs First, 2009a). Clearly, Ontario had lower costs based on better infrastructure, a more skilled workforce than southern US states, and a national health insurance system that didn't make manufacturers pay directly for health care as in the US. Ontario and Canadian officials had to accurately appraise the value of these advantages in order to win the investment without the highest subsidy. Observers such as Paul Krugman (2005, p. A19) and subsidy reform NGOs such as Good Jobs First (2009a) hailed the decision as proving that providing public goods like education and health care was a better policy than throwing incentives at companies. I, too, was pleased to see the decision. However, it turned out that one swallow didn't make a spring. Not only was Toyota's next assembly plant in Mississippi, receiving $291.6 million for a 2000-worker facility in 2006, no new assembly plants went to Canada even as Ford received $219.8 million from Michigan in 2006, Kia $353.1 million from Georgia in 2006 and Volkswagen $450.1 million from Tennessee in 2008 (all these subsidies are listed at present value; see Table 6.1 and its sources).

We see, then, that the automobile industry is another one in which companies will no longer invest without receiving incentives. The lure of high-paying jobs, plus indirect jobs at suppliers, has made them an attractive target for economic development officials. Ironically, supplier facilities usually end up receiving incentives as well, due to their ability to operate from across a subnational boundary from the assembly plant.

One example would be Toyota's Huntsville, Alabama, engine plant, which received $30 million in subsidies in 2001 (LeRoy, 2008).

Call centers

Call centers, also known as customer support centers or customer contact centers, are part of a quintessential service industry. In a typical call center, workers are connected to phone lines and computers to perform sales or service functions. They can range in size from a handful of people to several thousand, but a more typical range is from several hundred to 1000. They can be characterized primarily by ownership and directionality. With respect to ownership, call centers can be in-house, such that center workers provide service for that company's products and are employees of that company. Alternatively, there are a number of companies that provide call centers for firms on a contract basis, in which case the center employees are not employed by the firm whose products they are selling or servicing, but by the independent firm. Some of the major companies involved with this are EDS Contact Center Outsourcing Services, Convergys, West and Sitel.

Call centers can be outbound (calling customers or potential customers) or inbound (receiving calls).[4] These differences are significant for labor relations (Good and McFarland, 2004), but are not very important for investment incentives, and will not be considered further here. Finally, there are gradations in the level of service that a call center might provide: higher end services are, naturally, more attractive to governments and likely to obtain larger incentives. An example would be the Research in Motion technical support center in Halifax, where the jobs are expected to pay about C$45,000 per year (Moreira, 2005, p. B6).

Labor represents a large percentage of the cost of a call center, meaning that call centers generally are not located in high-wage regions, but tend rather to be concentrated in rural or high unemployment areas of industrialized nations, or in developing countries. In addition, call centers tend to employ staff on a part-time rather than full-time basis, pay below-average (but above minimum) wages, and have a largely female workforce (Good and McFarland, 2004). Whatever the location, however, governments have commonly used location incentives to attract call centers. Even in India, where workers might only earn $1/hour (Good and McFarland, 2004), state governments have deemed it necessary to use inducements to land these facilities.

1. In North America, there have been numerous instances of bidding wars and poaching (offering subsidies to a firm to relocate an existing facility). Some US companies have sought out 'near-shore' locations such as Canada or onshore location due to dissatisfaction with offshore facilities. Customers in the United States, for example, have often complained about the accents of call center personnel or otherwise had unsatisfactory customer service experiences, leading to the shift in some firms' location strategies (Finlayson, 2004, p. G1). Dell is one example of a company that expanded its use of North American call centers for this reason. Indeed, in 2004 and 2005, Dell opened a string of call centers in both the United States and Canada, prompting bidding wars among a number of cities.

In July 2004, Dell announced that it would locate a call center in Edmonton, Alberta. Edmonton triumphed over Calgary, Winnipeg and three cities in the United States.[5] It put together an incentive package worth about C$6 million, including $1/year land and a property tax reduction for five years (Goff, 2005, p. D1). According to Kent McMullin, Calgary did not offer incentives, while Winnipeg did. He believes it was possible to land this deal without offering incentives, citing Edmonton's success in attracting Ford, GE Credit, Neiman-Marcus and Convergys without incentives (interview, 21 March 2007). While the original announcement called for a 500-person center, the company decided by year-end to expand it to 750. By early 2007, it employed 1300, according to McMullin. However, Dell closed this facility and another one in Ottawa (see below) in 2008 as part of company-wide cost-cutting efforts (Fitzpatrick et al., 2008).

Alberta opted out of the subsidies game at the provincial level in 1995 with the Business Financial Assistance Limitations Act (the only exception was for film production),[6] choosing instead to focus on a low-tax strategy (Thomas, 2000, p. 181). The lower tax rate does make it easier to resist the incentive wars, and the province's low unemployment rate due to the oil sands boom further strengthens its municipalities' bargaining power with potential investors.[7]

In October 2004, Dell chose Oklahoma City from 125 cities in the central and eastern United States for a major customer service center, weeding out nearby Norman, Oklahoma after establishing a temporary facility in Oklahoma City that July. The city provided 68 acres of free land five minutes from downtown. The facility, expected to eventually employ up to 3000 workers, was located in a federal empowerment zone and was eligible for a 5 percent rebate on payroll taxes, $950,000 in training grants, and financing through tax-free bonds (Mecoy, 2004, p. A1; Streuli, 2004).

In August 2005, Dell announced a new 500-seat call center in the Ottawa suburb of Kanata, which beat out Kingston and Kitchener-Waterloo, also in Ontario.[8] Provincial law prohibits local governments from giving incentives (Reese, 1993), so incentives negotiations generally focus on what provincial programs a company may be eligible for. Most commonly, a firm will qualify for a C$5,000 training grant annually for three years for every employee hired (see Fisher, 2007, p. 78 and Thomas, 2000, p. 269 on the point that 'automatic' incentives are far more expensive than discretionary ones). In fact, that is what Dell received for its Ottawa call center (Mayeda, 2005). As with other locations to be discussed, Ottawa may well have benefited from relatively low wages, which resulted from its own version of the dot-com crash in the early part of this decade. According to one document from the Ottawa Centre for Research and Innovation, call center workers there made about C$4–5000 less than in Kitchener-Waterloo or Toronto, and a whopping C$16,000 less than in Dallas or Atlanta (Denley, 2005, p. C1).

Beyond Dell, a major North American bidding war took place in 2005 over the aforementioned Research in Motion (makers of the Blackberry) technical support center. In this case, two US and two Canadian finalist cities were competing head-to-head, before the intervention of Nova Scotia premier John Hamm, who flew to Waterloo to meet with company chairman and co-CEO Jim Balsillie. According to one report, the company had already decided to go to the United States, but reconsidered after Hamm's visit (Tutton, 2005, p. D1). Another province in which cities cannot give incentives, Nova Scotia put together a C$19 million package of training and wage support. The company was reportedly also to be considered for support by the federal government's regional aid program for the Maritime provinces, the Atlantic Canada Opportunities Agency (ACOA). Tutton writes: 'Carmi Levy, a research analyst with Info-Tech Research Group in London, Ont[ario], said government money was likely key to the deal, but the major factor was Ontario's tight labour market. "Waterloo and Ottawa are talent markets that have been tapped dry by the major technology vendors in Canada and the United States," he said. "For now RIM has Halifax mostly to itself."'

In some other cases, locations in the United States have managed to defeat locations in India, receiving location subsidies from state and local governments in the process. For example, Headway Corporate Resources, in the process of moving its headquarters from New York City to Raleigh, North, Carolina, visited three cities in India before deciding to locate its call center in rural Tarboro, North Carolina.

Headway received $2.6 million in tax incentives (Rives, 2005). Systems Technology Group received $4.8 million in state tax credits, and another $45,000 in local assistance, for a $2.2 million, 356-job expansion in Troy, Michigan. It, too, decided on the US location after considering India (Gallagher, 2005).

2. Outside of North America, the call center industry is also growing rapidly, usually fueled in part with investment incentives. Until recently, however, South Africa experienced rapid growth in call centers despite a lack of tax breaks, which some industry analysts blamed for inhibiting further growth (*Business Day*, 2006). This included in-house operations from firms such as Lufthansa and Fujitsu, and contract operators such as the United Kingdom's AvantiCall. However, by 2006, South Africa had only 6000 call center jobs, and the government began using tax breaks to further expand its presence in the call center industry. UK insurer Budget received a tax break of about $1.8 million for hiring 211 unemployed workers. Altogether, the government committed about $140 million to the program (Thornton, 2006, p. 46).

3. The Philippines had only 2400 call center workers in 2000 but, by various estimates, from 112,000 to 260,000 by the end of 2006 (Khanna, 2006; Villadiego, 2006, p. 15; Vitug, 2006). Considered a priority area for inward investment, call centers can receive a minimum of four years free of income tax, while companies locating in economic zones (ecozones) can follow this up with a permanent 5 percent tax rate on gross income, with other incentives available as well (Mondaq Business Briefing, 2004). Dell is one of many foreign companies to benefit from this, in the Pasay City Mall of Asia ecozone (Flores, 2006). The country is also investing $9.6 million in English speech courses for 'near hires' who have insufficient command of the spoken language (Vitug, 2006).

4. In the Caribbean, Jamaica and the Dominican Republic are the leading call center destinations. Jamaica's call center growth has been in the 'free zones' in the Montego Bay area, where tax and other incentives are available (Hemlock, 2005, p. 1E). Among them are perpetual zero tax on income and profits, exemption from import duties, and free repatriation of profits. The biggest operator was e-SGI, which employed 4100 at the end of 2007 (Jamaica Trade and Invest, 2010). In the Dominican Republic, call center employment tripled from 2005 to mid-2008, making it the largest in the Caribbean (Thomson, 2008).

5. The call center industry illustrates several important themes. Most obviously, investment incentives are widespread throughout the world, both in industrialized and developing countries. Nations that had

avoided the use of incentives, such as South Africa, came under political pressure to offer them, and often succumbed. Finally, it is difficult to determine the value of individual deals when they include open-ended benefits such as permanent tax-free status.

Conclusion

There are several lessons we can draw from these case studies. First, in some industries (automobiles and semiconductors from among our cases), companies simply will not invest without subsidies. Both are capital intensive, especially semiconductor fabrication, which has on occasion received incentives of $1 million per job, compared with the usual maximum in the auto industry of between $100,000 and $200,000. Second, locations without a history in a particular industry usually pay the most (consider the extraordinary $340,000 per job reported by Rodriguez-Pose and Arbix for a Mercedes-Benz factory, or even Alabama's $100,000+ awards to several auto companies). These huge subsidies then put pressure on existing locations to offer greater incentives in order to receive new investments.

Third, the largest subsidy does not always win, although that will be the usual case when locations are closely balanced. Sometimes it is even possible to receive an investment in a competitive situation without incentives, as Edmonton's experience in the call center sector illustrates. However, for this to be the case, a government must accurately estimate its cost advantage over competing locations. Yet, as Jones and Bachelor (1993, p. 14) argue, information asymmetries between firm and host make this difficult. In the European Union, companies negotiating to receive regional aid must document their cost disadvantages relative to other potential feasible sites.[9]

Fourth, contra Bartik (1991), the places with the most economic need are not always able to give the largest incentives. In many instances, poorer regions can only give aid in the form of tax holidays, rather than the cash grants available in richer jurisdictions. In the European Union, this is not so much the case, because the less affluent Member States can use money received through the EU's Structural Funds in order to supply cash grants to investors. Moreover, with its state aid rules, the European Union allows higher aid intensity in poorer areas and can enforce that on Member States, as the example of Hankook makes clear. The routine use of the Multi-Sectoral Framework has enabled the EU to reduce grants in multiple cases, including to zero in the most recent Intel case from Ireland. Despite the presence of state aid rules, the European Union has seen above-average performance in attracting FDI, whether compared with the world average or that of industrialized countries only (Dreyhaupt, 2006, pp. 152–3).

The next chapter turns to the case of Ireland, frequently touted as the proof that investment incentives and low taxes equals development. The truth, as we will see, is more complicated.

5 The Celtic Tiger: Incentives, Infrastructure, Tax Rates, Luck?

Ireland is often held up in economic development circles as the success story that proves the effectiveness of using investment incentives. Yet Ireland pursued essentially the same strategy of attracting foreign multinationals from the 1950s through the 1980s with little success. In the 1990s, the Irish economy boomed, creating the Ireland we know today. This chapter will analyze the relative contribution of incentives, EU infrastructure and training support, education and low tax rates to try to determine what finally went right.

The biggest difficulty to seeing Ireland's success as being solely due to the use of location subsidies and low taxes is the fact that it began this strategy in the late 1950s, and right through the 1980s, there was little progress in converging toward average EU living standards (Jacobsen, 1994; Ó Riain, 2004). As Ó Riain (2004, p. 9) puts it, 'Economists see... free trade and foreign investment producing growth – although the same formula had yielded only economic failure before the 1990s'. Major industrial policy reviews in 1982 (the Telesis Report) and 1992 (the Culliton Report) found that Irish economic development policy paid too much attention to attracting foreign investment and insufficient attention to developing indigenous enterprise. As a consequence of the latter report, the government restructured the Industrial Development Authority, focusing it solely on foreign investment attraction, while creating a new agency (Forbairt, now Enterprise Ireland) charged with the development of domestic industry, and a body to coordinate their efforts, Forfás.

In this chapter, it is necessary to consider not only investment incentives, but also tax competition. This is because Ireland's most powerful incentive has been its low corporate income tax rate applying to foreign multinationals, which has ranged from 0 percent before Ireland's accession to the EU (grandfathered until 1982 and, for some companies, until 1990), 10 percent from 1982 to 1998, and 12.5 percent today. Unlike the ability to offer grants or the receipt of Structural Funds, which have declined due to changes in EU state aid rules and Ireland's increasing prosperity, this is an incentive that is not affected directly by Ireland's rising income. However, other EU Member States' political tolerance of Ireland's low-tax regime has eroded badly, as we shall see.

Why should we care about Ireland? For one thing, Ireland is one of the OECD economies most dependent on FDI: As recently as 2002, inward FDI stock was 149.6 percent of Irish GDP, though it has fallen significantly since then. By contrast, another country where FDI has been a major issue for decades, such as Canada, recorded its FDI stock at 36.7 percent of GDP in 2007 (UNCTAD, 2008a).[1] That Ireland is seen as an example for other countries is shown by the veritable parade of foreign economic development officials coming to Dublin in the hope of replicating Ireland's model and success. In just the past two years, economic development officials from numerous countries and regions have either visited Ireland or hosted Irish officials, including the United Arab Emirates, Israel, Argentina and Uruguay, the US state of Virginia and Nigeria, to name just a few (Emirates News Agency, 2008; Krieger, 2007, p. 17; Kirby, 2007, p. 17; US Fed News, 2008; *This Day*, 2009). The Industrial Development Authority, now IDA Ireland, was a pioneer of investment attraction. As Sean Dorgan, former Chief Executive, put it (2006, p. 5), 'It was the first dedicated state agency in the world to undertake a massive and sustained campaign to establish a modern manufacturing base by attracting large-scale foreign investment.' IDA was an active suitor of foreign multinationals and one of the reasons for Ireland's economic success of the 1990s–2000s, with real GDP growth rates averaging 8 percent annually from 1994 to 2004 (Dorgan, 2006, p. 2). At the same time, Ireland's experience has some cautionary notes and has not been without its problems. Most pertinent to this book, Ireland demonstrates strongly that investment incentives (including low taxes) alone cannot make up for the lack of fundamental economic structures making a place a good location for investment. The Celtic Tiger, moreover, has seen a substantial increase in inequality, with the bottom three deciles losing 1 percentage point of disposable household income between 1987 and 1998 (Kirby, 2002, p. 58), and has a high level of poverty (and child poverty) for an industrialized nation, ranking 18th of 19 industrial nations on the UNDP's Human Poverty Index-2, ahead of only Italy (UNDP, 2007, p. 241). It remains very dependent on foreign investment and quite vulnerable to changes in the tax policies of foreign nations, particularly the United States.

Given this book's primary focus on investment incentives, I will sidestep the major debates over how to characterize the nature of the Irish state and society, whether as a 'developmental network state' (Ó Riain, 2004), a 'competition state' à la Cerny (Kirby, 2002) or as a peripheral state in a dependency theory analysis (O'Hearn, 1995, 2001). I will, however, draw on insights from all these traditions as I trace the history of Irish development, especially since 1958.

Lastly, the chapter asks what happens next to the Celtic Tiger: Even before the current crisis, the country's very success has caused a sharp reduction in its EU Structural Funds, substantial limitation on its ability to use state aid, a loss of cost competitiveness, intense resentment of its low-tax regime by other EU Member States, and its branding by the US as a tax haven. The crisis itself has led to greater questioning of the very premises of the Irish model (Kirby, 2010). This chapter will examine the strains these factors could cause in the future.

Early history

Ireland became independent in 1922, though the island was divided as six of Ulster's nine counties remained part of the United Kingdom. Shortly before independence, Ireland was an overwhelmingly agricultural country that, nonetheless, stood about average in terms of European income per capita (see Table 5.1).

Table 5.1 GNP per capita as a ratio of UK, 1910

Country	Ratio (%)
Belgium	75.6
Germany	70.3
France	69.6
Denmark	67.6
Ireland	62.0
Norway	60.4
Sweden	60.3
Italy	40.5
Finland	34.6

Source: Lee, 1989, table 12, p. 513, based on Crafts, 1983, and Cullen and Smout, 1977.

The country turned to a classic policy of import substitution in 1932, with the first election of Eamon de Valera's Fianna Fáil. The protectionist policies continued until the late 1950s, and ended in a crisis of high unemployment and substantial net emigration. Non-agricultural unemployment in 1958 was 9 percent (Kennedy et al., 1988, p. 62), while emigration was averaging over 40,000 per year (see Table 5.2). Moreover, the country's population fell from 2.97 million in 1926 to 2.82 million in 1961, as emigration more than offset natural population growth (Central Statistics Office Ireland, 2009b).

Table 5.2 Net migration in Ireland, 1946–51 to 2008 (thousands)

Year(s)	Annual average or annual net migration
1946–51	–24
1951–56	–39
1956–61	–42
1961–66	–16
1966–71	–11
1971–79	14
1979–81	–3
1981–86	–14
1986–91	–27
1991–96	2
1997	19.2
1998	17.4
1999	17.3
2000	26
2001	32.8
2002	41.3
2003	30.7
2004	32
2005	55.1
2006	71.8
2007	67.3
2008	38.5
2009	–7.8

Note: In all periods, both Census periods and annual data, data is calculated for the year ending in April (personal communication, Central Statistics Office Ireland, 2009). The 1976 Census was postponed until 1979 for budgetary reasons (National Archives of Ireland, 2009).

Sources: 1946–51 to 1991–96, Central Statistics Office Ireland, 2000, p. 14; 1997–2008, Central Statistics Office Ireland, 2009a; 2009, Central Statistics Office Ireland, 2009e.

The government decided in 1958 on a major reorientation of economic policy. Secretary of Finance T.K. Whitaker completed in May of that year *Economic Development*, which was the basis of the government white paper *Programme for Economic Expansion*, and both were published in November 1958. Lee calls them 'historic documents…signaling a shift from protection to free trade, and from discouragement to encouragement of foreign investment…' (Lee, 1989, p. 344). IDA, which had been created in 1949 (Ó Riain, 2004, p. 75) was strengthened during the 1950s and oriented to the attraction of foreign investment (Kennedy et al., 1988, p. 62).[2] However, the policy change initially was set up in a way to cause the least disturbance to domestic companies: foreign companies were targeted with generous investment incentives, but the major tax concession on offer was the introduction of Export Profit Tax Relief (0 tax on export earnings, also called Export Sales Relief), designed to ensure that foreign firms would not be competing on the domestic market (Lee, 1989, p. 352; Kennedy et al., 1988, p. 63). There was some hope that domestic firms would also take advantage of EPTR, but few were internationally competitive (Dublin interview #1, March 2009).

The liberalization of the economy began affecting domestic interests in the 1960s, with the Anglo-Irish Free Trade Agreement of 1965 being followed by Ireland's accession to the GATT in 1967 and its inclusion in the first enlargement of the European Union in 1973. Accession to the EU required a major change in the country's tax regime, because EPTR was an export subsidy, and export subsidies for intra-EU trade are a clear violation of EU state aid law (Thomas 2000, p. 95). As Jacobsen (1994, p. 99) points out, the accession agreement required Ireland to replace EPTR, but the EU allowed it to replace it with a tax incentive that was equally lucrative. The IDA proposed that the country should have a 0 percent rate of corporate income tax (Dublin interview #2, March 2009). However, the final outcome was a 10 percent corporate income tax rate on manufacturing, and firms already benefiting from EPTR could continue to do so through 1990. In 1981, some services firms also became eligible for the new 10 percent rate (Ó Riain, 2004, p. 71).

The accession compromise allowing Ireland's 10 percent manufacturing corporation tax ultimately led to difficulties. As the Irish economy grew more successful, more companies located or relocated there to take advantage of the low corporate income tax rate. Because Ireland has a number of double taxation treaties with its major trade partners, the fiscal situation allowed for creative tax planning. Other EU members, such as France, complained that the CIT regime constituted unfair tax competition (Brussels interview with French EU representation, July 2000). Ireland, meanwhile, preached the gospel of low taxes as a universally desirable policy (Liam MacGabhann interview, 24 July 2000). CIT rates did indeed fall overall within the EU, though CIT/GDP and CIT/total taxation did not (Stewart and Webb, 2006). Debate continues over whether this non-fall is a statistical artifact based on the conversion of personal income to corporate income to take advantage of the fact that CIT rates are lower than personal income tax rates (Ganghof and Genschel, 2007, pp. 9–11). But as Ireland's boom continued, it increased the ire of other EU members. As the Director-General of the Luxembourg Finance Ministry told me, Ireland's success meant that 'The political basis for the low tax rate no longer exists' (Gaston Reinesch interview, 25 July 2000).

1958–87

The results of the new policy orientation were somewhat disappointing. Though the advent of free trade and efforts to attract foreign investment brought some growth,[3] the entire period from 1960 to about 1988 appears as a virtually flat line on a graph of Irish GDP per capita in relation to EU-15 GDP per capita at purchasing power parity (Barry et al., 1999, p. 14). While there was a strong tendency for OECD economies to converge in terms of GDP per capita in the 1958–87 period or longer, Ireland did substantially worse than would be expected on the basis of its income level (Ó Gráda and O'Rourke, 1996, p. 392). As Table 5.3 shows, even in the early 1970s, Ireland received a low level of FDI inflows, with a noticeable increase after accession to the EU.

Moreover, as we saw in Table 5.2, the period 1961–71 was marked by net emigration (though much lower than in 1956–61), as was the period from 1979–91. In addition, this latter period saw a decline in employment in which 1979 levels were not reached again until 1993, after which Irish employment exploded (Barry et al., 1999, p. 17). Similarly, FDI inflows into Ireland tailed off after 1978, when it achieved a level that would not be reached again until 1990 (and not until 1998 as a share of world FDI inflows). Ireland's performance in the first 30 years of its low tax/high investment incentive regime was not impressive and, as with import substitution, it ended in a crisis. Ireland saw high unemployment (see Table 5.4), emigration averaged 27,000 annually (see Table 5.2), and the country had a massive government budget deficit of 12 percent of GNP or more in every year from 1980 to 1986. Government expenditure was at or near 60 percent of GNP in the same

Table 5.3 Inward FDI flows into Ireland (Millions of current US Dollars and Share of World Total)

Year	Amount	Share of World Total (%)
1970	32	0.240
1971	25	0.175
1972	31	0.208
1973	52	0.252
1974	51	0.212
1975	158	0.595
1976	173	0.785
1977	136	0.502
1978	375	1.092
1979	337	0.796
1980	286	0.530
1981	203	0.292
1982	242	0.417
1983	170	0.337
1984	121	0.214
1985	164	0.293
1986	250	0.290
1987	322	0.236
1988	257	0.158
1989	193	0.098
1990	622	0.300
1991	1362	0.875
1992	1458	0.875
1993	1078	0.485
1994	857	0.334
1995	1443	0.423
1996	2617	0.670
1997	2136	0.440
1998	8865	1.257
1999	18,211	1.688
2000	25,779	1.866
2001	9651	1.176
2002	29,324	4.657
2003	22,781	4.031
2004	–10,608	–1.443
2005	–31,689	–3.256
2006	–5542	–0.379
2007	24,706	1.249
2008	–20,030	–1.180

Source: UNCTAD FDI-Stat Interactive Database, date accessed 28 December 2009 at http://stats.unctad.org/fdi/ReportFolders/reportFolders.aspx?sCS_referer=&sCS_ChosenLang=en

Table 5.4 Unemployment rate (percent)

Year	Unemployment rate (%)
1983	14
1984	15.6
1985	16.9
1986	17
1987	16.8
1988	16.1
1989	14.6
1990	13.2
1991	14.6
1992	15.2
1993	15.5
1994	14
1995	12.1
1996	11.5
1997	10.3
1998	7.4
1999	5.5
2000	4.2
2001	3.9
2002	4.4
2003	4.6
2004	4.4
2005	4.4
2006	4.4
2007	4.6
2008	6.3
2009	11.8

Source: Central Statistics Office Ireland (2009c), 'Seasonally Adjusted Annual Average Standardised Unemployment Rates (SUR) (%) by Year'; Central Statistics Office Ireland (2010), 'Seasonally Adjusted Standardised Unemployment Rates (SUR)'.

period, and Ireland ended 1986 with a national debt of 122 percent of GNP (Smith, 2005, p. 112).

Pressure on IDA

As Ireland's economy underperformed in the 1980s and early 1990s, the government commissioned two studies on Irish economic development. Both the Telesis (1982) and Culliton (1992) Reports concluded that Ireland overpaid for foreign investment[4] and devoted insufficient attention to developing domestic industry. IDA came under criticism in both reports, with major policy changes recommended in the Telesis Report, and an actual breakup of IDA recommended by the Culliton Report.

1. The Telesis Report

The Telesis Report, commissioned by the National Economic and Social Council (NESC), was the first major investigation of Irish industrial development policy. It reviewed manufacturing in depth and gave some consideration to agriculture and other natural resource-based industries as well. The consultants conducted extensive interviews with officials of foreign multinationals, all of which had considered Ireland as a location and most of which had invested there (Telesis Consulting Group, 1982, p. 198). They made comparisons with similar EU locations as well as with the 'newly industrializing tax havens' of Puerto Rico and Singapore. For a range of typical projects, they concluded that Ireland's incentives were almost always the most generous, often by large margins. They calculated Ireland's market share for new investment by companies that had not invested previously in a particular country, finding that 80 percent of such new projects in 1978–79 went to Ireland as opposed to Northern Ireland, Scotland, Wales or Belgium. The conclusion from all of this evidence was that Ireland generally overpaid for foreign investment. As the report notes, 'in most businesses, if a company has an 80% market share and gives the largest discounts it is usually appropriate to consider "testing the water" by raising prices (in this case, reducing grants)' (Telesis Consulting Group, 1982, p. 197). As a result, Telesis recommended sharply cutting grants to foreign multinationals and shifting the savings to promoting indigenous industry (Telesis Consulting Group, 1982, pp. 226–7). However, a 1984 government White Paper on industrial policy rejected this recommendation (Smith, 2005, p. 111).

In addition, the report emphasized that Ireland's evaluation process for incentives was flawed by a focus on 'job approvals' as opposed to actual job creation: 'Irish industrial policy aims to create jobs. As it is now designed, it expends too much energy creating job approvals. The two are not synonymous' (Telesis Consulting Group, 1982, p. 220). Further, the report noted, 'Most IDA staff members can quote job approval figures "off the top of their heads," but few are as well versed on actual job changes in industry' (Telesis Consulting Group, 1982, p. 241).

In hindsight, some of the Telesis recommendations proved wildly inaccurate. Most striking was its denigration of the value of attracting chip fabrication plants, due to lack of linkages and the riskiness of the market (Telesis Consulting Group, 1982, p. 228). Of course, Ireland's attraction of Intel to build an eventual four fabrication facilities is one of IDA's proudest achievements. Nevertheless, the issues of value for money and actual job performance would continue to bedevil IDA.

2. The Culliton Report

Ten years later, the Culliton Report (Culliton et al., 1992) revisited many of these issues in a broad-based examination of Irish industrial policy. According to one official involved in drafting the study, one of the important background factors for the report was the realization that Ireland was vulnerable to tax policy changes in the US. This was brought home to the government by a dispute between the Internal Revenue Service and Bausch and Lomb, followed by attempted changes to the US tax code that would have weakened Ireland's tax advantages (Dublin interview #2, March 2009). Going beyond a narrow definition of 'industrial policy', the Industrial Policy Group supervising the report additionally studied 'overall macroeconomic and fiscal policy, the level and structure of taxation, the effectiveness of education and training and the provision of adequate infrastructure' (Culliton et al., 1992, p. 22). The report argued that manufacturing was dominated by MNC enclaves with little integration with the rest of the Irish economy (Ibid., p. 23). It applauded EU competition policy as a means for protecting Ireland from monopolistic abuses and from the need to give large amounts of state aid (Ibid., p. 28).[5] The report argued that taxation as a percentage of GDP was too high given its relatively low GDP/capita, and promoted a reduction in special tax exemptions which the Industrial Policy Group saw as having little coherence (Culliton et al., 1992, p. 38). One of the most important recommendations was that Ireland end the 10 percent rate for corporate income tax when it expired in 2010. As the report stated:

> The 10 percent regime (and previously Export Sales Relief) has been the single most effective tool in inducing inward foreign investment. Yet, it has not been without its drawbacks from the point of view of industrial development. For example, since costs incurred by manufacturing firms in Ireland attract little tax relief, firms rarely choose Ireland as a location for cost centers involving, for example, high-level management and support functions. The 10 percent rate, in

> combination with other measures, tends to encourage unnecessarily capital intensive production. It has led to a variety of complex tax avoidance schemes which tend to channel the benefits of the low tax rate away from manufacturing. Finally, the 10 percent rate has been far more valuable to foreign-based than to Irish-owned industry. It has clearly not acted as a spur to the development of the indigenous sector to anything like the same extent as for the foreign sector (Culliton et al., 1992, p. 40).

The Report found that IDA's performance on directing more grants toward indigenous firms and away from multinationals, recommended by the Telesis Report, had not been achieved: The proportion going to Irish firms had only risen from 51 percent in 1985 to 54 percent in 1989, rather than the Telesis target of 75 percent (Culliton et al., 1992, p. 62) Another important issue raised in the Culliton Report was job performance and cost per job. As with the Telesis Report (cf. Dublin interview #1, March 2009), Culliton again raised the issue of companies creating far fewer jobs than promised (Culliton et al., 1992, pp. 63–5). Citing a study carried out by the Department of Industry and Commerce, the report says plants existing at the end of 1980 received IR£ 946[6] million in 1990 prices[7] by the end of 1990; yet, instead of creating 61,500 jobs, they had collectively lost 45,000 jobs.[8] Grant-aided new start-ups in 1981–90 had promised 103,000 jobs, but created only 52,000 (Culliton et al., 1992, p. 63). The collective result was an expenditure of IR£ 1.6 billion for 7000 jobs (p. 65) which, though the Report does not say it, is over IR£ 228,000 per job. The Culliton Report then goes on to recommend reducing the amount of grants for foreign MNCs by providing a fixed budget rather than cost-per-job limits alone, and that most support for domestic firms should take the form of equity or venture capital rather than grants (Culliton et al., 1992, pp. 71–5). Finally, the Group recommended the creation of a new agency devoted strictly to promoting indigenous Irish industry (Ibid., p. 82), as had been recommended by Irish Congress of Trade Unions General Secretary Peter Cassells, a Group member, in 1987 (Dublin interview #2, March 2009). IDA opposed the breakup, favoring instead a group to coordinate work with foreign and domestic investors, which it foresaw as being under its control (Dublin interview #2, March 2009).

As one former official with experience in both IDA Ireland and Enterprise Ireland put it, 'The [Culliton] Report said we had a well-oiled machine for inward investment but not domestic companies'. An important aspect of this divergence was that 'the tax package was largely designed for MNCs, but sometimes fit poorly for domestic firms' (Dublin interview #1, March 2009). Moreover, the entire culture of pre-division IDA was directed toward attracting investment, and 'the creation of Enterprise Ireland released it from this dominant culture'. As one example of what this meant in concrete terms, the official pointed to Enterprise Ireland's (EI) success in providing R&D support for indigenous firms: 'With the benefit of hindsight, this would have been hard to achieve under the old culture' (Dublin interview #1, March 2009). Another official concurred, saying that IDA staff had 'found it more prestigious to work with MNCs rather than indigenous industry' (Dublin interview #2, March 2009). An IDA official admitted to doubts about its wisdom at the time, but 'FDI is a different business than developing entrepreneurs. We don't have to worry about firms' management expertise, whereas at EI, that's part of what they do' (Dublin interview #4, March 2009). Other views of the split are not as positive. One official said that the breakup of IDA meant that several competences were lost to Enterprise Ireland, especially in science and technology. 'There really were a lot of synergies lost with the breakup, and now Forfás has the job of coordinating them' (Dublin interview #5, March 2009).

The two functions were officially split into separate entities by the Industrial Development Act of 1993, which created IDA Ireland and Forbairt, under the coordination of Forfás (Forfás, 2009, p. 99). In turn, (EI) was created in 1998 through the amalgamation of Forbairt with the smaller Irish Trade Board and part of the training agency FAS (*Business and Finance*, 1998). Since EI works with Irish firms, it is essentially a support agency for small and medium enterprises (SMEs) rather than a provider of investment incentives like IDA Ireland, though it has at times instituted programs that arguably do constitute location incentives, such as a fund to attract Irish expatriates to start businesses back home (Creaton, 1998). Since its role in investment incentives is so small, Enterprise Ireland will not be considered in detail.

The Celtic Tiger

Ireland's growth from the late 1980s into the early 2000s was nothing short of extraordinary. As Table 5.3 shows, Ireland experienced several, increasingly large, surges in FDI inflows from 1990 to 2003. Most of the inflow came from the United States, with US multinationals currently accounting for about 95,000 of 130,000 jobs with foreign-owned firms (Dublin interview #4, March 2009). Ireland's GDP per capita surpassed the EU average in 1997, when its GDP per capita at purchasing power standards (PPS) reached €20,110 vs. the EU-15 average of €19,420 (Eurostat, 2002, p. 156). Note, however, that measured by gross national income (GNI), Ireland remained shy of the EU-27 average until 2000 (Kirby, 2010, p. 34). By 2004, it reached 139 percent of the EU-15 average; meanwhile, employment 'almost doubled from the early 1990s to 2007' (Ó Riain, 2008, p. 6). As can be seen from Table 5.4, the unemployment rate peaked at 17 percent in 1986, falling only to 15.5 percent in 1993, but after that it fell rapidly, declining by more than half of that in five years, and dipping below 5 percent in 2000. In addition, as Table 5.2 shows, emigration was finally reversed in the 1991–96 period, and net immigration grew rapidly thereafter.

At the same time, not everything was rosy in the Celtic Tiger period. Anti-poverty campaigners, such as the Conference of Religious of Ireland, argue that the government did not take advantage of Ireland's rapid growth to eliminate poverty. Rather, 17 percent of the population, almost 700,000 people, lived below the official poverty line in June 2008 (i.e., before the economic crisis hit), and 'growing prosperity has not delivered infrastructure, services or wellbeing on the scale required' (O'Brien, 2008, p. 3). Children's charity Barnardos reports that 7.4 percent of children lived in consistent poverty in 2007, meaning they lived in households with below 60 percent of median income and, in addition, suffered from at least one of eight measures of deprivation, such as not eating for 24 hours (Barnardos, 2009). Ireland's score on the UNDP's Human Poverty Index for industrialized countries (HPI-2) actually worsened from 1995 (the first year for which HPI-2 was calculated) to 2004, increasing from 15.2 percent to 16.0 percent (UNDP, 1998, p. 186; UNDP, 2007, p. 241). While some of the UNDP data is out of date (Smith, 2005, p. 49; e.g., functional illiteracy is given at 22.6 percent in every report from 1998 to 2007), Ireland's worsening outcome is due solely to a sharply increased level of poverty measured as below 50 percent of median income, from 11.1 percent in 1995 to 16.2 percent in 2004 (UNDP, 1998, p. 186; UNDP, 2007, p. 241). Nevertheless, scholars such as Smith (2005, pp. 51–2) and Ó Riain (2004, p. 9) argue, and I agree, that the Celtic Tiger was not a mirage, as demonstrated most strongly in employment numbers and the reversal of emigration.

Explaining the boom of the 1990s

Explanations for the success of the Irish economy abound, with competing accounts citing many of the same factors, but with major differences in emphasis. For the purposes of this book, I begin by focusing on one of the most central, and most obviously related to investment incentives, Ireland's increased ability to attract foreign direct investment (FDI) (see Table 5.3). I start with the views of the practitioners who helped make that happen, based on interviews conducted in March 2009. I then turn to a deeper inquiry into the competing explanations, honing in on the question of what changed at the end of the 1980s, the period when the crisis ended and the groundwork for the Celtic Tiger was laid.

1. Practitioners' view of Irish success

An important theme running through practitioners' views on Irish success is the increasing sophistication of the IDA in its investment attraction efforts. Over time, the agency improved its targeting techniques (Smith, 2005, p. 85, also cites this factor). Critical was the recognition that as an island on the periphery of the European Union, it was necessary to focus on products that were not strongly affected by distance; hence, the choice of industries such as computers, pharmaceutical and biotech, and financial services (Dublin interview #7, March 2009). Second, 'part of it was knowing what *wouldn't* come to Ireland', such as Japanese consumer electronics, which largely went to the UK (Dublin interview #1, March 2009). As the Telesis Report noted, Ireland also chose not to pursue low-wage manufacturing (Telesis Consulting Group, 1982, p. 173). One ex-official noted that many economists in the 1960s were telling Ireland to go low-tech, but IDA ignored them and aimed for high-tech firms. The first major high-tech firm was DEC in 1972 (Dublin interview #3, March 2009). A third element of targeting was knowing when not to do a deal. As one official put it, 'We walked away from many deals. Often the sector was implausible for Ireland or there was a bad business plan. DeLorean was the most famous case of this kind' (Dublin interview #1, March 2009). However, Jacobsen (1994, p. 112) argues the contrary, stating that 'the IDA rejected very few "realistic" projects. The DeLorean plant was one illustrious exception'.

Pricing was another important element of the FDI attraction strategy. 'IDA developed price per job limits that varied by sector', according to one official. Another point he emphasized was that it was necessary to pay more for firms coming to what is a new sector for your country (often called 'pioneers'). Having done that, however, 'It's hard to re-price. It's a challenge to pay less for followers, but we were able to do that in a number of cases.' He credits EU state aid policy with helping make it easier now to pay less for such follower firms (Dublin interview #1, March 2009). An IDA official says the country was able to pay less for investment 'partly because we were providing more of the inputs, better educational inputs, for example' (Dublin interview #4, March 2009).

An IDA Ireland official also emphasized the agency's speed, saying it was quicker than many of its competitors. 'We would get into things sometimes 80 per cent right, and then adjust. Even things that were problems, like Global Crossing, left us great infrastructure for Google, Facebook, etc.' One specific example of 'tweaking things as we went along' was in the area of R&D. Despite Ireland's low tax rate, 'we were disadvantaged against countries with high tax rates but big R&D write-offs, so we introduced a 20 per cent tax credit for R&D' (Dublin interview #4, March 2009).

The shift to a greater emphasis on R&D is a critical one for moving up the value chain. As several officials pointed out, IDA originally focused purely on employment (Dublin interview #4, March 2009). As one government official put it, 'When we started out, employment was the objective, but R&D has had more emphasis for the last 6–7 years.' In the current crisis, however, it is necessary for employment to 'stay on the radar' (Dublin interview #5, March 2009). This increased emphasis on R&D can be seen in Ireland's policy on state aid for research and development. Like the other Cohesion Countries, Ireland in 1995–97 devoted less of its state aid budget to R&D than the EU average, with just 5 percent of aid to manufacturing and services going to R&D versus an EU average of 10 percent (Thomas, 2000, p. 220). By 2008, however, 15 percent of Ireland's state aid went to research and development, only one percentage point shy of the EU average (European Union, 2010b).[9] In addition, the Irish government started putting much more of its own money into research and development, rather than simply relying on EU funding, including € 500 million for 2000–06 and establishing Science Foundation Ireland (Dublin interview #5, March 2009). According to the SFI (Science Foundation Ireland, 2009), total R&D funding for the 2007–13 National Development Plan came to € 8.2 billion, of which € 1.4 billion was allocated for SFI disbursement. IDA Ireland has claimed several recent successes in terms of attracting R&D facilities, such as Intel's announced expansion of its research center in Shannon in February 2009 (*Irish Independent*, 2009a).

2. What changed?

As we have seen, Ireland in 1987 was in the midst of a major crisis, marked by high unemployment, an enormous budget deficit and high levels of emigration. What, then, changed at the end of the 1980s?

Three factors stand out: in 1987, Ireland negotiated its first Social Partnership agreement; in 1988, the first reform of the Structural Funds took place, with Ireland receiving 2.5–3.0 percent of GDP in grants from the EU throughout the 1990s (Rodríguez-Pose and Fratesi, 2004, p. 99) and 1985–92 saw the completion of the Single Market. The Social Partnership was born out of the budget crisis. In exchange for reining in wage demands and agreeing to government budget cuts, labor was rewarded with tax cuts on wages that ultimately increased workers' real income. As mentioned above, inequality within Ireland increased substantially, leading some critics to describe it as an unequal partnership. Nevertheless, the agreements were renewed in 1991, 1994, 1997, 2000, 2003 (Smith, 2005, p. 120), and 2006 (Annan, 2008).[10] By reducing the size of its deficits, then beginning a string of government budget surpluses in 1998, Ireland steadily reduced its debt/GDP ratio to 25 percent in 2006 (Ó Riain, 2008, p. 7). The budgetary goals of the partnership agreements were also reinforced by the convergence requirements for adopting the euro as stated in the 1991 Maastricht Treaty (budget deficit of no more than 3 percent of GDP, and total government debt of no more than 60 percent of GDP). Peter Sutherland (2008, p. 16) identifies Ireland's decision to adopt the euro as a major advantage over the United Kingdom in attracting FDI.

There is considerable debate about the importance of Ireland's receipt of EU Structural Funds. As the poorest Member State at the time of its accession, it was eligible for money from the European Regional Development Fund, European Social Fund and European Agricultural Guidance and Guarantee Fund (Guidance Section)[11] from that time.[12] It was not until the 1988 reform and expansion of the Structural Funds (which doubled them in real terms) that this became serious money. Ireland was always very effective in negotiating for high levels of Structural Funding, receiving more per capita than any other Member State in both the 1989–93 and 1994–99 rounds of funding.[13] Ireland benefited in several ways. The money was used to strengthen training and education. It also funded infrastructure programs such as telecommunications and highways (Ó Riain, 2008, p. 15; Dublin interview #4, March 2009). Several sources (O'Donnell, 2000, p. 18; Dublin interview #5, March 2009; Dublin interview #6, March 2009) suggest that the country's administrative capabilities were strengthened by the requirements of the Structural Funds in terms of planning and oversight. The most frequently cited estimate of the economic effect of the Structural Funds was to increase Irish growth by 0.5 percentage points per year (Barry et al., 1999, p. 114). By contrast, Peter Sutherland writes, 'We largely wasted those funds. Much of them were spent on social programmes and training programmes, which were of limited real value. In my opinion, the money could have provided the infrastructure which we still noticeably lack' (Sutherland, 2008, p. 16).

Several sources cited the EU's Single Market program as contributing to Irish success. One source (a trade union official) suggested that it opened up continental markets, especially that of France, to Irish goods, allowing Ireland to reduce its dependence on the UK market (Dublin interview #6, March 2009). Two cited in particular the required liberalization of procurement rules system, which opened up opportunities for pharmaceutical firms manufacturing in Ireland (Dublin interviews #3 and #7, March 2009). Sutherland argues that the Single Market program improved Ireland's ability to attract FDI in two ways: by preventing countries from protecting their markets via non-tariff barriers (such as procurement rules); and the strengthening of state aid enforcement which kept richer Member States like France from handing out large investment incentives.[14] Indeed, he describes the Single Market program as 'probably [the] most important reason for our recent economic growth' (Sutherland, 2008, p. 16).

Yet the other Cohesion Countries (Greece, Spain and Portugal) also benefited from the reform of the Structural Funds and were 'present at the creation' of the Single Market, without having anywhere near the success that Ireland did (Smith, 2005, pp. 71–2). Her analysis gives us an important clue into what is needed beyond investment incentives and low taxes. She emphasizes the role of internal factors, such as the Social Partnership and improvements in education (Smith, 2005, pp. 74–6, 80–2).[15] Several officials I interviewed concurred on the importance of education in the country's ability to attract FDI (Dublin interview #2, March 2009). One noted that second-level education became free in 1966, and considered that science and technology education is key to any country's development. In Ireland's case, this meant the establishment of new technological universities (Dublin interview #3, March 2009) which competed with the established university system and pressured them into upgrading their own technological offerings (Ó Riain, 2004, p. 74). Moreover, Ireland adopted active labor market policies with spending levels on a par with the Scandinavian states, though the country's spending on these programs tailed off in the late 2000s (Ó Riain, 2008, p. 14).

One element that did not appear to figure in was the role of cutting personal income tax rates. As Ó Riain (2008, p. 17) states, 'The role of income tax cuts, often lauded as crucial to economic and employment growth, has been greatly exaggerated'. As he points out, the top income tax rate was cut from 52 percent to 48 percent from 1992 to 1993, but remained at 48 percent until 1999. He cites Sweeney (2004, p. 8), who shows further that in the six years when the top rate was 48 percent (1993–98), Ireland saw GNP growth rates generally over 7 percent and it added 309,000 jobs, with a further 177,000 jobs created in 1999–2000, when the top rate was 46 percent. Meanwhile, the decrease in the capital gains tax rate from 40 percent to 20 percent, which took place in 1998, unleashed a wave of property speculation (Ó Riain, 2008, pp. 17–18).

Finally, Ireland may have been lucky in that it achieved all the preconditions for growth just as the world economy began a growth spurt accompanied by a major increase in FDI. As one official put it, Ireland's growth coincided with the 'Clinton boom', adding that 'Nothing had changed but the environment' (Dublin interview #3, March 2009). O'Hearn largely concurs, saying there had been no 'essential change in industrial strategy by the Irish state', and that much of the reason for the FDI boom was the adoption of flexible production strategies by US multinationals, a part of which 'was often to move the final production process close to the final market' (O'Hearn, 2001, p. 191).

The future?

The current Irish situation is dire, with the country facing an unemployment rate of 13.7 percent (May 2010; Central Statistics Office Ireland, 2010), a bailout of the major banks, and a huge budget deficit, and more challenges loom on the horizon. One set of problems flows precisely from Ireland's recent success, which reduces its ability to receive Structural Funds and to offer investment incentives. Changes in EU state aid law have reduced the maximum aid that can be given anywhere in the Union, while the regional aid guidelines further reduce the incentives that can be given to large investment projects. Moreover, as Ireland has become wealthy, its cost competitiveness has been eroded, which has benefited the Eastern European Member States at Ireland's expense, particularly in the lower rungs of manufacturing. Finally, Ireland's success has reduced other EU Member States' willingness to tolerate its low-tax policy. Taxation is an issue with ramifications for Ireland beyond the EU, because a recent report by the US Government Accountability Office identified the country as a tax haven (GAO, 2008, p. 12), and the bulk of Irish FDI comes from the United States. Thus, there is a clear vulnerability on tax issues that could shake Ireland's low-tax policy to its core.

1. The perils of success

Ireland's very economic success has meant that it benefits much less from European Union policies designed to help poorer members of the EU. As we have already seen, Ireland was extremely successful in negotiating high levels of Structural Funds in the 1989–93 and 1994–99 programming rounds, for both of which it qualified in its entirety as an 'Objective 1' region. For the 2000–06 programming period, however, Ireland faced the prospect of completely losing Objective 1 status due to the fact that its rapid economic growth pushed it far above the 75 percent of EU GDP per capita limit for Objective 1 designation. While up to that time, Ireland had been a single region for EU statistical purposes, the government negotiated with Eurostat to split the country into two regions, so that the Border, Midlands and West regions could still qualify for Objective 1 funding levels. Even with that change, the country nevertheless lost over half of its Structural Funds (Thomas, 2000, p. 100).

State aid policy is a second area where rising income levels mean that Ireland no longer has benefits it enjoyed in the past. Since a region's allowed aid maximum is mainly a function of per capita income and unemployment, many parts of Ireland are no longer eligible to give the highest levels of regional aid[16] and some, such as County Kildare (where Intel is located) are no longer able to provide regional aid at all, although they can still provide aid for research and development. Furthermore, as a result of the State Aid Action Plan (see Chapter 8), regional aid maxima have been reduced across the board within the EU. The effect of these changes on investment incentives are magnified by the 1997 adoption of the Multi-Sectoral Framework for Large Investment Projects, which prohibits projects above €50 million from receiving a region's normal aid maximum, with progressive reductions as the size of the project increases (again, see Chapter 8 for details of these rules, which are now incorporated into the overall Regional Aid Guidelines). The final change to state aid law was that, beginning in the mid-1990s, the European Commission attacked Ireland's 10 percent corporate income tax as a state aid (Dublin interview #2, March 2009). In fact, the Commission even ruled that it constituted an operating aid, something that DG-Competition has strongly opposed in most cases (Thomas, 2000, p. 95). According to one official, Forfás surveyed foreign multinationals for their views on what would still be an attractive tax rate, with 12.5 percent being the result (Dublin interview #2, March 2009). The government adopted this as the corporate tax rate for all trading activities, and persuaded DG Competition that this was no longer a state aid (Thomas, 2000, p. 95).

All these factors played a role in the effective denial of regional aid to Intel in 2005 (Intel withdrew its request for aid when the European Commission opened an Article 88 (2) investigation of the subsidy) and in the reduced area where Ireland can give state aid at all. Intel was sharply critical of the Commission decision, warning it would 'have to "reassess" future Irish investment' (Smyth, March 2005a).[17] One IDA official is undeterred. 'Now we can't give grant aid in half the country and we're still winning business' (Dublin interview #4, March 2009). Irish officials have argued to the European Commission that these rules disadvantage them in competitions with non-EU locations, but so far the Commission has shown little inclination to change the regional aid guidelines (Wishlade, 2008a, p. 68).

Competition from other countries is another result of the boom, as rising wages make locations in other countries more attractive. Indeed, the International Monetary Fund has stated that Ireland 'has become the most expensive place to do business in the eurozone' (*Irish Independent*, 2009b). The biggest example of foreign competition so far is the January 2009 announcement that Dell would lay off 1900 workers in Limerick involved in manufacturing computers, transferring the work to Lodz, Poland, where lower wages were 'a deciding factor' (Quinn, 2009, p. 2; Agence France Presse, 2009a). Dell had been the largest employer in Limerick, with 3000 employees altogether at its manufacturing and research and development center there. An unpublished Forfás report estimated that as many as 9500 direct and indirect jobs could be lost if the company laid off 2510 employees in Limerick (*Irish Examiner*, 2009a). As with the 1994 collapse of Digital Equipment Company (DEC), the first major electronics firm to come to Ireland, task forces were assigned after Dell's announcement to help create spinoff firms. One official said the hope was that some of the logistics skills could be transferred into domestic firms in, for example, the food industry (Dublin interview #5, March 2009). Prior to the closure, Dell had accounted for a massive 5 percent of Irish GDP (Economist Intelligence Unit, 2009a).

The Polish government awarded state aid for the Dell Lodz plant of €54.5 million, projecting 3000 new jobs there. However, in December 2008 the European Commission announced that it would conduct a formal investigation into the aid under Article 88 (2) of the EC Treaty due to concerns about Dell's market share and the possible increase of production in a market segment in relative decline (Economist Intelligence Unit, 2009a). Such investigations often presage disapproval of the aid, as for instance in the Intel case in 2005. Nevertheless, after the investigation, the aid was approved for the full amount on 23 September 2009 over the objection of Ireland (*Limerick Leader*, 2009; European Union, 2009f). Irish politicians were quick to criticize the decision, noting that the unemployment rate was lower in Lodz than in Limerick (though obviously the standard of living is much lower in Lodz, or it would not have been possible to give such a large aid). European Commission President Jose Manuel Barroso softened the blow by announcing a €14.8 million support package for the laid-off workers of Dell Limerick (*Limerick Leader*, 2009). Surprisingly, the Commission announcement claimed that the loss of jobs in Ireland 'was not a consequence of the aid granted by the Polish authorities' due, apparently, to Dell's decision to expand somewhere in Eastern Europe, even if not Poland (European Union, 2009f). The issue of subsidized relocations will be discussed in detail in Chapter 8.

The pharmaceutical industry is another one where Ireland faces challenges from abroad. According to one senior development official, although pharmaceutical firms are less mobile than ICT companies due to the industry's high capital requirements, Ireland is seeing strong competition from Puerto Rico and Singapore, where there are fewer restrictions on what investment incentives they can offer firms (Dublin interview #5, March 2009).

2. Tax competition or tax haven?

The issue of Ireland's low corporate income tax, which I have previously described as a 'non-regulated means of competing for investment' (Thomas, 2000, p. 270), is by no means a new one, but it has become increasingly salient as Ireland has ceased to be a poor country. While the OECD had considered including Ireland in its initial list of tax havens (OECD, 1998), an OECD official stated that addressing low-tax jurisdictions for FDI was 'the political limit' the report could not touch because of a lack of consensus among the OECD's members (interview with OECD official, Paris, 1998).[18] The US Government Accountability Office issued a report in 2008 identifying Ireland as a tax haven (GAO, 2008, p. 12). It showed that of the 100 largest US corporations, 47 had subsidiaries there (GAO, 2008, Appendix II). One attraction of Ireland for US firms is based in the fact that they do not have to pay taxes on overseas earnings until they are repatriated, a tax loophole that

President Barack Obama has promised to close (Leonnig, 2009, p. D01). Several Irish observers suggested that the country could indeed be vulnerable to changes in US tax law, and one Irish trade union official said the country was vulnerable to changes in German law as well (Dublin interview #6, March 2009). One government official echoed the view that the government was vulnerable to US tax law changes: 'If the US is serious about keeping jobs at home, the effects on us would be substantial', noting that Ireland was heavily lobbying the US government on tax issues (Dublin interview #5, March 2009). Another government official confirmed that Ireland is 'constantly monitoring' changes in US tax law (Dublin interview #4, March 2009).

As one sign of Ireland's tax haven functions, it was revealed that Microsoft's Irish subsidiary, Microsoft Ireland Operations Limited (MIOL), accounted for more than 10 percent of the company's 2007 fiscal year pre-tax profit of $20.1 billion. This was accomplished with 1100 employees (Collins, 2008, Finance p. 1), a little over 1 percent of the company's worldwide employment of 79,000 as of 30 June 2007 (Microsoft, 2007, p. 14). This subsidiary's parent, Microsoft Ireland Research, was also an Irish company, with two shareholders, one in Bermuda and one in Dublin's International Financial Services Centre (Collins, 2008, Finance p. 1). Finfacts (2006) reports that Microsoft registered the latter company as an Irish unlimited company in 2006 to take advantage of the non-disclosure rules for unlimited companies. It quoted *The Wall Street Journal* as saying the subsidiary, Round Island One, has almost no employees but $16 billion in assets. These assets consist primarily of Microsoft patents, taking advantage of Ireland's exemption from tax of patent income (Finfacts, 2006). In fiscal year 2008, MIOL's profits dropped sharply as most of its business was transferred to Microsoft Ireland Research, which is also classified as an unlimited company and not required to file corporate accounts (Collins, 2009, Finance p. 21). Other high technology firms have availed themselves of Ireland's transfer pricing opportunities as well (Ó Riain, 2008, p. 17).

Pressure on Ireland's tax regime does not come solely from the United States. There are numerous proposals in the EU that would harmonize the corporate income tax base, the CIT rate, or both (van der Horst, 2007). Van der Horst conducts simulations of unilateral and multilateral tax rate reductions, various types of tax rate harmonization, tax base harmonization and combined tax base and tax rate harmonization. His results suggest that simply harmonizing the tax base, as the

European Commission has primarily focused on (van der Horst, 2007, p. 47), actually increases the incentives to follow beggar-thy-neighbor tax rate reductions (van der Horst, 2007, pp. 56–7). On the other hand, combining base harmonization and rate harmonization gives an increase in EU welfare of 0.14 percent of GDP (compared with a miniscule 0.02 percent of GDP for base harmonization alone), with most Member States seeing benefits (van der Horst, 2007, p. 59). This helps explain the popularity of harmonization among higher tax countries like France and Germany. However, the effect on Ireland would be negative, at –0.14 percent of GDP, which helps explain Ireland's continuing opposition to harmonization.[19] Barry criticizes van der Horst's finding of an overall increase in EU welfare, arguing that under US tax policy, which allows American MNCs to aggregate their taxes paid abroad for purposes of calculating their credits against US taxes, the existence of Ireland's low tax rate actually makes it possible for US MNCs to invest more in high-tax countries like Germany because it means that the tax in excess of US rates can still be credited in full because of the surplus generated in Ireland (Barry, 2007, pp. 3–4). However, this is implausible in view of the wide usage of the deferral provisions, meaning that there is no immediate need to generate tax credits at all.

Many present and former officials defend the country's low tax rate. The country has argued in multiple venues (OECD, EU and US) that the 12.5 percent rate is completely transparent. A common contrast made by Irish officials is with Dutch 'advance rulings' on tax, which set a company's tax rate on an individualized and confidential basis (e.g., Dublin interview #2, March 2009). One official emphasized that the country's choice of a lower corporate income tax has meant that the country has a higher value-added tax than most of the EU (Dublin interview #2, March 2009). At 21.5 percent, Ireland's standard VAT rate is exceeded only by Denmark and Sweden at 25 percent, and Finland and Poland at 22 percent (EU, 2009c, p. 3). As Kirby (2010, p. 63) notes, the VAT is a regressive tax. Moreover, in sharp opposition to the dominant view among political and policy leaders, he argues that the country's low corporation tax policy is one of the central flaws of the Irish model, inasmuch as it combines increased vulnerability to market fluctuations with a decreased financial capacity to ameliorate the effects of such fluctuations on individuals (Kirby, 2010, p. 169).

Despite its high VAT rate, Ireland's total tax burden as a percentage of GDP is only 31.2 percent, compared to the weighted EU-27 average of 39.8 percent and weighted euro-area average of 40.4 percent in

2007. Ireland's percentage is the lowest among the original 15 Member States, and fifth lowest among the EU-27 (EU 2009d). As James Wrynn presciently observed in 1998:

> Our European partners are now scrutinising our behaviour. What do they observe?
>
> They see a State which is rapidly approaching EU levels of income. However, we are unwilling to invest in our own society through taxation, and we expect other EU countries, which carry an average burden of tax of almost 50 per cent of GDP as against our 34 per cent, to fund key activities and infrastructure.
>
> We will build the Kinnegad bypass only if the Germans or Swedes pay. The self-help group in Tallaght will continue beyond 1999 if we can squeeze the money out of Europe in the next round of funding, but it is not a valid activity for Irish society to fund.
>
> Our European partners clearly see that we will not fund the essentials of a developed, fair and just society. As they see it, we create a tax climate which attracts industry from other EU countries, adding to their unemployment, attacking their social market model by attacking its taxation base, from which we ironically expect to draw benefit by way of structural funds. (Wrynn, 1998, p. 16)

This outlook underlies the pressure for tax harmonization coming from such higher tax Member States as France and Luxembourg (Thomas, 2000, 2002).

Moreover, there is a widespread view among foreign financial regulators that Ireland's 'light-touch regulation' is virtually no regulation at all, as several major scandals have been centered at Dublin's International Financial Services Centre (IFSC), including Italy's Parmalat in 2003 and the CologneRe/AIG scandal in 2005. Indeed, the UK Liberal Democrats' spokesman calls Dublin 'Liechtenstein on the Liffey' (O'Toole, 2009, p. 12). One official expressed skepticism at IDA's continued promotion of the IFSC 'when our regulation is evidently so bad' (Dublin interview #5, March 2009).

In terms of Ireland's current approach to economic development, opinions differ. One government official suggested, 'There is still a fascination with FDI that I think is inappropriate', arguing that despite all the reforms, the country was still not doing enough for indigenous firms. This official cited Finland and Austria as two countries that were at the cutting edge of indigenous firm support, but said that many country teams come to study Ireland for its work with FDI (Dublin interview #5,

March 2009). An IDA official said that the agency 'had not promoted the tax rate in a long time', noting that Ireland gives less grant aid than many of its competitors, 'and we have a worse tax situation than Singapore or Switzerland' (Dublin interview #4, March 2009).

Like the rest of the industrialized world, Ireland is in a deep recession, which is rapidly undermining the country's success. The country suffered a particularly serious housing bubble (a 188 percent increase in home prices from 1998 to 2007 [Burridge, 2009]) whose bursting contributed significantly to the Irish downturn. According to one trade union official, this bubble was driven in part by a number of tax schemes for property development (Dublin interview #6, March 2009). Other observers cite the lowering of interest rates that occurred when Ireland adopted the euro as the cause of the bubble (Lucey, 2009). One former government official said that already in the mid-1990s, Ireland 'lost the thread and went into property speculation' (Dublin interview #3, March 2009). As of May 2010, the seasonally adjusted standardized unemployment rate had reached 13.7 percent, compared with 4.8 percent in January 2008 (Central Statistics Office Ireland, 2010), its highest level since 1995 (see Table 5.3), the second highest in the eurozone (Pogatchnik, 2009), and 2009 saw net emigration return after 13 years of net inflows (Central Statistics Office Ireland, 2009e). Government revenues, which were heavily tied to taxes on real estate transactions, plummeted as a result. As Ó Riain (2008, p. 21) puts it, 'by 2008, the Irish political economy had constructed an institutionalized addiction to growth through the tax system. When growth slowed and real estate markets collapsed, government finances followed'.

Conclusion

What does the Irish case tell us about the use of investment incentives? First, it suggests that incentives alone, whether through subsidies or low corporate income tax rates, do not by themselves guarantee development (compare Aldaba, 2005, on the Philippine experience). The country experienced modest growth from 1958 to 1987, the first 30 years of its investment attraction policies, but it did not gain on EU-15 average GDP per capita until later. Ireland's success in the 1990s would have been impossible without, at a minimum, the substantial increase in third-level education that met the needs of foreign multinationals, the impact of social partnership and the full effects of joining the EU (free trade area, reform of the Structural Funds, the Single Market, and, arguably, adoption of the euro).[20] Even with EU accession in 1973 and the consequent use of Ireland as an export platform into the rest of Europe by US multinationals, there was only a modest bump in Ireland's share of world FDI inflows, which was reversed during the crisis of the 1980s (see Table 5.3). It took education and improved infrastructure to make investment incentives truly effective.

Second, the Irish experience shows us that if you have an attractive investment environment, being the first to offer incentives will yield an increase in investment, one that will persist if unmatched. Since Ireland had lower tax rates than its neighbors (not a low tax rate per se),[21] and it was able to provide large grants under the EU state aid rules, it had a potent pair of incentives that its competitors could not match. Indeed, Ireland benefited for decades from the existence of a large differential between its corporate income tax rate and those of other EU Member States or of the US. As a number of new EU Member States have adopted the low corporate tax rate model,[22] and have lower operating costs and greater ability to offer state aid than Ireland does, they have begun to attract investment away from Ireland (with Dell the most prominent example). Moreover, within the EU as a whole, corporate income tax rates have fallen by one-third in just 14 years, from an average of 35.3 percent in 1995 to 23.5 percent in 2009 (European Union, 2009e, p. 10). Taken together, these factors mean that Ireland enjoys a much smaller tax differential than in the past, which will reduce the attractiveness of low taxes as an incentive to invest in Ireland. In turn, this calls the economic sustainability of the low tax policy into question, and suggests that it cannot be replicated by latecomers. (This is not to say that it might not be required of latecomers who have to compete with Ireland, but that simply lowering taxes won't do anything for countries that don't have some other advantage over low-tax competitors.)

Similarly, Ireland's ability to give high levels of state aid has fallen substantially. In the last 10 years, changes in the state aid rules have sharply reduced Ireland's ability to give grants at all. Specifically, the EU has lowered the maximum levels of state aid in every region as part of the State Aid Action Plan's call for 'less and better targeted aid' (see Chapter 8), Ireland's prosperity has cost it the ability to give grant regional aid outside the 'BMW' (Border, Midlands, West) region of the country, and the regional aid guidelines on large investment projects further reduce the level of awards for large mobile projects like Intel or Centocor (*Irish Times*, 3 March 2005, p. 18), though the Commission did ultimately approve the latter project after effectively blocking Intel aid (Beesley, 2006, p. 20).

Third, Ireland's experience provides some support for Moran's claim that even attracting FDI does not guarantee developmental success unless the subsidiaries are integrated into the parent company's sourcing network, and not barred from such integration by tariff barriers or domestic content requirements (Moran, 2005, p. 282). Ireland's very liberal trade policies, strengthened of course by accession to the GATT and the EU, left the nation in no danger of throwing up protectionist barriers, which had been decisively rejected in 1958. Moreover, the pattern of FDI, with its overwhelming orientation toward exporting to the EU, ensured that local subsidiaries were fully integrated into global sourcing networks. On the other hand, in many cases there were few linkages with domestic firms, reducing spillover benefits to the Irish economy. The one exception may be software companies (documented in Ó Riain, 2004; Kirby, 2010, p. 40, also sees the sector as an exception, not the norm). Still, critics argue that Ireland's dependence on FDI could prove to be an Achilles' heel as other countries target Ireland's FDI (Kirby, 2002, p. 76), or due to potential negative effects on growth from having a large stock of foreign investment (O'Hearn, 2001, p. 193).

Fourth, and not mentioned above because it is wholly uncontroversial in Ireland, the country's experience shows that the use of clawbacks against grant-aided firms that fail to meet their job commitments does not scare off investment. IDA's decision to implement clawbacks came in 1987 (Smith, 2005, p. 130), which is to say right before Ireland's economic boom commenced. 'Grant refunds' are a routine aspect of IDA Ireland operations, with €14.6 million repaid in 2007 and €4.2 million repaid in 2008 (IDA Ireland, 2009, p. 37).

Does IDA Ireland overpay for jobs? This is an issue that has been debated at least since the Telesis Report of 1982. Interestingly, 2002 and 2003, which saw Ireland achieve its highest shares of world FDI inflows ever (see Table 5.3), were both marked by substantial net job losses in IDA supported firms, 4456 and 3346 jobs lost, respectively (IDA Ireland, 2009, p. 24). If we replicate the Culliton Report's approach to cost per job retained, we find that IDA-supported firms increased their full-time employment from 127,411 in 1999 to 136,043 in 2008, or a total of 8632 jobs (IDA Ireland, 2009, p. 24). From 2000 to 2008, IDA Ireland spent €879.7 million (calculated from IDA Ireland Annual Reports for 2000–08), or €101,911 per net full-time job increase. Of course, this is a substantial improvement over the IR£ 228,000 per job implied in the grant and jobs data of the Culliton Report. IDA Ireland is clearly paying less than half as much per job than in the 1980–90 period analyzed in the Culliton Report. Moreover, if we adopt IDA's method of calculating cost per job, we find that there has been about a 30 percent decrease from 1993–99 to 2002–08, from €18,730 in the first period to €13,202 (constant 2008 prices) in the tenth, most recent period (IDA Ireland, 2009, p. 22). It should be noted that this method of calculating cost per job is more demanding than what is usually seen in reports of individual projects in the press, which simply divide the incentive by the number of jobs expected. IDA Ireland's method only counts jobs in the denominator if they were maintained until the end of each seven-year period. By US standards, these would be considered low prices (Good Jobs First, the leading subsidy reform clearinghouse in the US, cites $35,000 per job as a federal benchmark; see LeRoy and Slocum, 1999, p. 1). However, there are two drawbacks to IDA's calculation: it does not include the tax benefits companies receive from Ireland's low taxes; and it excludes job losses at firms of jobs created before each seven-year reporting period. The latter reason is why IDA Ireland's numbers differ from those I calculated above.

Even with the reduction in grant aid, it is still worth inquiring about counterfactuals. Maybe Ireland would have done better putting €879.7 million into infrastructure and education rather than grants. We must also consider that in 1999–2008, Ireland was not a poor country, but above average EU GDP per capita for the entire period.

With the decline of grant aid in Ireland, the issue of corporation tax will become more acute. While Irish officials routinely praise the virtues of low tax rates, the political pressure on Ireland to raise its corporate income tax rate will continue, based on the view of a number of Member States that the low-tax policy is no longer acceptable because of Ireland's prosperity. However, since EU action on direct taxation (i.e., corporate and personal income tax) requires unanimity within the Council of Ministers, there is no direct way to force Ireland to change its CIT. Ireland has steadfastly refused to allow direct taxation to become subject to qualified majority voting.[23] Nevertheless, as one of the EU countries suffering the most from the current economic crisis, the possibility exists that it will be vulnerable to pressure. Moreover, the European Commission has shown itself in the past to be very creative in finding ways to achieve goals that would not appear to have Treaty support, the most obvious being the use of state aid rules to attack the 10 percent corporate income tax rate. Another relevant example is that the Commission persuaded the European Court of Justice that a maximum work week is a health and safety issue, which enabled the Commission (via a Council Directive adopted on a qualified majority) to force the UK government to adopt the 48-hour maximum work week even though the country had opted out of the Social Chapter of the Maastricht Treaty (*Financial Times*, 1996, p. 13; Perry, 1996). Like Ireland's low tax rate, the UK's opt-out was an example of an unregulated tool to compete for investment, though one that ended when the UK signed the Treaty of Amsterdam in 1997 (Thomas, 2000, p. 217).

While the Irish case shows us that incentives are not a sufficient condition for development, it does not solve the question of whether incentives are a *necessary* condition. Certainly being the first jurisdiction in your region with large incentives is beneficial to your growth, though at a cost to other states/provinces/countries. So it may be that the answer is no, *provided* you can achieve cooperation with neighboring jurisdictions to all refrain from the use of incentives, and otherwise yes, as a Prisoners' Dilemma analysis would suggest. But the continued co-existence of high-tax/high-service jurisdictions like Denmark and Sweden casts doubt on this answer. However, given the small number of such jurisdictions overall, it raises the question of what conditions make it possible to engage in such a 'high-road' strategy when other countries in your region are offering incentives.

In the next chapter, I move beyond Ireland to consider the European Union as a whole. There, I compare incentives in the EU with those of the US, to see which region gives higher incentives, and what that tells us about EU state aid control.

6
Who Provides the Most Investment Incentives: EU vs. US

Competing for Capital concluded that the EU's state aid policy was largely successful in its goals of controlling subsidies in general, and subsidies likely to go to mobile investment in particular. One then-recent development was the adoption of the Multi-Sectoral Framework, which for the first time specifically addressed investment incentives. Now over ten years old and incorporated into the EU's regional aid guidelines, it is necessary to ask if it really has affected the incentives received by large investors. The strategy of this chapter will be to compare both the largest incentives and aggregate incentives (to the extent it can be estimated) in the EU and the US. Preliminary work (Wishlade, 2008a) suggests that the EU has indeed lowered incentives relative to those in the US, but I propose to calculate US incentives on a net present value basis as the EU does, and to compare the aid intensities (incentive as percentage of investment, incentive per job) in both regions.

The second element of this comparison is to estimate investment incentives and total subsidies given by state and local governments to business in the United States. While the data for doing this are very fragile, they suggest that in 2005 US subnational governments give approximately \$47 billion in incentives and as much as \$65 billion in total subsidies (\$70 billion if accelerated depreciation is included). By contrast, regional aid (the type most commonly used for investment incentives) in EU Member States in 2005 was €9.6 billion (approximately \$12.9 billion).

Largest investment incentives in the US and the EU

First, we contrast the use of investment incentives in the United States and the European Union. This comparison provides something of a natural experiment for the effectiveness of EU state aid control, insofar as the two polities are of comparable size economically and both have no restrictions on capital movements within their borders. Given the number of smaller political units within each, both see competition for investment within their borders with its attendant potential for transfers from taxpayers to investors and simultaneous threats of economic distortion and inefficiency. Yet the regulatory response in the two regions has been sharply different.

The EU has made comprehensive efforts to control bidding wars for investment; indeed, the EU's rules on regional aid were designed in part specifically to keep Member States from outbidding each other for investment[1] and a Multi Sectoral Framework was introduced in 1997 specifically to address investment incentives given to large projects. As Wishlade (2008b, pp. 497–8) shows, the original version of the framework ('MSF 1998') produced little reduction in maximum aid intensities, whereas the second version ('MSF 2002') created sharply lower aid awards through the use of what she calls a 'reduction matrix' applying to all investment over €50 million (see Chapter 8 for details). This led to a significant decrease in the size of investment subsidies approved under the MSF 2002 than under the MSF 1998 (see Table 6.2 and discussion below). The MSF rules are now part of the overall Regional Aid Guidelines (RAG) as of 2007. A well-known example of these rules in action came in 2005 when Ireland wanted to award Intel €170 million in regional aid for a new, €1.6 billion chip fabrication facility in Leixlip, outside of Dublin. The Competition Directorate notified the government that it would open an investigative procedure under Article 88(2) EEC to determine if the aid was allowable under the rules of the Multi Sectoral Framework because of Intel's dominant position in the microchip industry and because the location was scheduled to lose all eligibility for regional aid; as a result, Ireland withdrew the proposed aid (Staunton, 2005, p. 18). Interestingly, despite holding a highly public 'opening' of the facility in June 2006 (Shoesmith, 2006, p. 1), the project was not completed, but may be finished under a new round of Intel investment (Lyons, 2009, Business p. 1).

In contrast with the regulated nature of competition for investment in the European Union, there are no rules governing location tournaments in the United States. While previous evaluations of the effectiveness of EU state aid law have been increasingly positive (Thomas, 2000; Dreyhaupt, 2006; Wishlade, 2008a, among others), there has been little work done to date on the extent to which the rules have affected the size of investment incentives. Wishlade (2008a) is the most extensive effort along these lines, but is hampered in that the size of incentives in the US and EU are not usually expressed in comparable terms: that is, while the Commission expresses all aid amounts in terms of their present value, neither the press nor subsidy reform campaigners in the US routinely do so. As a result, the values of incentives in the US have been overstated relative to those in the EU. Here, I calculate the largest 25 incentives given in the US since 1999 on a present value basis to give a more accurate comparison with the largest EU incentives. Besides comparing the incentives in currency amounts, it also compares them in terms of cost per job and aid intensity. The basic answer is that marquee projects in the US receive more money than do similar projects in the EU, as shown in Tables 6.1 and 6.2.

Perhaps the most obvious observation is that the largest incentives mainly occurred under the MSF 1998,[2] which accounts for four of the top five incentives as given in Table 6.2. With the introduction of the MSF 2002, there was a significant decline in the amount of awards given (Wishlade, 2008b, pp. 497–8). This improvement is even clearer when we compare the size of MSF 2002 and RAG 2006 incentives with those in the United States.

For example, the award American Micro Devices received in New York State dwarfed that received in Dresden under the MSF 2002 ($1.1 billion vs. approx. $354 million). The next largest post-MSF 1998 computer-related aid in the EU, Qimonda's DRAM facility in Germany, received approximately $190 million, compared to $533 million for IBM in New York in 2000, and less than even the third-largest US computer industry incentive, $269 million for Sematech. In terms of aid intensity (incentive as a percentage of the investment), the levels in Germany (all in Dresden) were 11.99 percent for AMD and 13.25 percent for Qimonda, compared to 34 percent for AMD, 21.32 percent for IBM, and 44.8 percent for Sematech in New York State (all in the Albany area).

The situation is similar for marquee projects in the automobile industry. To take the largest deal in each area, Volkswagen's 2008 deal in Chattanooga, Tennessee, for a $450 million subsidy is 45 percent of the investment and approximately $225,000 per job; Ford's deal in Craiova, Romania, includes approximately a $193 million subsidy, amounting to 23.8 percent of the investment, at a cost of about $62,250 per job. Kia's $353 million incentive package in Georgia is 29.4 percent of the investment and $141,200 per job, whereas Hankook Tire's incentive in Hungary is about $125 million, 20.55 percent of the investment and $83,350 per job. Initially, the plant was to be built in Slovakia, but the Multi Sectoral Framework limited the aid intensity there to 15 percent,

Table 6.1 Twenty-five largest incentives in the US since 1999

Company	Year	City	State	Amount
Boeing	2003	Everett	WA	$1,984,000,000
Advanced Micro Devices	2006	Malta	NY	$1,118,000,000
ThyssenKrupp	2007	Mount Vernon	AL	$734,304,000
Scripps Research Institute	2003	Palm Beach County	FL	$566,500,000
IBM	2000	East Fishkill	NY	$533,083,333
Volkswagen	2008	Chattanooga	TN	$450,139,048
Kia	2006	West Point	GA	$353,083,333
Toyota	2006	Blue Springs	MS	$291,634,000
Nissan	2000	Canton	MS	$289,666,667
Sematech	2007	Albany	NY	$269,444,444
Hyundai	2002	Montgomery	AL	$233,936,363
Ford	2006	Detroit	MI	$219,780,000
Toyota	2003	San Antonio	TX	$218,100,000
International Sematech	2002	Albany	NY	$175,636,364
Dell	2004	Winston-Salem	NC	$174,230,401
Goodyear	2004	Akron	OH	$173,099,088
Samsung Austin Semiconductor	2006	Austin	TX	$171,244,444
Eli Lilly	1999	Indianapolis	IN	$150,916,667
Marathon Oil	2007	Detroit	MI	$148,800,000
Honda	1999	Lincoln	AL	$144,221,818
General Motors	2000	Lansing	MI	$138,844,542
Alenia/Vought	2004	Charleston	SC	$133,133,333
Dell	1999	Nashville	TN	$132,373,334
Hemlock Semiconductor	2007	Hemlock	MI	$124,226,666
Google	2007	Lenoir	NC	$114,637,037

Sources: See appendix; author's calculations based on details of each agreement; list updated from Good Jobs First (2009b).

so the company decided to seek a higher subsidy elsewhere in the region (Thomas, 2007c, p. 38).

The US locations giving investment incentives were substantially more prosperous than comparable EU regions. For example, let's compare locations receiving automobile assembly plants. Alabama per capita income in 2006 was $29,414 in chained 2000 dollars (Bureau of Economic Analysis, 2009, p. 74). By contrast, the Czech Republic's gross national income per capita in 2006 was $12,680 at current exchange rates and $21,470 at purchasing parity (World Bank, 2007, p. 334), while

Table 6.2 Twenty-five largest incentives in the European Union since 2000

Company	Year	Country	Amount (million €)	Legal basis comm. decision
Advanced Micro Devices	2004	Germany	545	MSF 1998
ST Microelectronics	2002	Italy	542	MSF 1998
BMW	2002	Germany	363	MSF 1998/MV
Advanced Micro Devices	2007	Germany	262.40	MSF 2002
Infineon	2002	Germany	219	MSF 1998
Hyundai	2007	Czech R.	194.49	MSF 2002
Ford Craiova	2008	Romania	143.00*	RAG 2006
Qimonda	2006	Germany	140.94	MSF 2002
Wacker Siltronic	2004	Germany	120.904	MSF 1998
Wacker Chemie	2001	Germany	119	MSF 1998
Iveco	2002	Italy	109	MSF 1998/MV
Repsol Polimeros	2007	Portugal	103.32	MSF 2002
Hankook Tire	2006	Hungary	92.61	MSF 2002
Atlantica Invest AG	2007	Italy	89.56	MSF 2002
De Tomaso	2005	Italy	81	MSF 1998/MV
Artensa	2007	Portugal	80.09	MSF 2002
Volkswagen	2001	Germany	74	MSF 1998/MV
HighSi GmbH	2006	Germany	73.45	MSF 2002
Solar World	2003	Germany	73.15	MSF 1998
Propapier	2008	Germany	72.15	RAG 2006
DHL Airways GmbH	2004	Germany	70.8	MSF 1998
Autoeuropa Portugal	2003	Portugal	69.4	MSF 2002
CELBI	2007	Portugal	68.07	MSF 2002
Intico Solar	2008	Germany	65.62	RAG 2006
Peugeot Citroën	2004	Spain	58.3	MSF 2002

Sources: European Union (2001); European Union (2007a); Haufler and Mittermaier (2008), table 1 (author corrected currency conversion on Volkswagen decision); Wishlade (2009), figures 17 and 20. *Gross value, not present value. MV=Motor Vehicle Framework. At the time of this writing, €1=$1.35 approximately.

Romania's was $4850 at current exchange rates and $9820 at purchasing power parity (PPP) (World Bank, 2007, p. 335). In the microchip fabrication sector, we can compare Dresden's GDP per capita at PPP of approximately $27,894 in 2006[3] with New York State's $47,135 in chained 2000 dollars (Bureau of Economic Analysis, 2009, p. 74).

Overall, 17 projects in the United States since 2002 have received over $100 million (€74.1 million) in subsidies, compared to eight projects in the European Union since the introduction of MSF 2002. Considering, as shown above, that many of the US incentives were given in prosperous jurisdictions, whereas those in the EU were all given in poorer regions of the Union (often especially poorer ones, such as in eastern Germany, Portugal and the new Member States, which together account for 12 of the 14 MSF 2002 and later projects listed in Table 6.2), it seems fair to conclude that investment incentives are under better control in the EU; the Multi Sectoral Framework/Regional Aid Guidelines are doing their job at reducing the incentives given to large investment projects.

A related area of interest is whether EU regional aid guidelines might hamper the EU in its competition for mobile investment (Wishlade, 2008a, pp. 67–8). Ireland has been particularly vocal in its concern on this issue, especially in cases in which it might be the only EU location being considered (i.e., Intel).[4] After the effective denial of aid for Intel in 2005, the company twice warned that the country would be considered less competitive in the future (Smyth, 2005a, p. 1; Staunton, 2006, p. 4). As Wishlade (2008a, p. 68) notes, it is not surprising that the Commission does not want to expand the scope for aid to deal with a few exceptional situations, but it is probably wise to monitor this issue in the future.

One measure that would shed light on this is FDI performance. Comparing the United States with the EU-15, for example, shows that the former's share of inward FDI has declined substantially, while the reverse is true of the latter. As Dreyhaupt (2006, p. 152) says, '... the EU today remains the most vibrant destination for global FDI'. Table 6.3 shows the details.

Based on these results, the original judgment appears to stand: The EU has greater control of locational tournaments than does the US, without a cost in inward investment. While certainly the institutional

Table 6.3 Share of world FDI flows and stock (%)

	United States		EU-15	
Year	**Flow**	**Stock**	**Flow**	**Stock**
1985	36.663	19.164	28.602	28.580
1990	23.361	20.343	46.472	39.055
1995	17.233	18.376	34.110	38.196
2000	22.458	21.720	48.226	35.979
2005	10.932	16.052	46.844	41.167
2007	12.702	13.760	40.336	41.582

Source: UNCTAD FDI-Stat Database, consulted 10 April 2009 at http://stats.unctad.org/FDI/TableViewer/tableView.aspx

environment is very different in the two jurisdictions, there may well be lessons the US can learn from EU experience.

Estimating aggregate US State and local incentives and subsidies

Estimating aggregate state and local subsidies in the US is a difficult proposition because of the lack of transparency at all subnational levels of government. *Competing for Capital* made an important leap forward in this process by finding reasonable estimates by state-level budget organizations in eight states comprising 30 percent of US GDP, and adjusting them to exclude items that would not be considered subsidies internationally (Thomas, 2000). Extrapolating on the basis of share of GDP, it produced a final estimate of $48.8 billion (Thomas, 2000, p. 159), of which some $26.4 billion was investment incentives as opposed to operating subsidies (Thomas, 2003). Peters and Fisher (2004) estimated that US incentives amounted to $40–50 billion in 2002. Here I repeat the approach take in *Competing for Capital* to provide a new estimate.

Partial estimates do exist. The Associated Press surveyed states in 2009 and found that they gave $1.8 billion in tax breaks to film and TV production in 2006–08, $1 billion of that in 2008 alone (Nuckols and Waggoner, 2009).

The ideal way to calculate total investment incentives by state and local governments would be to take a complete list of every year's investment projects, calculate the present value of the location subsidy given to each one, and sum them. Given that not only every state, but thousands of cities large and small, undertake such projects each year, this is an impossible task in the absence of reporting requirements such as those which exist in the European Union and US states like Minnesota and Illinois. Some states, such as Missouri, do have reporting requirements for certain local subsidies, such as tax increment financing (TIF; Missouri Department of Economic Development, 2010) and transportation development districts (TDD; Missouri State Auditor's Office, 2010), and these requirements are largely though not completely followed, but other large programs such as local tax abatement have no such reporting. Moreover, even if a comprehensive list existed, it would also be necessary to determine if projects qualify for automatic tax incentives such as exemptions of machinery from state sales and use tax. Consequently, the data requirements for creating an ideal calculation cannot possibly be met, so I have relied on information on state subsidies plus fragmentary data on local subsidies.

Even focusing on the states, the estimation procedure is hampered by the fact that so few states provide a so-called 'unified development budget' that shows both expenditure programs and tax expenditures related to economic development. Moreover, none of these is written with the goal of international comparability of the data in mind, and the studies that do exist, most authored by subsidy reformers, tend to err on the side of including too many provisions. Therefore, in completing this estimate, I have relied on the few existing state estimates that have been made, and adjusted them to try to include only those items that would be considered a subsidy in previous EU or OECD studies (the latter of which had been published from 1990 to 1998; Thomas, 2000, pp. 256–7). Certain issues were repeated in almost every state estimate: almost all, for instance, included data for the cost of the state's net operating loss (NOL) provisions. However, NOL rules are clearly part of the general structure of corporate taxation and are absolutely nonspecific (in the sense of the WTO Agreement on Subsidies and Countervailing Measures; see Chapter 8) as they apply to every corporation. While I exclude NOL figures from my estimates, it is important to note that some states have changed their rules recently to allow companies to lengthen the time period for the use of NOL credits (for California, see Sibley, 2008). I do, however, count the cost of states' changing their apportionment formulae for multi-state corporations because of the clearly competitive use of the apportionment rules to attract investment. While the standard for decades was to tax a share of a multi-state corporation's income equal to the average of the firm's share in a state of its sales, assets and employment (or payroll), since at least the early 1990s, a number of states have increased the weighting of the sales factor, most commonly double-weighting it, but some using it exclusively in what is termed 'single sales factor' apportionment (Mazerov, 2005). Apportionment rules apply to multi-state firms and are thus not quite as nonspecific as NOL rules, but the deliberate nature of changes to the formulae to attract investment leads me to include tax expenditures based on these changes. A less clear-cut rule is accelerated depreciation. In the US, accelerated depreciation is generally available, which means that it would not be counted as a state aid in the European Union. However, because generally available accelerated depreciation does not exist in the EU, I argue that it is an incentive for investing in the US as opposed to other countries and should be counted (Thomas, 2000, pp. 157–8). At the state level, we find that it is not reported for most states because they allow companies to calculate their tax based on their federal taxable income, meaning that accelerated depreciation is factored in before state tax expenditures kick in. For states, moreover, accelerated depreciation is not an incentive to choose one over the other. As a result, I estimate state incentives and subsidies without accelerated depreciation, but I also include an estimate for accelerated depreciation for analysts who are interested in defining subsidies to include it.[5]

For local subsidies, I have followed the same procedure as used in *Competing for Capital*, using local estimates where available (Michigan and Missouri), but otherwise estimating them to equal state subsidies due to the ubiquitous use of local tax abatements, tax increment financing and other tools, based on interviews with state budget expert Iris Lav of the Center on Budget and Policy Priorities and site location consultant Jeff Goodman (Thomas, 2000, p. 158). In Missouri, local incentives vastly outweigh state subsidies, with $770 million committed in tax increment financing and transportation development districts alone in 2005, whereas the biggest state incentive was single sales factor at $77 million. Moreover, a study of the counties in the St. Louis region conducted by the East-West Gateway Council of Governments (the regional planning agency) estimated that the value of tax abatements issued by municipalities in the St. Louis region was about the same as that of TIF subsidies (East-West Gateway Council of Governments, 2009, p. iii), which means potentially hundreds of millions of more dollars per year given by local governments and not accounted for here. On the other hand, TIF and TDD commitments need to be discounted since they are paid out in multi-year periods, as are tax abatements. Furthermore, a few approved TIF projects never take place. However, many TIF projects should have little or no discounting because they are financed through bonds, allowing the investor to receive the subsidy as soon as eligible expenditures are made. Missouri is without doubt an outlier with its 7:1 local/state subsidy ratio, but it reinforces the plausibility of imputing to local governments a level of subsidies equal to that of state governments. Finally, it is important to note that I treat all local subsidies as investment incentives because all of them function to affect location, whether they are part of a larger state incentive package or a stand-alone subsidy given only by the city or county government.

Table 6.4 shows the details. State and local subsidies total $64.8 billion when calculated on the same basis as *Competing for Capital*, while state and local investment incentives are $46.8 billion, with state accelerated depreciation of just over $5 billion.

Table 6.4 Estimates of state (or state/local) corporate subsidies, ca. 2005 ($ million)

Investment incentives and operating subsidies, excluding accelerated depreciation

State	State IIs	State Op.	State Total	S/L Total
California	1506	2725	4231	8462
North Carolina	433	739	1172	2344
Massachusetts	256	533	789	1578
Michigan	691	61	752	1426*
Missouri	107	N/A	107	877*
Kentucky	177	365	542	1084
Rhode Island	61	5	66	132
Vermont	16		16	32
Total				15,935

Notes: Implied national total (based on 24.5881% of US GDP) 64,808
N/A: Information not available.
*Uses actual data on local subsidies.
Totals may not sum due to rounding.

Incentives only

State	State incentives	Local incentives	Total
California	1506	4231	5737
North Carolina	433	1172	1605
Massachusetts	256	789	1045
Michigan	691	675	1366
Missouri	107	770	877
Kentucky	177	542	719
Rhode Island	61	61	122
Vermont	16	16	32
Total			11,503

Note: Implied national total (based on 24.5881% of US GDP) 46,783

Accelerated depreciation	
California	542
Massachusetts	219
Michigan	149*
Missouri	104
Total	1,014

Note: Implied national total 5043 (based on 20.1090% of US GDP).
*FY 2009.

The caveats applicable to the estimate in *Competing for Capital* are equally relevant here. States might have tax expenditure budgets precisely because subsidies have become a political issue, thus lending an upward selection bias to the numbers (Thomas, 2000, p. 188). The local estimate is, as I said there, 'poorly grounded' (Thomas, 2000, p. 160) given that it is mostly an imputed figure based on the judgment of fiscal and site selection experts. Yet, as the case of local incentives in Missouri shows, it is possible that local subsidies could exceed state subsidies in some states. Moreover, we should remember that *Competing for Capital* estimated state and local subsidies to be 0.65 percent of 1995 US GDP, whereas the seemingly high local estimate for California, as shown in Table 6.4, yields an overall estimate that is less than 0.5 percent of California's $1.8 trillion economy.

At the same time, there are factors that tend to bias this estimate downward. First, the absence of operating subsidy data and tax abatements information for Missouri suggests the possibility that substantial amounts have been omitted. Second, 19 of the largest 25 incentives shown in Table 6.1 were given in states not represented in Table 6.4. Third, except for North Carolina, there is no good data (and hence I have made no estimate) for the amount of project-specific infrastructure in incentive packages. Thus, it is quite possible that the real totals exceed the estimates here. All things considered, I believe these figures are more likely to be underestimates than overestimates, but there is no way to know for sure.

The overall results, then, imply $46.8 billion in state and local incentives in 2005 (which I had estimated as $26.4 billion for 1996), $64.8 billion in overall subsidies (vs. $48.8 billion in 1996), $69.8 billion with accelerated depreciation included. Keep in mind that these estimates are not comparable enough to say that subsidies or incentives have 'grown' by the differences in 2005 and 1996 estimates, since they are based on different states, have highly uncertain margins of error and there is no way of telling whether the estimates are overestimates or underestimates in 1996 or 2005. For example, I would expect incentives and subsidies to grow at least as rapidly as GDP, and while that is the case with my new estimate for incentives, my new estimate for subsidies in only about 0.5 percent of 2005 GDP, rather than 0.65 percent as in 1996. The most we can say is that my present estimate is the best possible given the continuing poor state of data availability.

Conclusion

This chapter has examined US incentive use compared with that in the European Union. As we have seen, on marquee projects there is no doubt that US state and local governments provide larger incentives than EU Member States. Moreover, the states using incentives in the US are significantly wealthier than comparable regions in the EU. However, this appears not to have brought the US relatively more FDI; indeed, the data show that the US share of global FDI flows have fallen substantially while those of the EU-15 have grown. We will return to EU state aid control in Chapter 8, focusing specifically on the rules for mobile investment.

Finally, using the best data available, I estimate US state and local investment incentives to be approximately $46.8 billion in 2005, while total US state and local subsidies reached $64.8 billion, $69.8 billion if accelerated depreciation is included.

In the next chapter, I move beyond the 'Europe and North America' focus of *Competing for Capital* and this chapter to analyze the spread of investment incentives to developing countries, focusing in particular on China, Brazil, India and Vietnam.

Appendix: Sources for Table 6.1

Associated Press (2007) 'Comparing Incentive Packages', Associated Press State and Local Wire, 19 May.

Bowermaster, D. and R. Thomas (2004) 'What the state promised Boeing', *Seattle Times*, 21 January, A1.

Bradsher, K. (1999) 'Honda plans to build plant in Alabama for larger vehicles', *The New York Times*, 7 May, C20.

Bruns, A. (2008) 'Chattanooga stands and delivers', *Site Selection Magazine*, September.

—— (2005) 'Dell goes Carolina Blue', *Site Selection Magazine*, May.

—— (2007) 'The extra mile', *Site Selection Magazine*, May.

—— (2008) 'Staying power', *Site Selection Magazine*, May.

CanagaRetna, S. M. (2007) 'Driving the economy', *State News*, August, http://www.slcatlanta.org/Publications/EconDev/drivingtheeconomy.pdf, date accessed 10 February 2009

Center for Nanoscale Science & Engineering-State University of New York at Albany (2007) 'The Troy record: Sematech poised to move operations to Albany', 10 May, http://cnse.albany.edu/News/index.cfm?InstanceID=573&NewsID=649&step=sho9w_detail, date accessed 1 February 2009.

Cox, J. B. (2007) 'Google could cost $260 million; Lenoir and Caldwell County tax breaks exceed incentives offered by the state; the full costs hadn't been disclosed', *Raleigh News & Observer*, 8 February, A1.

Feder, B. J. (2000) 'Courted by state, I.B.M. plans huge chip factory', *The New York Times*, 11 October, B1.

Fox, W. F., M. N. Murray and A. B. Watts (2008) 'Economic & sales tax revenue effects of Volkswagen's location of its automobile assembly plant in Chattanooga, Tennessee', Center for Business & Economic Research-University of Tennessee Knoxville.

Lam, T. (2008) 'Marathon refinery gets OK to expand, but concerns expressed: It'll create more jobs, but pollution a worry for some', *Detroit Free Press*, 21 June, Biz 1.

Lyne, J. (2006) 'New York's big subsidies bolster upstate's winning bid for AMD's $3.2 billion 300-MM Fab', *Site Selection Magazine*, 10 June.

—— (2003) 'Toyota picks Texas for 2000-employee, $800M assembly plant', *Site Selection Magazine*, 10 February.

Malaysia Industrial Development Authority (MIDA) New York (2006) 'Weekly Situational Report', 25–29 September, http://digitalibrary.mida.gov.my/equip-mida/custom/situational/New%20York/2006/NY/WEEK%2039.doc, date accessed 10 February 2009.

Mackinnon, J. and P. Trexlerand (2007) 'A great day for Akron: goodyear is staying; new HQ to be built', *Akron Beacon Journal*, 6 December.

Man, A. (2004) 'Palm Beach County, Fla., approves $ 200 million land deal', *South Florida Sun Sentinel*, 4 February.

McCurry, J. W. (2005) 'An aviation cluster takes off in S.C.', *Site Selection Magazine*, March.

McDermott, J. P. (2004) 'State investing millions in plant AH…', *The Post & Courier*, 8 December, 1A.

Michigan Strategic Fund Board (2007) 'Adopted meeting minutes', 19 December, http://ref.themedc.org/cm/attach/C1A2AEBD-21E0–4033-A212-C031CF54A244/Dec_19_2007_MSF_Minutes.pdf, date accessed 15 February 2009.

Ohio Department of Development (2007), 4 December, http://media.ohio.com/documents/stategoodyear.pdf, date accessed 15 February 2009.

Perez-Pena, R. (2002) 'Albany chosen as hub for the next generation of chips', *The New York Times*, 18 May, A1.

Sigo, S. (2006) 'Kia's arrival in Georgia City to be partly financed by GOs', *The Bond Buyer*, Vol. 355, No. 32338, 30.

Site Selection Magazine (2000) ''99's top deals: case studies in fast-track strategies', May.

Site Selection Magazine (1999) 'An (Eli) Lilly Blooms in Indianapolis…', September, http://www.siteselection.com/ssinsider/incentive/ti9909.htm, date accessed 10 February 2009 .

Site Selection Magazine (2003) 'Florida Legislators squabble but OK scripps subsidies', November.

South Florida Sun Sentinel (2004) 'Price tag for Palm Beach County, Fla., Property May Rise in Scripps Deal', 3 February.

Starner, R. (2007) 'How the East won "The Next Big Thing"', *Site Selection Magazine*, July.

—— (2003) 'Fast track', *Site Selection Magazine*, May.

—— (2004) 'The tex-mex effect', *Site Selection Magazine*, May.

—— (2001) 'Top deals of 2000: chip plants deliver big bucks', *Site Selection Magazine*, May.

Times Union (2008) 'Tug of war over Empire zones', 31 December, http://timesunion.com/AspStories/story.asp?storyID=755369&category=BUSINESS, date accessed 17 March 2009.

7

The Spread of Investment Incentives to Developing Countries

In contrast to the long-standing use of investment incentives in developed nations, the use of incentives in developing countries is, for the most part, a more recent phenomenon. Some see this as largely a defensive reaction to their use in the North (Oman, 2000; Mora et al., 2005), while another important driver is fiscal decentralization in countries such as Brazil, India, China (Markusen and Nesse, 2007) and Vietnam (Hong et al., 2009). In these decentralized countries, we see a number of cases of subnational competition for investment comparable to those in the US. As in the United States, there is very little regulation of this competition, even though in the Brazilian case the main incentive used by the states was technically illegal. Vietnam actually has made the greatest efforts to regulate subnational incentives, with differentiated aid maxima à la the European Union, but in 2005 newspaper reports revealed widespread violation of these maxima by provincial governments (Hong et al., 2009).

At the same time, developing countries do use investment incentives against each other. The Press Trust of India (2008) reports that the Chinese city of Wuxi, Jiangsu Province, organized a five-day tour of India offering incentives to Indian information technology and other firms to locate there, including free and reduced rent. Wuxi Minister Yang Weize told the PTI, 'We want to make Wuxi the Bangalore of China.'

Oman (2000) presciently observed that the expansion of the use of incentives followed, rather than preceded, the expansion of foreign direct investment (FDI) in various areas of the world. This pattern has mostly held up in developing countries, with the partial exception of

China, where its opening to the world economy was accompanied from the beginning with incentives in a small number of special economic zones or SEZs (Zhou et al., 2002).

China

Investment incentives in China began with the original SEZs designated by the Chinese government (in Shantou, Shenzhen, Xiamen and Zhuhai) when it first opened up to foreign investment in 1979 (see Table 7.1). The main incentive was a two-year tax holiday followed by three years of taxation at half the normal rate (Zhou et al., 2002, p. 64). In 1984 and 1985, the government designated 14 Open Coastal Cities where foreign investment was allowed, though with smaller incentives than in the SEZs, and in 1988, a fifth SEZ was opened in Hainan (Zhou et al., 2002, p. 65).

China's early FDI was largely in the form of joint ventures. In 1990, almost all inward FDI was in the form of joint ventures, but even as late as 2000, about half of inward FDI consisted of joint ventures with Chinese firms. With China's accession to the WTO in late 2001, wholly owned foreign subsidiaries came to predominate, accounting for about 75 percent of China's FDI by 2005 (Bishop, 2007, p. 90).

China's opening to the world economy was accompanied by political and fiscal decentralization, which some observers, notably Qian and Weingast (1996), saw as critical to its overall economic transformation. This is disputed by Cai and Treisman (2006), who argue that it was not decentralization which explained the dynamics of the move to a market economy, but centralized political battles that continued to favor economic reform even after a certain amount of political recentralization in the 1990s. Chin (2010, p. 15) expands on this, arguing that the appearance of decentralization must be qualified in 'pillar industries' such as the auto industry, where the 1990s saw the reassertion of 'a greater degree of centralized coordination to China's auto development process, especially in utilizing foreign investment' (Chin, 2010, p. 15). All investments above $30 million had to be approved by the State Planning Commission and other central government agencies, which 'enabled central authorities to contain some of the interjurisdictional competition for FDI between provinces' (Chin, 2010, p. 25). What is beyond doubt, however, is that today investment incentives are given by both provincial and municipal governments (Du et al., 2008, p. 421), as nationally designated investment zones have now been complemented

Table 7.1 Inward FDI flows into China (Millions of current US dollars and share of world total)

Year	Amount	Share of world total (%)
1980	57	0.105
1981	265	0.381
1982	430	0.741
1983	916	1.822
1984	1419	2.497
1985	1956	3.500
1986	2244	2.599
1987	2314	1.694
1988	3194	1.961
1989	3393	1.725
1990	3487	1.682
1991	4366	2.805
1992	11,008	6.607
1993	27,515	12.371
1994	33,767	13.150
1995	37,521	10.998
1996	41,726	10.687
1997	45,257	9.316
1998	45,463	6.446
1999	40,319	3.738
2000	40,715	2.947
2001	46,878	5.714
2002	52,743	8.376
2003	53,505	9.467
2004	60,630	8.250
2005	72,406	7.439
2006	72,715	4.977
2007	83,521	4.221
2008	108,312	6.381

Source: UNCTAD FDI-Stat Interactive Database, consulted 28 December 2009 at http://stats.unctad.org/fdi/ReportFolders/reportFolders.aspx?sCS_referer=&sCS_ChosenLang=en

with zones sponsored by municipal and provincial governments. 'In the city of Dongguan, both municipal and township governments are particularly willing to offer financial incentives such as reduced land prices, factory leases and utilities charges to Taiwanese investors' (Chen, 2006, p. 27). Chen credits their use of incentives as a major factor in the city's status as the main destination in China for FDI from both Taiwan and Hong Kong, though he acknowledges that the lack of coordination among municipalities raises the possibility that cities are giving excessive subsidies to firms (2006, pp. 27–8).[1] In the Greater Shanghai area, numerous local governments have established at least 20 special zones competing with each other for foreign investment. Bishop (2007, p. 100) credits this competition with a reduction in rent-seeking behavior by municipal governments. At the same time, his study presents evidence of rent-seeking by firms: 'Si and Bruton's study (1999)...discuss...a joint venture in the fast food industry in Shanghai where the Chinese joint venture partner was not in the food business and was primarily interested in the profit to be gained, whereas the European partner wanted the excellent contacts that the Chinese partner was able to provide' (Bishop, 2007, p. 94). More telling still, he writes, 'A study of the role of FDI in technology transfer in Dalian (Young and Lan, 1997) found that more than one-third of Chinese joint venture partners did not hope to gain any technology from the joint venture arrangement. Rather, they were involved in it because it enabled them to take advantage of favorable tax policies applicable to joint ventures' (Bishop, 2007, p. 94). Thus, even in the presence of what he sees as fairly high administrative capabilities in Shanghai's governments (2007, pp. 99–100), rent-seeking by firms appears to be a problem.

Overall, it is impossible to estimate the use of investment incentives in China. While it is obvious that scores of nationally designated zones (SEZs and ETDZs), provincial and even municipal economic zones are active in the attraction of investment to their jurisdiction, the measures themselves are not transparent, particularly in the case of tax holidays and sub-market priced land and inputs. Moreover, solid data on the cost of any individual incentive agreement is sparse,[2] even for a high-profile firm like Intel (see Chapter 4). Chien and Gordon consider that Chinese competition for investment may be more dysfunctional than that in the US, because of high levels of inter-provincial protectionism (2008, pp. 39, 44). Given the nondemocratic nature of the government, it is no surprise that there has not been a subsidy reform movement or effective pressure on governments to disclose incentive terms.

Brazil

Brazil has been an important destination for FDI for over 40 years (see Table 7.2). The country received a major influx of FDI in the automobile industry in the late 1950s and early 1960s. For the most part, these investments occurred in the São Paulo region (Rodríguez-Pose and Arbix, 2001, p. 140). The only exception was Fiat's assembly facility in

Table 7.2 Inward FDI flows into Brazil (Millions of current US dollars and share of world total)

Year	Amount	Share of world total (%)
1970	392	2.935
1971	449	3.144
1972	460	3.080
1973	1181	5.719
1974	1208	5.007
1975	1203	4.527
1976	1391	6.323
1977	1827	6.733
1978	2180	6.346
1979	2408	5.693
1980	1910	3.532
1981	2522	3.625
1982	3115	5.366
1983	1326	2.638
1984	1501	2.641
1985	1418	2.538
1986	317	0.367
1987	1169	0.856
1988	2805	1.723
1989	1130	0.575
1990	989	0.477
1991	1102	0.708
1992	2061	1.237
1993	1291	0.580
1994	2150	0.837
1995	4405	1.291
1996	10,792	2.764
1997	18,993	3.910
1998	28,856	4.091
1999	28,578	2.650
2000	32,779	2.372
2001	22,457	2.737
2002	16,590	2.635
2003	10,144	1.795
2004	18,146	2.469
2005	15,066	1.548
2006	18,822	1.288
2007	34,585	1.748
2008	45,048	2.655

Source: UNCTAD FDI-Stat Interactive Database, consulted 28 December 2009 at http://stats.unctad.org/fdi/ReportFolders/reportFolders.aspx?sCS_referer=&sCS_ChosenLang=en

Minas Gerais in the 1970s, in a joint venture with the state government (Evans, 1979, p. 228). In the 1990s, however, a new wave of automotive investments came to Brazil as part of the 'New Automotive Regime', a policy connected to the Real Plan that reduced the nation's long-standing problems of inflation. Since the late 1990s, Brazil has seen high-profile incentive wars in the auto industry (note the big spike in inward FDI beginning in 1996, in Table 7.2). However, the fiscal war was not confined to the auto sector and, indeed, continues to this day.

Like the United States, investment incentives are mainly provided at the subnational level, rather than at the federal level. However, the Brazilian Development Bank, BNDES, (Banco Nacional de Desenvolvimento Economico e Social) provides loans for numerous investment projects. It also manages the Amazon Fund, which provides grants for sustainable production, research and development, and reforestation in the Amazon region (BNDES, 2009a). In the first ten months of 2009, BNDES disbursed R$ 107.5 billion, approximately $62.5 billion (BNDES, 2009b). Support to micro, small and medium enterprises (MSMEs) plays a substantial role in BNDES' operations, with R$ 21.8 billion in disbursements to MSMEs in 2008, 24 percent of the bank's total of R$ 92 billion in disbursements (BNDES, 2009c, p. 102).

In addition, the federal government provides regional incentives in the north, northeast and center-west regions of the country. These have been significant in Ford's original investment and expansion in Camaçari, Bahia (Cavalcante and Uderman, 2004, p. 3; Reuters, 2009).

It is among Brazil's states (frequently in combination with municipalities) where investment incentives have most come into play. The 'fiscal war' involves the rebating of value-added tax (ICMS in Portuguese) at the state level. Although such rebates are usually provided for investment, São Paulo state also provides ICMS exemptions for research and development expenditures (Economist Intelligence Unit, 2008). According to the Brazilian Constitution and administrative rules, any exemption or incentive based on the ICMS 'are supposed to be regulated and approved by a national council of finance secretaries' (Afonso and Barroso, 2007, p. 27). In other words, the incentives are technically illegal. To get around this, states have used the technique of making long-term loans at nominal interest rates to provide the rebate. Brazilian tax experts point out that despite attempts to stop this through legal channels, the Supreme Court has left the issue to the political arena; states have also re-enacted laws struck down by the Supreme Court (interviews, São Paulo, 28 and 29 July 2009).

Mora and Varsano (2001, p. 13) argue that states' large investment incentives do not appear to be necessary to bring the investments to Brazil, at least in the auto industry. By far the largest economy in South America and in Mercosur, the country would attract these facilities in any event, except for a tiny possibility of going to Argentina. As with the US or EU, they argue that while it is rational for any individual state to offer incentives, their widespread adoption is collectively irrational for Brazil.

The case of Ford's investment in Camaçari, Bahia, provides a good example of the dynamics of the fiscal war in the automobile industry.[3] In 1997, Ford had announced that it would build a new facility in the state of Rio Grande do Sul at a cost of $1 billion. However, in 1998, elections brought the Workers' Party (PT) to power and it promptly announced its intention to renegotiate the incentives packages provided by its predecessor to Ford and General Motors. While the new PT administration was able to reach agreement with GM, it was unable to do so with Ford, which canceled the project in April 1999. Over the next six weeks, Ford engaged in a high-profile auction in which seven states were finalists although all but four states submitted bids. In June, the company announced it would put the project, now substantially larger at $1.9 billion, in one of the poorest states in the country, Bahia. According to Cavalcante and Uderman (2004, p. 24), the total incentives package came to R$2,642 million ($1.428 billion at the exchange rate they use, $1 = R$1.85), 75 percent of the cost of the investment. Alternatively, we can calculate that this equals $285,600 per job for the 5000 jobs the investment was expected to create. By either measure of aid intensity, the cost is far more than for an assembly plant in the EU or even the US (see Chapter 6). For a developing country like Brazil, this is an extraordinary cost. As in the US, subnational competition for investment undermines the country's bargaining power it would have with multinationals based on the large size of the market. Other 1990s auto investments were large as well: Volkswagen was estimated to have received $54–94,000 per job from Rio de Janeiro state in 1995, Renault $133,000 per job in Paraná in 1996 and Mercedes-Benz an eye-popping $340,000 per job from Minas Gerais in 1996 (Oman, 2000, p. 32). Huge incentives have been given in the biodiesel manufacturing sector as well. In April 2009, Goiás state gave tax breaks worth five times the amount of the investment, approximately $209,333 per job to Canadian ethanol producer Usina Canada. The R$53 million, 600-jobs facility was to locate in the city of Acreuna, and receive R$273 million, about

$125.6 million at the time of the announcement (Latin America News Digest, 2009).

Fiscal wars can also break out between poorer states. In February 2009, the toy company Estrela announced a new R$20 million factory in Ribeirópolis in Sergipe state. The company already had an agreement to build the facility in Pernambuco state. It received tax incentives for locating in the interior of Sergipe, and was negotiating for loans from the Bank of the Northeast and the Bank of the State of Sergipe (Filho and Silveira, 2009).

Afonso and Barraso (2007, p. 39) argue that once the fiscal war became generalized (i.e., the richer states offered incentives to counter the efforts of poorer states), the distribution of investment reverted to what would be expected on the basis of the relative locational advantages, with investment incentives merely offsetting each other, just as Guisinger (1985) argued. In the case of the automobile industry, this meant that assembly plants tended to go where the market, skilled labor and infrastructure were the best, São Paulo state. Toyota's 2008 decision to locate in Sorocaba, São Paulo state (Newton, 2008), would be an example of this reconcentration.[4] As evidence that the fiscal war halted the deconcentration of industry generally, Afonso and Barraso (2007, p. 39) note that from 1994 to 2005, São Paulo state's GDP grew faster than the national average, 31.5 percent vs. 29.7 percent. However, according to another source, the state's share of *industrial* GDP had fallen from 49 to 41 percent over the 1998–2009 period (interview, São Paulo, 29 July 2009).

What caused the fiscal war?

A large number of factors came together that led to the 'fiscal war'. First, Brazil's 1988 Constitution was the source of expanded budgetary power for state and local governments, and it was designed in that way as a means of consolidating the end of the 1964–85 dictatorship by decentralizing government (Mora and Varsano, 2001, p. 3; Afonso and Barraso, 2007, p. 2). Second, a legacy of the dictatorship meant that the states had little experience in negotiating with foreign multinationals (Rodríguez-Pose and Arbix, 2001, p. 150). This made them less capable of achieving favorable outcomes in the course of such bargaining, leaving them vulnerable to demands for higher subsidies. Third, the level of inequality between the states drove the poorer ones to inaugurate the fiscal war. Regional inequality in Brazil is notably higher than, for example, the United States: in 2007, GDP per capita ranged from R$22,667 in São Paulo state to R$4662 in Piauí (IBGE, 2010), a ratio of 4.8:1 excluding the Federal District. By contrast, in the US, real state GDP per capita in 2008 (in 2000 dollars) ranges from Delaware's $56,401 to Mississippi's $24,403 (Bureau of Economic Analysis, 2009), a ratio of 2.3:1 excluding the District of Columbia. The trigger was Brazil's hyperinflation crisis,[5] in the course of which the federal government ceased its use of regional policies. The poorer states saw no alternative to offering incentives to attract investment (Afonso et al., 2005, p. 105). Fourth, the physical mobility of production within Brazil increased with the upgrading of the country's road infrastructure (Rodríguez-Pose and Arbix, 2001, p. 143). Fifth, auto companies were willing to consider states other than São Paulo because of high labor costs and their perception of high worker militancy there (Rodríguez-Pose and Arbix, 2001, pp. 142–3). With the opening of the Brazilian economy under the Real Plan, the still relatively protected automobile industry (Oman, 2000, p. 31) attracted tariff-jumping FDI to its rapidly growing market, making the auto industry one of the first to see the consequences of the fiscal wars.

These consequences were substantial. Rodríguez-Pose and Arbix (2001, pp. 149–50) argue that the fiscal war in the automobile industry constituted 'pure waste', due to the extremely high levels of incentives going to firms that would have located in Brazil anyway, incentive packages that made it easier for firms to import components rather than buy them in Brazil, jobless growth due to the higher productivity of new factories,[6] poor bargaining ability among state governments, lack of strong non-governmental organizations to oppose them (though they do note some recent politicization of the issue),[7] and the lack of an effective regulator like the European Commission. Seven Brazilian states (including Rio Grande do Sul, Rio de Janeiro and Minas Gerais, all active in the recruitment of auto firms) declared bankruptcy in 1999, a sign of the fiscal strain placed on them by the competition for investment (Rodríguez-Pose and Arbix, 2001, p. 151). In addition, in a sign that the fiscal war had indeed caused 'global inefficiency' in Brazil, there was substantial overcapacity in the industry, with Farrell et al. (2004) reporting an astonishing 80 percent overcapacity in 2002, which raised prices for cars by 20 percent. Even in 2008, the industry had 25 percent greater capacity than its production (calculated from ANFAVEA, 2009, pp. 10 and 56). Finally, the fiscal war has had broader consequences in Mercosur, prompting Argentina already in the late 1990s to promote rules on subnational investment incentives throughout the region (Oman, 2000, p. 35), though with no success.

Trying to end the fiscal war

The irrationality of the fiscal war is widely recognized in Brazil,[8] but distributing the costs and benefits of tax reform has made progress on it extremely slow. The Cardoso administration came into office in 1995 pledging to change the tax system, but by the end of its two terms of office in 2003, its only major accomplishment was exempting exports from the state ICMS (Werneck, 2006, p. 78). This fell far short of the goal of replacing the ICMS with a federal-level value-added tax, which was taken up again by the Lula administration.

President Lula held a two-day meeting with all 27 state governors in early 2003 to negotiate a consensus proposal on reforming taxes and social security. What emerged was a compromise that allowed states to continue to administer the value-added tax, but they were to be restricted to only five tax rates and future ICMS tax incentives were to be banned entirely (Werneck, 2006, pp. 82–3). That, however, faltered in Congress, while governors made new demands on extending the Manaus Free Zone, on social security taxation, and on compensation to states that would lose from the ICMS reforms. While the federal government extended the Free Zone for 10 years, it otherwise 'muddled through' with extensions of temporary turnover taxes (Werneck, 2006, pp. 85, 92–3).

After the failure of reform in 2003, the Lula administration returned to the issue in 2008, presenting a package for a constitutional amendment that included consolidation of three federal taxes, the unification of the ICMS and levying it in the source rather than destination state (Kerr, 2008). This proposal further combined an end to ICMS-based incentives with an expansion of the National Regional Development Fund from R$2.8 billion to R$3.5 billion, about $1.466 billion in November 2008 (Seabra, 2008). However, by late 2009, the proposal had not been approved by the Brazilian Congress and it was speculated that reform would have to wait until after the country's 2010 elections (Economist Intelligence Unit, 2009c). According to officials from Rio de Janeiro state, São Paulo state opposed this agreement because it argues that the amounts proposed for the fund are far too large. Meanwhile, the poorer states would not agree to the reform without the increase in the development fund (interview, Rio de Janeiro, July 2009).

Conclusion

Brazil's fiscal war is now 15 years old and has spread from the auto industry to virtually every sector and state. Many of the problems seen with investment incentives in industrialized countries have occurred now in Brazil, from consultants' inflated job predictions[9] to fiscal crises, to the politicization of the incentives issue. With the repeated failure of tax reform, however, there is no immediately evident solution to the fiscal war. While there is increased concern about the cost of incentives among some civil society groups, as long as richer and poorer states remain at loggerheads, it is impossible to predict when the impasse will end.

India

As Table 7.3 shows, India, for much of its history, had little FDI. It was not until economic reforms beginning in 1991 that India began attracting significant amounts of FDI and, at the same time, beginning a series of location tournaments for investment among the states. The situation was flagged at least as early as Oman's (2000, pp. 55–8) OECD Development Centre report on FDI incentives, particularly for several high-profile subsidies provided to multinational auto makers. As he wrote, 'To varying degrees, India's 25 [now 28] state governments have moved since 1991 to woo private investors, particularly foreign investors, with a broad range of incentives' (2000, p. 55). Indeed, a Ford factory in India received from $200,000 to $420,000 per job, depending on the discount rate used in the calculation (Oman, 2000, p. 80).

A more recent example has been the saga of homegrown multinational Tata Motors' Nano project. Billed as the least expensive car in the world, the Nano was originally announced to be built in the state of West Bengal (Coffin, 2008, p. 14). Opponents of the $350 million plant claimed that the state government had taken the land from unwilling farmers and given it to Tata,[10] and held a series of sometimes-violent protests against the planned 750-worker plant. After two years of protests by the farmers (Kinetz, 2008), which saw demonstrators physically surround the facility and block roads to it, Tata threw in the towel in October 2008 on the 85 percent complete plant (Coffin, 2008, p. 14). The company then was offered incentives by at least eight other states to locate the project in their jurisdiction (Mitra, 2008), with Gujarat finally being awarded the project a mere four days after the closure in West Bengal was announced (Leishemba, 2008). One estimate said the firm had received incentives in West Bengal of 25–30,000 rupees (USD 500–600) per car, on a car that was to sell for only 100,000 rupees (Mitra, 2008)! Ratan Tata said the deal in Gujarat was 'as good as or slightly better than the one we had previously' (Leishemba, 2008).

Table 7.3 Inward FDI flows into India (Millions of current US dollars and share of world total)

Year	Amount	Share of world total (%)
1970	45	0.341
1971	48	0.334
1972	18	0.119
1973	38	0.184
1974	57	0.236
1975	85	0.320
1976	51	0.232
1977	–36	–0.133
1978	18	0.053
1979	49	0.115
1980	79	0.146
1981	92	0.132
1982	72	0.124
1983	6	0.011
1984	19	0.034
1985	106	0.190
1986	118	0.136
1987	212	0.155
1988	91	0.056
1989	252	0.128
1990	237	0.114
1991	75	0.048
1992	252	0.151
1993	532	0.239
1994	974	0.379
1995	2151	0.631
1996	2525	0.647
1997	3619	0.745
1998	2633	0.373
1999	2168	0.201
2000	3585	0.259
2001	5472	0.667
2002	5627	0.894
2003	4323	0.765
2004	5771	0.785
2005	7606	0.781
2006	20,336	1.392
2007	25,127	1.270
2008	41,554	2.448

Source: UNCTAD FDI-Stat Interactive Database, consulted 28 December 2009 at http://stats.unctad.org/fdi/ReportFolders/reportFolders.aspx?sCS_referer=&sCS_ChosenLang=en

Blakely (2008, p. 73) estimates that Gujarat gave the automaker £500 million, and that Tata requested a £1 billion bailout from the British government for Jaguar and Land Rover, which it had acquired from Ford. In addition, leaked Gujarat government documents suggest that the state is giving vastly more support to Tata – for moving the equipment there from West Bengal, low land prices, huge infrastructure expenditures and a $1.95 billion, 20-year loan at 0.1 percent interest, with an estimated face value of 30,000 crore rupees, an amazing $6 billion at early 2009 exchange rates (Inter Press Service, 2009).

Another area in which is India uses investment incentives (and sees interstate bidding wars) is call centers and other back-office operations. In addition to wages as low as $1/hour (Good and McFarland, 2004) and large numbers of educated English-speaking workers, the country offers both investment incentives and tax treaties that create tax avoidance[11] opportunities. National legislation created SEZs in 2005 that allow tax 100 percent deductions of profits from export activity (Krishna, 2007). State governments in India provide their own incentives, as for instance in the state of Bihar (Indo-Asian News Service, 2006). The Chennai government offers automatic capital grants for investments under 300 crore rupees [3 billion rupees, or about $68 million at 2005 exchange rates], and special packages for larger investments (*Business Line*, 2005). More recently, Punjab has jumped into the incentive game as well, setting up IT zones with cheap land and tax breaks (Sarin, 2008). Similarly, West Bengal has incentives in the call center sector, including start-up capital for small and medium-sized enterprises (United News of India, 2007).

In the pharmaceutical industry, as well, Indian states have actively been using tax incentives to attract investment. As *India Business Insight* (2004) reported, 'Pharmaceutical companies are moving out of their traditional manufacturing hubs in Gujarat and Maharashtra to States that offer tax concessions', including Himachal Pradesh, which attracted Torrent Pharmaceuticals and Alembic Ltd. The state offered both a 100 percent excise tax exemption (ten years) and 100 percent income tax exemption (five years), attracting large foreign multinationals like Colgate-Palmolive and Samsung. Gujarat responded by setting up its own tax-free zone in Kutch (Mathew, 2004).

As befits the world's most populous democracy, investment incentives provoke substantial political organizing. The Special Economic Zone legislation was opposed by a vast array of interests, from farmers who feared losing their land to the zones to state government officials worried about the cost of foregone taxes (Aiyar, 2006, p. 53). Passed by Parliament in June 2005, by September 2006, 267 SEZs had been approved fully or in principle. Unlike in China, the SEZs are privately owned, not state-owned. As Aiyar relates, one of the first groups to object was the Communist Party of India (Marxist), the leading political party in the Left Front government of West Bengal. In October 2006, the West Bengal governing parties called for substantial revisions to the SEZ law, especially in the areas of land transfer to private developers, rules to prevent real estate speculation, attention to possibly increasing regional inequality and the revenue loss to state governments (Communist Party of India [Marxist], 2006). As Coffin (2008, p. 14), points out, with 2/3 of India's population living in rural areas, transferring farmland to industrial uses has been politically explosive. This was the case when Tata was trying to build the Nano in West Bengal; however, it was the Left Front supporting the development and the opposition Trinamool Congress that led the farmers' protests (Coffin, 2008). Various opposition parties organized protests attacking the program as a whole or specific projects, such as the SEZ in Navi Mumbai, Maharashtra, run by Reliance Industries (Aiyar, 2006, p. 53). The SEZs carry a dizzying array of tax incentives. Only 35 percent of the land area actually has to be used for processing, with the rest available for residential, recreational and retail development, raising the specter of land grabs and real estate speculation (Aiyar, 2006, p. 53; *The Economist*, 2006). The National Institute of Public Finance and Policy, the Reserve Bank of India and the International Monetary Fund have all raised concerns about the magnitude of possible revenue losses, estimated by the first of these organizations at 175,000 crore rupees (Aiyar, 2006, p. 53), or $35 billion.[12] According to a Press Trust of India (2006) report, there were clashes between the Commerce Ministry and Finance Ministry over the cost of SEZ's though Finance Minister P. Chidambaram downplayed them.

The economic downturn has had an effect on India's investment incentives. DLF, an Indian real estate developer, requested that four of its SEZs be de-designated. In June 2009, the government approved this request but required the company to repay all of the tax credits it had received in connection with the start-up of the IT zones (Press Trust of India, 2009).

Vietnam

The Vietnamese case is striking due to the ambitious control provisions attempted by a developing country. These arrangements were severely tested in 2005 when investigations revealed that more than 30 provinces had offered illegal incentives.

Background

Since Vietnam began market reforms beginning with the Doi Moi period in the mid-1980s, FDI has played a substantial role in the economy. As Table 7.4 shows, Vietnam first began receiving sizable FDI inflows

Table 7.4 Inward FDI flows into Vietnam (Millions of current US dollars and share of world total)

Year	Amount	Share of world total (%)
1980	2	0.003
1981	18	0.026
1982	13	0.022
1983	0	0.000
1984	1	0.001
1985	−0	−0.000
1986	0	0.000
1987	10	0.008
1988	8	0.005
1989	4	0.002
1990	180	0.087
1991	375	0.241
1992	474	0.284
1993	926	0.416
1994	1945	0.757
1995	1780	0.522
1996	1803	0.462
1997	2587	0.533
1998	1700	0.241
1999	1484	0.138
2000	1289	0.093
2001	1300	0.158
2002	1200	0.191
2003	1450	0.257
2004	1610	0.219
2005	2021	0.208
2006	2400	0.164
2007	6739	0.341
2008	8050	0.474

Source: UNCTAD FDI-Stat Interactive Database, consulted 28 December 2009 at http://stats.unctad.org/fdi/ReportFolders/reportFolders.aspx?sCS_referer=&sCS_ChosenLang=en

in 1990, growing rapidly until the East Asian financial crisis starting in 1997. It was not until 2007 that the country surpassed the level of inflows it received in 1997, and data from the Ministry of Planning and Investment (MPI) showed that 2008 was a record year for disbursed FDI, at $11.5 billion compared to 2007's $8.3 billion (Vietnam News Briefs, 19 March 2009).[13]

In terms of sectoral distribution, the 1987–91 period was dominated by investment 'in off shore oil and gas projects' (Malesky, 2008, p. 99), while in 1991–98, there was an increased emphasis on manufacturing and tourism (Richards et al., 2002, p. 91; Malesky, 2008, p. 99). Already by 2000, and despite the effect of the East Asian financial crisis, foreign invested enterprises (FIEs) accounted for an eighth of Vietnamese GDP and a quarter of tax revenues (Freeman and Nestor, 2004, p. 179).

Vietnam has worked hard to move up the value chain. In particular, the country has attracted four investments from Canon, including the world's largest laser printer facility (Vietnam News Briefs, 23 December 2008; Vietnam News Briefs, 25 August 2008), and in 2006 Intel announced a chip assembly plant and test facility in Ho Chi Minh City, with an investment certificate granted for $605 million (Muoi, 2006). In November 2006, the company announced that it was expanding the project from a $300 million initial investment to a $1 billion, 500,000 sq. ft. facility, making it the largest foreign investment the country had received to that point (Mason, 2006). The plant is now scheduled to open in July 2010 (Vietnam News Briefs, 29 January 2010).

Vietnam's regionally differentiated investment incentives

Vietnam is a poor country, with an estimated GDP per capita of $2800 (CIA, 2009) at purchasing power parity, $1024 at official exchange rates (US Department of State, 2009). Nevertheless, there are significant regional differences, so the Common Law on Investment of 2005 designates two levels of allowable regional incentives, 'locations with extremely difficult socio-economic conditions' and 'locations with difficult socio-economic conditions', or Location 1 and Location 2, respectively. Each of these has a menu of corporate income tax holidays, value-added tax exemptions, reductions on import duties and natural resource royalties and land tax reductions (Hong et al., 2009, p. 13).[14] This stands in contrast with the European Union which, while it has only two legal bases for regional aid authorization, Articles 88 (3) (a) and 88 (3) (c), has numerous levels of aid maxima (European Union, 2009). Fifty-four of the country's 64 provinces have areas that qualify for Location 1 or Location 2 preferences (for the full list, see Hong et al., 2009, pp. 53–4). In addition, there is a long menu of incentives available for specific industries and activities, which dilutes the attractiveness of the regional aid since these incentives can be received anywhere in the country and are in many ways as generous as the regional incentives (Hong et al., 2009, p. 13). Further complicating the 'complex web of incentives', all industrial parks qualify for Location 2 preferences and all high-tech parks and economic zones qualify for Location 1 preferences, and there are also incentives for hiring and training, particularly women and ethnic minorities (UNCTAD, 2008, p. 53). UNCTAD notes, 'Although the GDT [General Department of Taxation] appears capable of administering the incentives, their complex structure imposes a very high administrative burden both on investors and the tax authorities'. Moreover, virtually all new investments qualify for incentives, diluting their impact. UNCTAD thus argues for simplification of the tax system and a far more focused incentive system (UNCTAD, 2008, pp. 55–6). The fiscal cost of the incentives has been estimated to equal 0.7 percent of Vietnam's GDP in 2001 (Fletcher, 2002, p. 13).[15] By comparison, the most recent estimate of US state and local government incentives, $40–50 billion in 2002 (Peters and Fisher, 2004, p. 28) equaled about 0.4–0.5 percent of US GDP.

Subnational competition for investment

Given the regional variations in income, it is not surprising that officials in the country's poorer provinces would want to promote investment in their territories. Moreover, the dilution of regional policy by the proliferation of incentives for all sorts of industries, employment and training would further motivate such efforts. As a result, provincial officials engaged in pitched battles for inward FDI projects, and many offered investment incentives beyond what was allowed by law.

In addition to the use of fiscal incentives, there is also anecdotal evidence of pollution haven behavior. According to one press report, 'because of trying to attract investment, some local authorities ignored regulations on requiring environmental protection measures. As a result, the environment has been abused, while the money collected from investments is not enough to fix the pollution. The recent Vedan case is a prime example' (VietNamNet, 13 October 2008). Vedan, which had dumped untreated wastewater into the Thi Vai River, was hit with $7.7 million in fines and threatened with closure of its monosodium glutamate production by the government (Vietnam News Briefs, 13 February 2009).

Fence breaking by the provinces

Depending on the source, 31, 32 or 33 provinces broke the rules regarding the limits on incentives (VietNamNet, 4 January 2006; Vu et al., 2007; and Hong et al., 2009, respectively). According to the Department of Planning and Investment, there were 1135 projects altogether that received excessive incentives (VietNamNet, 21 November 2006). Some typical violations of the investment regulations included rebating taxes such as corporate income tax and VAT, providing rent-free land, and higher or lengthier exemptions on land tax than provided for by the central government (Hong et al., 2009, p. 11). For example, Ben Tre province extended the corporate income tax exemption by four years and provided a 50 percent reduction for a further nine years (Hong et al., 2009, p. 11). A majority of the violators also gave incentives to industries that were not eligible to receive them (Vu et al., 2007, p. 15).

The most extensive analysis of the fence-breaking outbreak is that of Vu et al. (2007). First, they show that fence-breaking provinces had lower investment, lower incomes and larger budget deficits than non-fence breaking provinces did. Indeed, the average non-fence breaker had a substantial budget surplus (Vu et al., 2007, p. 14). Second, they recount specific examples of provinces responding to illegal incentives nearby with their own illegal incentives; Phu Tho pledged to have the lowest land use fees after its neighbor, Vinh Phuc, announced a series of incentives exceeding those allowed by the central government (Vu et al., 2007, p. 15). They also perform a regression and panel analysis of FDI inflows into the provinces, finding that provinces which adopted extralegal incentives actually *reduced* the amount of FDI per capita they received in the year after adoption of those incentives. This was statistically significant for registered FDI, but not for implemented FDI (Vu et al., 2007, p. 26). Malesky, analyzing economic reform fence-breaking in 1990–2000 more generally, also finds that provinces breaking the rules do not increase the amount of implemented FDI they receive, with negative but statistically non-significant results (Malesky, 2008, p. 111–2). In an interesting contrast, he finds that provinces with high levels of FDI are more likely to engage in fence-breaking economic reforms (in a total of 13 categories, such as land, labor and legal policies, in addition to investment incentives). However, as we have already seen, the provinces that engaged in fence-breaking on investment incentives tended to have lower levels of per capita FDI than non-fence breakers. Taken together, these two findings could suggest that high-FDI provinces engaged in fence-breaking in areas other than investment incentives. It is hard to claim this with certainty, however, because his data precedes the more recent investment incentive fence-breaking, which occurred from 2001 to 2005 (Vu et al., 2007, p. 17). This also implies that investors were not responding to incentives with greater investment. Indeed, two studies have found this in the case of Vietnam. The first, conducted by the Vietnam National University-Ho Chi Minh City and the Vietnam Competition Initiative in 2004, concluded that 'Nearly 85% of firms said they would have made the same investment decision even without incentives' (VietNamNet, 6 November 2004). In a small 2008 survey of foreign firms in quarrying and mining, seven companies said that Vietnam offered better investment incentives than other countries in which they did business; nonetheless, five of those seven would have invested in Vietnam without incentives, even accounting for the incentives they would have received in other countries (Hong et al., 2009, p. 25).[16] This implies the incentives were not 'decisive' in the investment decision, in the sense used by Guisinger and Associates (1985). In this instance, firms said they would have invested in Vietnam anyway because of the low level of royalties on natural resources and low labor costs (Hong et al., 2009, p. 25).

Exposure, debate and the end of the fiscal war

The story of provincial fence-breaking on investment incentives broke in a series of newspaper articles in the summer of 2005 (Hong et al., 2009, p. 11) and an investigation by the Ministry of Finance (Vu et al., 2007, p. 15). Some provinces defended their use of higher incentives, arguing that the government's policy was inadequate to the specifics of every province and that it would reduce foreign investment (vnexpress.net, 22 June 2005). The controversy was capped by a decision of Prime Minister Phan Van Khai on 29 December 2005 ordering the provinces to immediately end the illegal subsidies (VietNamNet, 4 January 2006 and 10 January 2006). The central government required the provinces to provide reports on these incentives and on corrective actions (Vu et al., 2007, p. 18), and threatened legal consequences for the provincial officials who authorized them (VietNamNet, 10 January 2006). Despite a deadline of 1 March 2006 for the reports, only 14 provinces had filed them by mid-March, 'and only six of these provinces acknowledged violations'. Even after a second order to provide reports, by 2 August 2006, there were still 22 provinces which had not done so, and many of those reports were unsatisfactory (Vu et al., 2007, p. 18). In November 2006, however, the Ministry of Planning and Investment announced that there had been 1135 cases of excessive incentives (VietNamNet, 21 November 2006).

Evidence on compliance

Even the EU, with its long experience and extensive case law, does not achieve full compliance with its state aid rules, especially with newer Member States. How well has Vietnam, which has far fewer resources and less experience, been able to regain control over the situation since 2005? As noted above, there were substantial initial compliance problems, with some provinces not providing the required reports on violations, not admitting violations if they did submit reports, and other provinces submitting very sketchy reports with few details. However, following Malesky's (2004, p. 311) point that senior Vietnamese officials use press releases to criticize provincial programs, we can examine press reports to see whether the provinces have complied with the crackdown on excessive incentive programs. Some press reports do show cases of compliance. In July 2006, Da Nang repealed its incentives which were incompatible with the Common Investment Law effective 1 July 2006 (VietNamNet, 12 July 2006). Gia Lai province also complied with the central government rules, replacing tax and land incentives with increased infrastructure spending (VietNamNet, 5 October 2006). Another report suggested that decentralization was leading to overproduction of competing facilities, although the problem with illegal incentives was under control: 'Excessive investment incentives given by local authorities in an effort to attract more investment *once* gave the Government and central management authorities a terrible headache' (VietNamNet, 3 April 2007, my emphasis). At the same time, it was clear that the scramble for investment had not abated: In October 2008, Deputy Minister of Planning and Investment Nguyen Chi Dung noted that there were numerous instances in the southern provinces (from Thua Thien-Hue south) where local governments were offering reductions in land costs, taxes and other incentives. There were 60 investment promotion agencies in those provinces alone, and an official from the IPA of Thua Thien-Hue said, 'Local authorities have been scrambling to offer investment incentives to lure investment. Every province and city is trying to build steel mills, airports, seaports, and even oil refineries' (VietNamNet, 14 October 2008). One example of this is the $7.9 billion steel mill/seaport facility being built by Taiwan's Son Duong Formosa in the Vung Ang Economic Zone in Ha Tinh province, where it was slated to receive a 10 percent corporate income tax rate (Vietnam News Briefs, 24 December 2008) instead of the standard 32 percent rate (Fletcher, 2002, p. 9). For their part, Hong et al. see the problem as largely solved with the adoption of the 2005 Common Law on Investment (i.e., the end of separate regimes for foreign and domestic investors) and the Prime Minister's decision of 29 December 2005 (Hong et al., 2009, p. 11). A review of news articles in the Vietnamese-language press (Lam Toi Consulting, 2009) revealed only one report of new fence-breaking (Nguoi Lao Dong, 20 July 2009). Whether this is an isolated incident or just the first in a new outbreak of violations remains to be seen.

Vu et al. ask an important question: If there is so much fence-breaking going on, maybe the problem is not the fence-breakers, but the fence. They suggest that the government investigate the causes of such widespread fence-breaking to see if, rather than punishing the violators, the policies adopted should be applied to the country as a whole (Vu et al., 2007, p. 18). This resembles the battle among richer and poorer states in Brazil, where the latter are demanding the establishment of special funds for their development as the price for ending the country's fiscal war (interview, São Paulo, 29 July 2009).

Conclusion

Subnational competition for investment in Vietnam has been particularly fierce, at times leading to the use of illegal incentives by many provinces. This bears significant similarities with Brazil, in terms of the 'fiscal war' being instigated by the poorer provinces (poorer states in Brazil), in the resort to extralegal methods of investment attraction, and in the widespread nature of these legal violations. In both cases, we see unlawful activities related to the perception that increasing integration was leading to the exacerbation of regional inequality. In Brazil, repeated efforts to resolve the fiscal war have foundered on debates over the establishment of a large development fund similar to the EU's Structural Funds. In Vietnam, the central government has been able to reassert the limits it imposes on investment attraction activities, even as it has further decentralized them. Whether it maintains control, as the EU's Directorate-General for Competition has been able to do for investment incentives there, remains to be seen.

At the same time, it is difficult to make comparisons of the incentives in Vietnam with those in other developing countries. While the country is gaining a reputation as one that is willing to bend over backwards for foreign investors, the tax holidays and other incentives it gives are, by their very nature, not transparent. Moreover, since the country is not a democracy, the government has no requirements to publish the details of investment subsidies, and there is no popular organizing on subsidy issues as there is in India.

The cost to developing countries of investment incentives

As this chapter has shown, the use of investment incentives has spread to developing countries with great rapidity. What is striking in the three cases for which there are estimates of the costs of (some) incentives (Brazil, India and Vietnam) is that developing countries are paying higher costs than industrialized nations. As we have seen, both Brazil and India have spent well over $200,000 per job for automobile assembly plants, far above the highest amount recorded in much richer US states like Mississippi or Alabama. Vietnam has been estimated to spend 0.7 percent of its GDP on incentives (Fletcher, 2002), compared to at most 0.5 percent by US state and local governments. Why should this be so? All three countries are now seen as attractive destinations for FDI, with wages far lower than in the US or EU. All three, of course, see subnational competition for investment, and surely that is part of the explanation. Yet these are tremendous costs for developing countries to shoulder, which no doubt reduce their growth from what it might otherwise be. As Maffini and Marenzi (2007, p. 2) point out for Latin America, general investment attraction policies like these are not geared toward investments that can promise technological spillovers and help the host countries move up the value chain. In fact, I would contend that at such high levels of cost, these incentives detract from the more important goal of upgrading education in developing countries than we see in US states, precisely because of the substantially greater cost.

8
Controlling Incentives and Maximizing the Value of Inward Investment

This chapter analyzes the ways that policymakers around the world have tried to control investment incentives and evaluate their success. As discussed earlier, a number of studies, such as that of Head, Ries, and Swenson (1999) and Albornoz and Corcos (2007), offer theoretical justification for multilateral control of incentives. Here we consider several real-life attempts in that direction. First, I will discuss the rules and effectiveness of the most comprehensive disciplinary effort, that of the European Union. This section begins with a general outline of rules, followed by the most important framework applying to investment incentives *per se*, the Multi-Sectoral Framework on Regional Aid for Large Investment Projects. As we will see, these comprehensive controls have achieved the most success in disciplining investment incentives and bidding wars, but they lack a complete ban on the use of relocation subsidies. The various rules in the GATT Uruguay Round agreements that affect subsidies, including the Agreement on Subsidies and Countervailing Measures (SCM), the General Agreement on Trade in Services (GATS), and the Agreement on Trade-Related Investment Measures (TRIMS), are then explained. These constitute a relatively blunt tool for controlling investment incentives, and the transparency provided by the reporting requirements of the Agreement on Subsidies and Countervailing Measures is far less than that achieved in the EU. Third, we consider two subnational agreements on incentives among Canadian provinces and territories, and among Australian states. While Canada's Code of Conduct on Incentives has failed to prevent provinces from using relocation incentives, the size of the relocating projects has declined from the 1990s when the provisions were adopted. Australia's

Interstate Investment Cooperation Act has done a better, though still not perfect, job preventing subsidized relocations. Fourth, we will examine the contentious politics of subsidy control in the United States. While essentially all federal programs prohibit their use in funding relocation incentives, the two voluntary attempts by groups of states to ban such incentives both quickly failed. There is, however, a substantial amount of political organizing on subsidy issues in the US. The chapter finishes with an analysis of the disciplines that exist in a small number of the many bilateral investment treaties (BITs) and investment incentive agreements (IIAs) in force around the world, as well as in bilateral or regional free trade agreements. As these are aimed primarily at protecting investors' rights, they do not really address control of incentives.

European Union state aid control

'State aid' is the term the European Union uses to refer to subsidies. Thus, state aid law applies to far more than investment incentives, but to all types of selective government support to business, even state-owned firms. Of particular interest for this report are the rules on regional aid, most notably the formerly stand-alone Multi-Sectoral Framework on Regional Aid for Large Investment Projects ('Multi-Sectoral Framework' or MSF). EU state aid rules begin from the presumption that subsidies should not be used by Member States unless they contribute to a goal of the European Union as a whole (not just that of a Member State) and do so in a way that is least distorting of trade within the EU. In other words, there must be a *quid pro quo* (the French term for this principle is *contrepartie*; it is sometimes translated into English as 'compensatory justification' or, more literally, 'counterpart'): if a government gives subsidies to a company, it must contribute to the goals of the EU. Contributing to the development of backward areas, restructuring of firms in difficulty, research and development, controlling pollution, and employment support can all potentially serve this function.

A second critical element of state aid control is oversight: all subsidies must be notified to the European Commission in advance, and may not be implemented until they are approved by the Commission, which can prohibit or modify them if they are in violation of EU law.[1] In the mid-1980s, the Commission began requiring the repayment of aid incompatible with Articles 87–89 of the Treaty of Rome that had been given without respecting the notification rules as the ultimate deterrent of non-notification. Since then, aid recipients and the Member States have fought against this in cases before the European Court of Justice (ECJ), only to see all their substantive arguments struck down (Thomas, 2000, pp. 115–21, 233–8). In the 2000s, however, aid recipients continued to delay repayment by making appeals in national courts against the repayment orders, which led in some cases (in Germany, for example) to dragging out the process for more than eight years (Tucker, 1998; Thomas, 2000, pp. 236–7). In a major decision (Commission v. France, Case C-232/05) in October 2006, the ECJ ruled that such appeals to national courts could not be allowed to suspend the repayment action, which was effective immediately unless Community Courts (the Court of First Instance or the ECJ) ruled otherwise (Willemot and Fort, 2007). As the Court put it, 'Thus, by failing to have regard to the objectives pursued by the Community rules on State aid, that national procedure has prevented the immediate restoration of the previously existing situation and prolonged the unfair competitive advantage resulting from the aid at issue' (Commission v. France, 2006, paragraph 52). This decision greatly strengthens the Commission's hand in dealing with recalcitrant Member States because they can no longer hide behind the alleged rights of the aid recipient as an excuse to not secure repayment.

The backlog in non-implemented aid repayment orders is falling rapidly: the Commission reports that the number of pending recovery cases had fallen from 94 in 2004 to 43 in mid-2009, that €7.1 billion had been recovered over the same period (compared to just €2.3 billion between 2000 and 2004), and that unrepaid aid fell from 75 percent at the end of 2004 to 9 percent in mid-2009 (European Union, 2009h, p. 13).

The regional aid rules are central to state aid control because they designate a maximum aid intensity for every location within the European Union (Thomas 2000, p. 89). The key idea is that poorer areas of the EU can give larger subsidies than richer ones; indeed, the most prosperous regions cannot give regional aid at all.[2] Governments can only give support to firms in proportion to the disadvantage of the region (Thomas 2000, p. 57). Eligible areas are determined primarily by the region's GDP per capita in relation to that of the EU average[3] or national average,[4] but actual maps are negotiated between the Commission and each Member State. As Wishlade (1997, pp. 22–3) relates, drawing up these maps has at times been highly contentious. Regional aid is the most likely form to be used for attracting mobile investment and, with that in mind, the Commission adopted the Multi-Sectoral Framework on 16 December 1997. The 'MSF 1998' was replaced with the 'MSF 2002', while beginning in 2007 the MSF rules were incorporated into the guidelines on regional aid. These provisions now apply to projects with over €50 million in eligible expenditures (fixed investment plus first two years' wage costs), with the effect of reducing the aid maximum to 50 percent of the normal maximum for expenditures between €50 and €100 million, and 34 percent of the normal maximum for expenditures above €100 million.[5] Thus, in a region where the normal aid maximum was 30 percent of eligible expenditures, an investment of €200 million could receive up to €32.5 million ([50 × 0.3] + [50 × 0.15] + [100 × 0.1]). Investments receiving more aid than the maximum allowable for a €100 million investment must be individually notified to the Commission; in this example, a project receiving more than €22.5 million in aid would need to be notified individually. In addition, the Commission's decision also takes into account the competitive situation of the industry in question (demerits for a dominant producer) and employment. Thus, the Commission in 2005 informally indicated to the Irish government that it would not approve a proposed €170 million aid to Intel for a €1.6 billion chip fabrication plant at Leixlip, and the Irish authorities withdrew the aid notification. Though Intel built the first facility included in the application, Ireland feared the decision would make it less competitive in the future for such major investments, a view encouraged by Intel's chairman, Craig Barrett (Smyth, 2005a; Staunton, 2005, 2006; Shoesmith, 2006).[6] Indeed, the bulk of the aid rejected was for later projects which to date have still not even begun (Lyons, 2009, Business p. 1). Similarly, in 2008 an EU decision under the MSF 2002 to open an investigation of a proposed investment subsidy of €37.4 million to steel-maker Dunaferr prompted Hungary to withdraw the aid proposal (European Union, 2008a). And in 2002, the UK withdrew a proposed €17.4 million aid to Ford after the Commission opened an investigation under the MSF 1998 (European Union, 2002a, 2002b). All of these cases show the effectiveness of the MSF rules in controlling investment incentives.

Also important to an understanding of the state aid rules are the rules on aid for environmental purposes. The EU first introduced such rules in 1974 (European Union, 2005a, p. 27), staking out a policy generally supportive of using subsidies to promote energy conservation and the environment. Prior to the 2001 Guidelines on State Aid for Environmental Protection, such support was 'of limited importance', comprising only 1.85 percent of state aid to manufacturing and services in 1996–98 (European Union, 2004b). Beginning in 1999, however, the subsidies given in this category rose steadily, mostly in the form of tax exemptions rather than grants (European Union, 2005a, p. 37, table 12). In 2008, aid for environmental protection and energy saving was the second highest category of all aid excluding crisis measures, making up 24 percent of aid to manufacturing and services, just behind the 26 percent devoted to regional aid (European Union, 2010b).

Much of this aid is in the form of partial exemption from new energy taxes. Introduced to provide incentives for reduced use of fossil fuels, such 'ecotaxes' also raised fears that they would make European industry uncompetitive internationally. As a result, many of the taxes included provisions to exempt manufacturers and other large-scale users from part of the new tax. For example, effective 1 April 1999, Germany introduced an ecotax with both a general rate reduction for businesses and a rebate for manufacturing (this discussion is based on European Union, 2007c). These reductions were considered state aid, with the amounts for 2005 being €1.85 billion for the rate reduction and €1.9 billion for the rebate. As the Commission noted in its decision, even after these provisions, German manufacturers had to pay rates that were above the minimums set in the EU's 2003 Energy Tax Directive, which led the Commission to approve the proposed aid. Since Germany, by far the biggest absolute user of environmental aid in 2005, spent €7.1 billion for this purpose (European Union, 2006b, table k5_4), it can be seen that these two measures alone accounted for more than half of that. As the Commission admits, 'only a relatively small proportion comprises aid to make investments that reach higher environmental standards than community standards or to undertake further investment to reduce pollution or for the development of renewable energy sources' (European Union, 2005a, p. 39). The vast majority is exemption from ecotaxes to make them politically palatable.

As discussed in Chapter 4, some aid for environmental purposes in the EU consists of investment incentives for biofuel production facilities. Under the 2008 Guidelines for State Aid to Environmental Protection, capital grants of up to 60 percent of 'extra investment costs borne by the beneficiary compared with a conventional power plant' are permitted for investment in renewable energy sources (European Union, 2008b, points 103 and 105). While information is available on some specific projects, aggregate amounts of incentives are harder to determine. Kutas et al. (2007, pp. 54–6) report that Germany spent €1.75 billion on all investment aid to bioenergy, while in other Member States for which a total amount can be estimated, it is at most in the tens of millions of euros.

The European Union has seen a general downward trend of state aid, falling from about 2 percent of GDP in the 1980s to 1 percent and under in the 1990s, to about 0.5 percent in 2007 (European Union, 2009h, p. 5) and 0.54 percent in 2008 (European Union, 2009h, p. 4).[7] This is one indication of the success of state aid control. Another is the fact that the largest incentives in the EU are smaller than those for comparable projects in the US, as we saw in Chapter 6. Moreover, not only are the incentives smaller, but they are going into poorer areas than comparable US projects. Furthermore, while in 2000, state aid trends appeared to undermine long-run cohesion because the 11 central Member States gave far more of their state aid to research and development than did the four Cohesion countries (Ireland, Portugal, Spain and Greece; Thomas, 2000, p. 220), both Spain and Ireland have now converged on the EU-27 average, as have a number of the new Member States (European Union, 2010b).

Recent developments in EU state aid control (aside from crisis aid, which applies mostly to the banking sector and not to investment incentives) stem from the State Aid Action Plan for 2005–09 (European Union, 2005b). In this document, the Commission announced its goal of 'less and better targeted state aid', simplified procedures, greater responsibility on Member States for carrying out the rules and the concomitant requirement for them to respect the rules. In particular, the action plan included the incorporation of the Multi-Sectoral Framework within the regional aid guidelines (effective in 2007), the General Block Exemption Regulation (adopted in 2008 as Commission Regulation (EC) 800/2008 of 6 August 2008; European Union, 2009h, p. 11), and a discussion of how to ensure compliance by Member States, including the possibility of seeking financial penalties as provided under Article 228 of the European Community Treaty.[8] Naturally, the economic crisis has caused big changes in state aid, but this does not affect the control elements relevant for investment incentives. State aid to bail out banks equal to 1.7 percent of GDP was approved over the course of 2008, and a Temporary Framework was approved by the Commission in December 2008 for improving access to credit, especially for small and medium enterprises (European Union, 2009h, p. 4; Campos, 2009, p. 2).

One attractive element of the EU state aid regime is that the notification requirement ensures wide availability of information on subsidies in the European Union. Moreover, the Commission (more precisely, the Directorate-General for Competition) publishes a tremendous amount of data, all of which is available on its website at ec.europa.eu/comm/competition/index_en.html.[9] Particularly notable were the 'Surveys' on state aid, beginning in 1989, which made public a database on state aid going back to 1981. The Surveys have now been superseded by the online state aid 'Scoreboard'.

On the other hand, there is a glaring hole in state aid control: relocation incentives are not banned. For example, the relocation of Renault's Vilvoorde, Belgium, plant to Spain prompted union demonstrations at the home of then-Competition Commissioner Karel Van Miert in 1997 (Damme, ed., 1997, pp. 61, 115) leading to the cancellation of European Regional Development funding for the Spanish subsidy (Lillie, 1999, pp. 8–9).

The most recent case of a subsidized relocation is the January 2009 axing of 1900 jobs at Dell's manufacturing facility in Limerick, Ireland (Quinn, 2009, p. 2; Agence France Presse, 2009a), and the transfer of these operations to Lodz, Poland, where the company received €54.5 million in state aid (Limerick Leader, 2009; European Union, 2009f). This relocation has been subject to substantial dispute. Although the Limerick and Lodz plants both serve the Europe-Middle East-Africa (EMEA) market (*Foreign Direct Investment*, 2009), the European Parliament approved a European Globalization Fund package for the Irish Dell workers of €14.8 million based on a supposed relocation of Dell's activity to 'China and other Asian countries' (States News Service, 2009).[10] In the EP's press release, it was noted that 'the European Commission wrote Parliament a letter stating that there was no connection between the redundancies in Ireland and a new Dell plant in Poland, the Polish factory having been planned long before the closure in Limerick' (States News Service, 2009). Similarly, in the Commission's decision on Dell aid in Lodz, the Commission stated that the job losses in Limerick were not caused by the state aid at Lodz because the new Dell investment would have taken place in any event, if not at Lodz then at Nitra in Slovakia, although it would not have received aid at the latter location (European Union, 2009g, p. 38). However, this explanation that Dell was moving within the EU anyway is not consistent with the claim that the production moved to Asia. Moreover, while a non-subsidized relocation often generates substantial political conflict (e.g., Nokia's move from Germany to Romania; Seveanu, 2008), it does not implicate the state aid rules. The Commission concluded that aid in Lodz was justified because it was €40 million cheaper for Dell to produce in Nitra than in Lodz if there were no state aid at Lodz (European Union, 2009g, pp. 32–3), an admission that it was less efficient to produce at Lodz. The Commission justified its decision to allow the aid based on the fact that per capita income, unemployment, and risk of poverty were all worse in Lodz than in Nitra (European Union, 2009g, pp. 39–40). For this reason, the Commission considered that the investment was of greater benefit to the Community in Lodz than in Nitra

(European Union, 2009g, p. 39; cf. Bartik, 1991). What it does not explain is why this benefit justifies state aid greater than the difference in the aid limits of the two regions: the difference in aid limits between Lodz and Nitra is only 10 percent GGE (50 percent vs. 40 percent), but the Commission authorized aid of 27.81 percent (European Union, 2009g, p. 41). This seems on its face to violate the principle of proportionality (see Thomas, 2000, p. 57).

Despite approving the globalization fund support for Irish Dell workers, MEPs expressed a great deal of anger at the Commission's actions. While criticism from Irish MEPs was predictable, Socialist and Democratic caucus MEPs from the UK and France were equally vocal. Stephen Hughes (UK, Labour) said the state aid decision on Lodz was 'simply not acceptable' and added, 'Dell cannot close a plant relying on EU funds to help the workers who lose their jobs, then reopen another in another member state with subsidies from public funds.' Similarly, the French chair of the EP's Employment and Social Affairs Committee, Pervenche Berès (Parti Socialiste), said, 'The Dell case must never happen again.... The EU recovery plan (in the wake of the economic downturn) commits EU institutions to maintain jobs whenever possible; obviously, the Commission did very little to implement this policy in the Dell case' (Meade, 2009). In the Polish government's submissions to the Commission on the criticism of the relocation, it noted that the Commission had previously approved an aid for a company, Getrag Ford in Slovakia, which was reducing production in Germany (European Union, 2009g, p. 17). The Commission's response was that this was not relevant because the Getrag closure in Germany was part of a single investment project, which was not the case with Dell (European Union, 2009g, pp. 25–6).[11] Perhaps more to the point from the view of an outside observer, it was also the case that there were no job losses at Getrag Ford's plant in Germany, as the 100 employees affected were to be transferred to another assembly line there (European Union, 2006e, pp. 5–6), unlike the 1900 jobs lost at Limerick. Moreover, whereas Getrag's German facility that was being closed had received no state aid (European Union, 2006e, p. 6), Dell had received €55 million in grants since its arrival in Ireland in 1991 (*Irish Examiner*, 2008).

The latest twist in the Dell saga is that in early December 2009, less than three months after the European Commission approved Dell's state aid in Lodz, the company sold the Polish facility to Taiwan's Foxconn Group (Agence France Presse, 2009b; M2 EquityBites, 2009) for an undisclosed sum. Dell planned to purchase its computers from the factory, and it was anticipated that there would be no layoffs in Lodz.

Approval from the European Commission was pending at the time of this writing.

Subsidized relocations have led to major political battles in the EU, as in the US, Canada and Australia (see further below on Canada's Code of Conduct on Incentives and Australia's Interstate Investment Cooperation Agreement). While the US has largely banned the use of federal funds for subsidized relocation by state and local governments (Thomas, 2000, pp. 164–6), Oxelheim and Ghauri fear that 'The worst-case scenario is that the race [for FDI] becomes so strong that it makes a threat to the cohesion of the entire EU' (2008, p. 369).

World Trade Organization subsidy rules

The World Trade Organization has three agreements that touch on investment incentives, the Agreement on Subsidies and Countervailing Measures (SCM), the General Agreement on Trade in Services (GATS), and the Agreement on Trade-Related Investment Measures (TRIMS), all adopted as part of the Uruguay Round negotiations. In terms of disciplining incentives, the Agreement on SCM is the most important. This agreement also requires the notification of subsidies, which is important in its own right.

1. Like EU state aid rules, the Agreement on Subsidies and Countervailing Measures applies to all subsidies, not just location incentives. While previous GATT rounds had contained subsidy provisions, the ASCM defined a subsidy for the first time, and provided that a subsidy had to be specific to 'an enterprise or industry or groups of enterprises or industries' (WTO, Agreement on Subsidies and Countervailing Measures, Article 2.1) to be considered actionable (export subsidies are automatically considered specific). One intriguing aspect of this agreement was its classification of subsidies according to a traffic light scheme: red-light, or prohibited, subsidies; yellow-light actionable subsidies, and green-light non-actionable subsidies. The support measures that could potentially fall into the green-light category largely followed European Union practice on subsidies that could be considered compatible with the Treaty of Rome – that is, regional aid, R&D aid, and aid for meeting new environmental requirements.

Despite pushing for generous allowances for research and development support, the Clinton administration was generally hostile to the idea of green-lighting certain aid, and the designation expired in 1999, although this was due more to objections from developing countries (Thomas 2000, pp. 261–2). Now, all subsidies can be classified as either prohibited (the former 'red-light', i.e., based on exports or domestic content) or actionable (all other subsidies, provided they are specific).

Also expiring in 1999 were provisions establishing criteria for a rebuttable presumption of serious prejudice. In Article 6.1, one factor which could lead to a presumption of serious prejudice was ad valorem subsidization of 5 percent. This linked to Annex IV, which set forth the method of calculation and, in a provision relevant to investment incentives, stated that for companies in a start-up situation, a subsidy of 15 percent of the investment would also satisfy the presumption (WTO, Agreement on Subsidies and Countervailing Measures). When Article 6.1 and Annex IV expired in 1999, there was no longer any guidance specifically for location subsidies, hence incentives are to be incorporated into an overall calculation of subsidy levels.

Investment incentives have long been a part of WTO jurisprudence on subsidies. In the 1996 case of Italian pasta (termed 'Certain Pasta from Italy' in the US countervailing duty case), the United States found that a number of Italian pasta makers had received subsidies from the Italian government, regional governments, the European Regional Development Fund, and the European Social Fund (Department of Commerce, 2007, p. 2). While some of the alleged subsidies were for export, several were investment aids.[12] More recently, the European Communities have argued that state and local investment incentives to Boeing in the state of Washington (the result of a 20-state bidding war, as recounted in LeRoy, 2005, pp. 87–8), valued at $3.2 billion over 20 years, constituted a violation of subsidy rules (WTO, 2009). In September 2009, the panel ruled against EU launch aid to Airbus, but the ruling on the EU's complaint was not expected until June 2010 (*Daily Post*, 2010, p. 22).

Article 27 of the Agreement established 'special and differential' rules for developing countries. As Mutti (2003, pp. 83–5) points out, an important consequence of this is that it enables poorer countries to maintain export processing zones, which would otherwise run afoul of the prohibition on export subsidies. The list of nations qualifying for this exemption includes all of those designated by the United Nations as 'least developed' plus 20 nations with a GNP per capita under $1000 at current exchange rates, of which the largest were India and Indonesia (WTO, Agreement on Subsidies and Countervailing Measures, Annex VII).

2. The General Agreement on Trade in Services (GATS) may have an eventual effect on investment incentives. Unlike the TRIMS agreement (below), which applies to trade in goods, the GATS applies to the

provision of services across borders in any of four 'modes' of supply: (1) remote; (2) consumer presence in supplying country (especially tourism); (3) commercial presence (a bank); or (4) personal presence of a supplier in the purchasing country (a consultant, for instance).[13] Investment incentives could easily occur for any of the first three modes: A call center could be either mode 1 or 3, depending on whether it served foreign or domestic customers (and obviously, it could be both), while hotels and other tourism-related investments have certainly received subsidies as well. Article XV of the GATS provided for future negotiations on the status on subsidies to services; however, there have been no agreements to date on this contentious issue (Global Subsidies Initiative, 2010). Should such negotiations ever come to fruition, the 'eventual' effect on incentives might finally arrive.

3. The Agreement on Trade-Related Investment Measures (TRIMS) forbids governments granting incentives from making them conditional on domestic content or trade-balancing rules, and prohibits foreign-exchange balancing rules, restricting the import of inputs, or restricting the recipient's exports (Agreement on Trade Related Investment Measures, Annex). Indeed, TRIMS is not a regulation of incentives so much as it a regulation of performance requirements on any investment; however, it is important to highlight that such measures cannot be imposed even when the investor receives a subsidy.

With China's accession to the WTO, the TRIMS agreement has assumed greater significance in its effect on host state policies for ensuring benefits from foreign investment. Bishop (2007, pp. 95–6) argues that China's policies on mandatory technology transfer and local content requirements had been successful in building up the capacity of Chinese firms in Shanghai. Both of these avenues have now been prohibited in China's TRIMS-plus accession agreement (Beijing interview, June 2009), but Bishop is sanguine that Chinese firms may have already obtained sufficient success from these former policies to make progress on their own, going so far as to say that 'the "demonstration effect" might have been the major benefit of joint ventures' (2007, p. 96). In addition, China continues to try to skirt the letter of the TRIMS rules by making approval of foreign investment 'unofficially' contingent on technology transfer or local content (Beijing interview, June 2009).

4. The Agreement on SCM includes the provision that all members must notify their subsidies to the WTO Secretariat. Unlike the situation in the European Union, this entails *ex post* notification as opposed to *ex ante* notification. In principle, these submissions should cover all subsidies given within a country, at all levels of government, and

include the amounts spent on such support. If adhered to, this would be a valuable transparency exercise. However, by October 2009, a number of large countries had submitted neither their 2009 nor their 2007 'new and full' notifications, including India, Mexico, Israel, South Africa and Indonesia (WTO, 2009b). On the other hand, the United States had improved the timeliness of its notifications, submitting its report on time[14] but the report only covered FY 2005–06 and was still plagued by incomplete reporting of subnational subsidies including, by my count, only nine individual incentive packages in the entire notification.

Three important differences stand out between the EU state aid regime and WTO subsidy rules. First, the European Commission can act on its own initiative against subsidies it believes may be incompatible with the Treaty. It can act before a harm has even taken place if a proposed aid is properly notified. By contrast, World Trade Organization subsidy disputes (and countervailing duty measures at the national level) are complaint-driven. Second, because of the notification requirement, subsidy discipline in the European Union is *ex ante* (except in the important case of non-notified aid), whereas WTO control is always *ex post*. Third, aid repayment is a common remedy for illegal subsidies in the EU, whereas it has only been used once in the WTO (in a 2000 complaint by the United States against Australia; see Thomas, 2000, p. 260), but is now being advocated by the US in its complaint against Airbus (Alden, 2005).

It is also important to note that not all investment subsidies have trade effects. If a local government provides an incentive to Wal-Mart[15] or other retailer, this will be irrelevant to trade and thus fall outside of the terms of reference for the Agreement on Subsidies and Countervailing Measures. However, if and when subsidies disciplines are inaugurated under the General Agreement on Trade in Services, such incentives could be regulated under the GATS.

Subnational agreements on incentives

Canada and Australia are two federal states where competition for investment at the subnational level has at times been severe. In both instances, the pressures have led provinces and states to attempts to control incentives. The United States, with its much larger economy, has seen numerous battles over this issue.

1. In Canada, the subsidized relocation of investment, or poaching (usually called 'piracy' in the United States) was a major problem in the 1990s, with Nova Scotia and Manitoba both losing existing call centers

to New Brunswick (DeMont, 1994, p. 26), and Crown Life Insurance moving 1200 headquarters jobs from Toronto to Regina in 1991 with a C$250 million provincial loan guarantee (Kelly, 1991, p. 44). It was in this context that the Code of Conduct on Incentives was agreed in July 1994 as part of the Agreement on Internal Trade (AIT), whose parties include the federal government, all 10 provinces, and two of the country's three territories.[16] The Code (Annex 607.3) explicitly prohibited relocation subsidies in Article 3, Prohibited Incentives (Internal Trade Secretariat, 1994):

> No Party shall provide an incentive that is contingent, in law or in fact, and would directly result in an enterprise, located in the territory of any Party, relocating an existing operation into its territory.

Moreover, under Article 4, Avoidance of Certain Incentives, the governments agreed to make 'best efforts' to avoid bidding wars; however, unlike Article 3, this was not legally binding.

Thomas (2000, p. 177) argued that banning poaching could be seen as a useful way of breaking down the Prisoners' Dilemma of investment competition into smaller steps, as suggested by Axelrod (1984, pp. 131–2):

> Of all location subsidies, however, the problems inherent in relocation incentives are most evident because no new jobs are created by such moves. By tackling a small but significant and clearly egregious part of the overall problem, U.S. states might be able to similarly launch themselves into greater cooperation in avoiding investment subsidies.

The Code has now been in existence for 15 years. Has it been a success? The short answer is 'no.' Its only legal test came in 1995, when United Parcel Service (UPS) relocated 870 jobs from British Columbia, Manitoba, and Ontario to New Brunswick, receiving C$11 million in training grants in the process (Thomas 2000, p. 178; Brown, 2006, pp. 62–3). British Columbia filed a complaint in September 1996 under the AIT. After charge and counter-charge between the two provinces, the dispute was never resolved. No other poaching case has been raised under the AIT since.

However, this does not mean that the use of relocation incentives has disappeared. In fact, New Brunswick gave BBM Bureau of Measurement C$594,000 to lure 62 jobs from Toronto, even as the UPS dispute was taking place (Canadian Press, 1996, p. 69). Since then, poaching has continued (though New Brunswick stopped after McKenna left office), but on a smaller scale than in the 1990s. The largest occurred in 2005, when Clarke Inc., a trucking company, moved its headquarters from Concord, Ontario, to Halifax, Nova Scotia, for which it received C$1.9 million in payroll rebates (Nova Scotia Business, Inc., 2007; Richer, 2005; Thomas, 2007b), a deal that is even posted on the province's investment attraction website. Nova Scotia gave a C$2 million equity injection to Impath Networks to move 10 headquarters jobs from Ottawa to Halifax (Canadian Press, 2008). Quebec has offered incentives to small high-tech companies in the Ottawa area to move across the river to Gatineau (Tuck, 1999). Ontario offered Sobeys incentives to relocate its headquarters from Nova Scotia, causing the latter to give a retention subsidy (interviews). Finally, Prince Edward Island gave relocation subsidies to three small companies, one in 2000 and two in 2005 (Canadian Press, 2000; Bornais, 2005, p. 12; *Guardian*, 2005, p. A3). Nonetheless, it must be noted that these occurrences were quite small compared with the UPS relocation of 1995. Clarke only moved 95 jobs, and the other deals are smaller still. Moreover, it appears that Ontario takes a benign view of poaching; as one interviewee put it, 'They see themselves as playing on a much larger stage.' Thus, the loss of 95 jobs to Nova Scotia is not too significant.

Within provinces, however, Canada has cut down the competition for investment. In eight of Canada's ten provinces, local governments are prohibited from giving incentives (Reese, 1993; Thomas, 2000; interviews). The two still allowing municipal incentives (Manitoba and Saskatchewan) have just over 2 million in population and few major cities. Thus, compared with the United States, where thousands of municipal governments join the 50 state governments in competing for projects, the cooperation problem faced in Canada is far more tractable.

Canadian provinces do seem to use incentives far less than US state and local governments. The prohibition of municipal subsidies in most provinces means that the retail sector is rarely subsidized.[17] In industries where the two compete directly, Canada appears to benefit from its universal health insurance system and can pay less in incentives. In the auto industry, for example, in 2005 Ontario landed a Toyota assembly plant with a package worth US$100.5 million at the exchange rate prevailing at the time, or 15.5 percent of the cost of the investment. Meanwhile, new assembly plants in the United States from 1999 to 2008 were receiving packages worth from $133 million (16.6 percent) for Toyota in Texas to $450 million (45 percent) for Volkswagen in Tennessee (see Chapter 6).

At the same time, competitive pressures are clearly at work. Ontario's Conservative Party governments of the 1990s and early 2000s cut subsidies to the auto industry, and the province received no new assembly facilities, and several were closed, in the period from 1995 to 2003 (Keenan, 2003, p. B1; Woodcock, 2006, p. D3). As a result, the Liberal government elected in 2003 established a C$500 million Auto Investment Strategy Fund, which funded the new Toyota plant, reinvestments by the Big Three (General Motors, Ford and Chrysler), and new parts facilities by Honda and Linamar (*Site Selection*, 12 June 2006). However, if we look at the overall pattern of incentives, they are falling in Canada while, as we saw in Chapter 6, they have risen in the United States since 1996.

One possible exception is support for research and development, which is generous in Canada. For example, the British Columbia government provides 100 percent deductibility of both current and capital R&D costs, and a 10 percent tax credit added on top of a federal 20 percent tax credit (BC Ministry of Economic Development, 2006). Québec provides a tax credit of 17.5 percent (Larson, 2006, p. 5D). Whether any of this qualifies as a subsidy depends on the *de jure* or *de facto* specificity of each particular program.

The most recent development in Canada has been the Trade, Investment, and Labour Mobility Agreement (TILMA) between Alberta and British Columbia. This pact was negotiated under Article 1800 of the Agreement on Internal Trade, which allows the parties to reach additional agreements that need not apply to all of them. The agreement, which came into force on 1 April 2007, bans business subsidies in the two provinces under its Article 12. These provisions apply to all levels of government (interview).

It is unclear whether these policy changes (fall in incentives, and New Brunswick ending poaching) are actually due to the Code of Conduct. One provincial official involved with internal trade did not think so; instead, changes in governments brought in leaders less inclined to offer subsidies. Even in relatively interventionist Québec, incentives have fallen over the last several years. The same has been true in New Brunswick (interviews).

2. In Australia, bidding wars and poaching were also considered to be a problem for the states and territories. In 2000, South Australia offered auto parts firms A$15,000 per job to relocate from Victoria (Wallace and O'Brien, 2000, p. 5). The following year, Victoria returned

the favor by offering A$2 million to South Australia parts maker Castalloy (Field, 2001, p. 7). Reform movements started as early as 1996, when the Community and Public Sector Union endorsed a New South Wales government initiative to end the poaching and bidding wars (Millett, 1996, p. 7), and an Industry Commission report criticized state incentives and recommended that they be cut back or abolished entirely. The Industry Commission's successor, the Productivity Commission, published further estimates of state incentive spending in 2002 (Productivity Commission, 2004, p. 87). Following this, five of the country's six states (New South Wales, Victoria, Tasmania, South Australia and Western Australia), plus the Northern Territory and the Australian Capital Territory (ACT), reached an agreement in 2003 to end bidding wars among them. In addition, the parties provide annual reports to each other on their investment attraction. Queensland was the only state that refused to go along. Stimulated in part by an A$100 million subsidy to Fox News in Sydney (Markusen and Nesse, 2007, p. 5), the signatories banned relocation incentives and pledged not to use subsidies for investments that were clearly coming to Australia (State of Victoria, 2003). According to Victorian Treasurer John Brumby, the 'Interstate Investment Co-operation Agreement' (IICA) built on an information exchange program with New South Wales.[18] He said: 'Victoria has already exchanged information with NSW on 30 projects, and companies have been caught out overstating the incentives offered by the potential "rival" location. It's estimated that this action alone has already saved taxpayers around $20 million.' The three-year agreement was renewed for another five years in 2006 (State of Victoria, 2006). A year later, Brumby said the signatories had saved 'tens of millions of dollars' as a result of the agreement and that '...some jurisdictions [were] noticing a decrease in the number of companies seeking incentives to relocate from one State or Territory to another' (State of Victoria, 2007). The agreement remains largely informal, with no monitoring or enforcement mechanisms, a weakness criticized by the Productivity Commission in 2005 (Insight Economics, 2006, p. 24). Further, the fact that Queensland has not signed is considered a problem by the IICA's parties, with some going so far as to say 'that unless there is a uniform agreement they will start to undertake "poaching" activities in a certain jurisdiction', (Insight Economics, 2006, p. 25), presumably Queensland.

As with Canada, the annual report is not publicly available, reducing the transparency of incentives offered by the states and territories. In contrast to Canada, however, the agreement seems to be more closely adhered to. A newspaper search of the premium Nexis database turned up only one instance of poaching, when the New South Wales government provided undisclosed incentives for the relocation of a Regional Express Airlines pilot training school from Mangalore, Victoria, to Wagga Wagga, NSW (Macdonald, 2009). Furthermore, according to a State of Victoria Treasury official, there have been 'a few' relocations among the signatories that received incentives, but he argued that the companies had decided to move anyway (interview). However, this would mean the agreement is only a partial success: if the facilities were moving anyway, it was a waste of money to subsidize the firms' relocations.

3. In the United States, there are three main aspects of disciplines on incentives. The first is controls on federal subsidies used by subnational governments. Second, there have been formal relations among states, including two regional no-raiding agreements, plus the work of the National Governors Association (NGA). Third, the most significant force for reform in the United States has been private non-governmental organizations (NGOs).

Two main federal issues have been important: industrial revenue bonds, which the federal government subsidizes through their tax deductibility; and campaigns for no-raiding provisions in the main federal subsidy programs available to state and local governments.

Industrial revenue bonds are tax-exempt bonds issued by local governments to fund a wide variety of projects. Since the dividends from these bonds are exempt from federal tax, issuers can pay a lower interest rate than would be the case with a taxable bond. Until 1986, there were few restrictions on them; they were very popular with local governments because the entire cost was borne by the federal government through their tax deductibility. In the 1986 tax reform, caps were put on the amount of bonds that could be issued and restrictions placed on their use (Thomas, 2000, p. 164).

As Greg LeRoy (1999) has said, 'Behind every reform, there lies a horror story: a company that failed to deliver or a company that got subsidies but then did something to offend the public.' This is true for all of the cases examined here. For example, in May 1994, Briggs and Stratton accepted subsidies from cities in Missouri and Kentucky to relocate lawnmower production from Milwaukee, Wisconsin. In both Missouri and Kentucky, the local governments used their federal Community Development Block Grant (CDBG) subsidies from the federal government. Moreover, in both instances, the workers losing their jobs were unionized, while the new locations were non-union. Wisconsin's Congressional delegation spearheaded the reform of

CDBG: it was successful as early as July 1994 in getting the US House of Representatives to place no-raiding requirements into the legislation, but a filibuster threat in the Senate by Missouri Senator Kit Bond prevented its passage. The ban was finally adopted in November 1998 (Thomas, 2000, p. 166). Similar stories lie behind the anti-piracy provisions that were eventually placed into the Urban Development Action Grant, Economic Development Administration, Small Business Administration, and Workforce Investment Act programs (Thomas, 2000, p. 165).

State governments have entered into two voluntary no-raiding agreements. In the 1980s, the Council of Great Lakes Governors approved an anti-piracy pact, but it collapsed even before it came into effect. A 1991 agreement among New York, New Jersey and Connecticut met the same fate a few days after it started (Schweke et al., 1994, p. 70). New York City has been a particular target of nearby jurisdictions, and has been subject to local companies threatening to move out of the city in order to receive retention subsidies (LeRoy, 2005, pp. 38–43).

The National Governors Association (NGA) has played an important political role in the United States. State governors are quite aware of the dangers of bidding wars for investment. However, the NGA has consistently argued that there should be no federal intervention to stop incentives, and that states should refrain from bidding wars because avoiding them is good policy (Kayne and Shonka, 1994, pp. 25–6). However, the track record of state behavior in using relocation subsidies and taking part in bidding wars makes this view implausible (Thomas, 2000, p. 168).

The main impetus for enacting disciplines in the United States has come from civil society organizations. Washington-based Good Jobs First has built itself into the nation's clearinghouse for NGOs involved in subsidy reform, and has expanded to offices in New York. Its website, www.goodjobsfirst.org, should be consulted by any researcher interested in the state of play of US subsidy reform.

One of the main demands of state-level organizations has been transparency. As noted already, many incentive deals are shrouded in secrecy, making it impossible to monitor their operation. Beginning with Minnesota in 1995, some 10 states now have firm-level disclosure of subsidy deals. The Minnesota law required that all state and local government subsidies must be reported, that the granting authority set job and wage standards for those subsidies, and requires them to use clawbacks if the job goals have not been met within two years. Along with Minnesota, Maine and Illinois have the most comprehensive reporting requirements, and Illinois even posts its reports on the Web (Good Jobs First, 2007b).

A second major issue has been the Living Wage movement. Its goal is to have cities enact ordinances that require subsidy recipients and city contractors to pay wages above a threshold often related to the US poverty line (Martin, 2001, p. 471). ACORN (Association of Community Organizations for Reform Now) is a national organization that was active in a number of local campaigns and helped aid its national diffusion (Martin, 2001, p. 473). The goal of this campaign has been to extract benefits from the investments made, rather than directly controlling the offering of subsidies.

Building on the idea of extracting concrete commitments from investors are Community Benefit Agreements. According to Good Jobs First (2007c):

> The community benefits movement is founded on the premise that economic development should create tangible improvements for local residents, particularly those in low-income neighborhoods. Community benefits agreements (CBAs) are legally enforceable contracts, signed by community groups and by a developer, which spell out a set of community benefits that the developer has committed to provide as part of a development project.

Typical provisions include 'first source' hiring (i.e., neighborhood residents), training funds, job quality provisions (wages, benefits), affordable housing if there is displacement, and environmental commitments, to name a few. CBAs have been negotiated in Los Angeles, Denver and Milwaukee (Good Jobs First, 2007c).

Reflecting the environmental critique of subsidies is the Green Scissors campaign. This campaign brought together organizations from both the Left and Right. Its core groups were Friends of the Earth, Taxpayers for Common Sense, and the US Public Interest Research Group. Beginning in 1993, the groups released their first report titled 'The Green Solution to Red Ink', which was later changed to 'Green Scissors Report'. The reports targeted projects such as the TPX fusion reactor and Advanced Neutron Source project, both of which had substantial waste disposal problems (Thomas 2000, pp. 169–70). According to the group's website, it 'has succeeded in cutting funding for wasteful federal programs by more than $26 billion' (Green Scissors, 2003). Unfortunately, the organization now appears defunct, with no updates on the website since 2006.

The Commerce Clause of the United States Constitution prohibits states from interfering with interstate commerce. In December 1999, a group of citizens in Ohio and Michigan challenged tax credit programs that partially funded the retention of a Jeep factory in Toledo, Ohio (Cuno v. Daimler-Chrysler). While the District Court ruled in favor of Ohio and Daimler-Chrysler, the 6th US Circuit Court of Appeals ruled that the state tax credits (but not local property tax abatements) did violate the Commerce Clause. However, in 2006, the US Supreme Court ruled that the plaintiffs lacked the standing to bring the case and dismissed it, sending the plaintiffs back to square one. Prior to the Supreme Court decision, US Senator George Voinovich from Ohio had introduced legislation to effectively overturn the ruling had the Supreme Court upheld the Appeals Court decision; he stated after the decision that he still intended to pursue it to stop such cases from being filed again (Koff, 2006, p. C1).[19]

Bilateral investment treaties and investment incentive agreements

Bilateral investment treaties (BITs) are agreements for the protection of investors in a particular host country. They are typically negotiated when firms in the investing country perceive political risk (such as expropriation or currency inconvertibility) to be a problem in the host nation. BITs commonly prohibit expropriation without proper compensation (as well as lesser adverse actions toward the investor), and provide that disputes will be subject to international arbitration rather than host country courts. The claimed attraction for developing countries is that by agreeing to BITs they will become more likely to receive investment from their treaty partners (an issue beyond the scope of this book). Beginning in 1959 (Elkin et al., 2004, p. 37), there are now over 2200 bilateral investment treaties in effect (Houde and Yannaca-Small, 2004, p. 3). BITs rarely address the disciplining of investment incentives, because their purpose is to protect the investor rather than placing limits on benefits that the investor might receive from a host government. As Houde and Yannaca-Small (2004, p. 7) put it, '...investment incentives are not usually an issue covered by BITs, even when they include provisions on the making of an investment...'

In the United States, investment incentive agreements (IIAs) are entered into by the Overseas Private Investment Corporation (OPIC) with host governments. As Sheppard et al. (2005) point out, these differ from BITs by the fact that they are designed to protect OPIC rather than the investor. There are over 150 IIAs between the United States and foreign governments. 'In general terms, these agreements provide for operation of OPIC's programs in foreign countries, recognition of OPIC's rights as transferee, assignee, and subrogee, and international arbitration between governments if disputes arise that cannot be settled by negotiation.' The 'investment incentive' in IIAs is the permission for OPIC to operate in the country, offering benefits to the investor such as political risk insurance, loans, or equity investment. An important example is the investment incentive agreement between India and the United States (Indian Embassy, 1997). This IIA was invoked when OPIC sought arbitration in 2004 over a claimed expropriation of the Dabhol power plant, which was owned by Enron, Bechtel and General Electric (Sheppard et al., 2005). Again, this is not a discipline on incentives in the sense of preventing or regulating the host government's ability to offer inducements to an investor, but rather a protection against political risk.

Indeed, bilateral investment treaties and investment incentive agreements, especially those with TRIMS+ restrictions on performance requirement, threaten to reduce the benefits developing countries can receive from foreign investment. It is easy to see why: essentially, BITs freeze bargains struck when a multinational investor had the most leverage, that is, before making the investment. To use Vernon's (1971) term, BITs prevent the 'obsolescing bargain' from obsolescing. Unless we are going to say that 'might makes right', there is no reason to privilege agreements signed when only one side is at its strongest. While many developing countries sign them in hopes of increasing their foreign investment, the evidence they actually do increase investment is mixed and the restrictions on host country policies could be very deleterious down the road (Hallward-Driemeier, 2003). Thus, I have recommended that developing countries avoid restrictions on their performance requirements whenever possible (Thomas, 2009, pp. 6–7).

Free Trade Agreements (FTAs)

The long-standing failure of the Doha Round trade negotiations has shifted the emphasis of many countries to the use of bilateral and regional free trade agreements to advance their trade and investment agendas. Typically, these FTAs have imposed stronger disciplines on performance requirements than the TRIMS agreement. The 2004 Australia-United States Free Trade Agreement (Department of Foreign Affairs and Trade, 2007) goes beyond the TRIMS agreement by additionally banning export requirements, requirements or preferences for host country purchases, conditioning domestic sales on export performance, technology transfer requirements, and requirements that the investment be the exclusive supplier of its products to any market (chapter 11.9, paragraph 1). However, the investment chapter at the same time explicitly permits governments providing investment incentives to enforce 'compliance with a requirement to locate production, supply a service, train or employ workers, construct or expand particular facilities, or carry out research and development, in its territory' (chapter 11.9, paragraph 3a). In addition, several of the 'TRIMS Plus' bans mentioned above are not enumerated in paragraph 2 (performance requirements that cannot be combined with subsidies), that is, export requirements, technology transfer requirements, and exclusive supply arrangements.

Conclusion

The European Union's state aid rules address subsidies comprehensively, but only in 1997 did the EU set up a framework specific to large mobile investment projects. The Commission's rules and procedures provide transparency and enforce a preference for poorer jurisdictions via the differential aid maxima allowed in the various regions. The Multi-Sectoral Framework, now incorporated into the Regional Aid Guidelines, sharply reduces the amount of aid available to large corporations, no matter what the location's aid maximum is. The MSF's rules directly target investment incentives, and have been used to stop the award of location subsidies to Intel in Ireland. The Commission has substantial monitoring and enforcement capacity, which the European Court of Justice has consistently upheld, most recently with its ruling in Commission v. France that appeals to national courts cannot suspend repayment orders for illegally granted subsidies.

Why has the European Union regime been such a success? Sinnaeve (2007, pp. 97–8) emphasizes that the existence of an independent monitoring and enforcement authority is crucial. She believes that attempts to achieve subsidy control without an independent entity are unlikely to have much effect. This is certainly consistent with what some scholars such as Lipson (1984, p. 7) have said regarding factors that increase the likelihood of international cooperation (see also Thomas, 2000, 250–3).

World Trade Organization subsidy rules are not crafted with a specific focus on investment incentives and are consequently a blunt tool for dealing with them. The European Union's challenge to state and local incentives to Boeing may create a useful precedent. The notification requirements would be useful if they were followed by the major nations; however, some countries are behind in their notification filings (such as India), while many federal countries (such as the US and Canada) do not report their subnational expenditure data. While the Agreement on Subsidies and Countervailing Measures has little effect on the granting of incentives, the Agreement on Trade-Related Investment Measures has virtually none, and the General Agreement on Trade in Services does not yet have subsidy rules.

Canada's Code of Conduct on Incentives has largely failed in terms of ending the poaching of investment; the most that can be said in its favor is that recent cases have been much smaller (all less than 100 jobs) than some of the 1990s cases that prompted the Code's adoption. While the Code requires the provinces to make reports on their location incentives to the Secretariat on Internal Trade, this information is not publicly available. However, reasonable proxies do suggest declining use of subsidies (Brown, 2006), and this author's interviews in the spring of 2007 reveal a general sense that incentives are less of a problem, in part because several provinces have reduced their use. However, incentives for R&D are widespread and often generous, due to the happy combination (for economic developers) of spinoff potential and the reduced countervail risk of that type of subsidy. Australia's newer interstate agreement was renewed in 2006, but one state, Queensland, still refuses to join. It appears, however, to have been complied with better than Canada's Code.

In the United States, the presence of thousands of local governments in the incentive game, in addition to the 50 states, creates a collective action problem that at times seems intractable. However, even interstate agreements with only a few parties have failed, suggesting it is not simply a problem of numbers. The failure of the Commerce Clause challenge to Ohio's tax credit programs is further grounds for pessimism. Still, citizen pressure is slowly providing more transparency on incentives and also mandating the types of commitments governments must obtain from investing companies.

Bilateral investment treaties, even when they do address investment incentives, have little disciplinary effect in the sense of restricting or regulating when such subsidies can be given. Instead, consistent with their purpose of investor protection, a few do guarantee that promised investment incentives must be paid, and leave their non-payment open to international arbitration claims as a potential breach of the investor guarantees in the treaty. Recent bilateral and regional free trade agreements are creating a patchwork expansion of the TRIMS disciplines on performance requirements, but do not restrict whether governments can provide subsidies in the first place. Ultimately, all of these agreements hinder host governments from maximizing their gains from foreign investment.

9

A Policy Agenda for the Twenty-first Century: Transparency and Beyond

Competition for investment using investment incentives is a genuine strategic interaction, not a figment of policymakers' imagination. Whether analyzed with Prisoners' Dilemma or more complex games, the studies have found that optimal regulation of incentives improves overall efficiency and welfare. The European Union has shown what the broad parameters of 'optimal' regulation look like: banning investment incentives in rich regions, and holding them as low as possible in poorer regions. With rules that explicitly address incentives (rather than all subsidies) in place since 1997, the EU has managed to effect a reduction in the size of location subsidy packages, as we saw in Chapter 6.

Despite this example, and its dissemination to the United States and other industrialized countries, there is little regulation of location subsidies outside the EU. Moreover, the use of investment incentives has spread to developing countries in the last 20 years. As a result, the agenda for incentive policy reform differs widely from country to country. Yet the reasons reform is needed are many.

Outside the European Union, it is clear that investment incentives can be expensive (and some incentives in the EU may still be excessive). Awards of more than \$1 million per job have now been documented in a number of cases in the United States, in such industries as semiconductors, steel and a banking data center. Awards in the \$100–200,000 per job range have been common for the automobile industry in the United States, and even higher amounts have been recorded in India and Brazil. Total spending by governments is harder to pin down, but various estimates have put the cost at 0.7 percent of Vietnam's GDP (Fletcher, 2002), 1 percent of Philippine GDP (Botman et al., 2008) and at least $46.8 billion by US state and local governments alone (see Chapter 6).

Location subsidies are widespread. They are used on every continent, in most countries, and at multiple levels of government. They take a variety of forms, including grants, tax credits and exemptions, subsidized loans, tax holidays, free land and infrastructure, reduced price inputs such as power and so on. This plethora of instruments reduces transparency substantially.

Poor regions cannot consistently outbid rich regions for FDI, despite their greater need for it. This has been shown for the United States by Fisher and Peters (1998, p. 26) and for the European Union by the Commission of the European Communities (1990, p. 8–2; 1991, p. 8) and Yuill et al. (1994, pp. 100–2). The main reason is that richer countries are much better able to give cash grants, while poorer regions must rely much more on tax holidays and other tax advantages whose multiyear spread degrades their present value (see Chin, 2010, pp. 37–8, for China). Obvious exceptions are poor regions of rich countries (eastern Germany, the Italian Mezzogiorno; see Thomas, 2000, p. 270), or poorer countries within the European Union, which now have access to Structural Funds that can be used for cash grants to inward investors.

There is a tendency for programs targeted to poorer areas to lose their focus over time, whether the programs form part of a centralized regional policy or a decentralized economic development policy. Greenbaum and Bondonio have shown this in their work on European Union Objective 2 regions and enterprise zones in the United States, and the Bill Lee Act in North Carolina (which provided differential support limits based on locations' economic circumstances) saw successive weakenings of its targeting (Craver, 2005, p. 1).

Most incentive competitions remain regional. Whether it is the auto industry, steel, biofuels or (almost all the time) call centers, a potential investor is rarely looking at multiple regions for a given investment. Consider the European Commission's rejection of a cost comparison between Wales and Ohio, cited in Chapter 6; this illustrates perfectly the understanding that locating an engine plant for the European market in the United States made no sense. By contrast, the luxury car market is worldwide, and Ford was able to extract much higher than usual aid for its Jaguar unit in 1996 when it threatened to move production to the United States, where half of the vehicles were sold (Thomas 1997, pp. 133–4). The industry most likely to see global incentive competition is the computer industry, especially silicon fabrication.[1]

The rise in capital mobility in the last 30–40 years, combined with the substantial information asymmetries of negotiations over incentives, means that the site location process itself generates rents for a firm. The numerous instances in which firms have admitted that the site was chosen before incentive negotiations (or even a sham auction) began provide strong evidence for this (LeRoy, 2005, enumerates many examples). Companies have become more sophisticated in their understanding of this fact, and the rise of site location consultants has helped speed the diffusion of this knowledge. But the underlying factor is that increasing capital mobility has made more sites economically viable for any given investment. As Thomas (1992, 1997) argued, this implies an increasing bargaining power for companies vis-à-vis host governments. The international relations literature provides us with important concepts for understanding this process. Consider Markusen and Nesse's (2007) focus on the importance of site location consultants and devolution: these have clear analogues in bargaining power theory, MNC learning and greater difficulty of government cooperation, respectively (Thomas, 1997, pp. 9–18, especially table 1.1). Indeed, I would argue that any theory of MNC location that does not include both corporate rent-seeking and bargaining power is incomplete.

Controlling investment incentives is difficult. Even agreements to prevent subsidizing the relocation of existing businesses have failed in two instances in the United States. Whether approached through Prisoners' Dilemma analysis or more complicated games, control does appear to be desirable theoretically. The best example of control's feasibility is the European Union, which benefits from favorable institutional rules and an independent monitoring and enforcement body. The latter sets it off from other jurisdictions, such as Australia and Canada, which have agreements among states or provinces to head off poaching and bidding wars, but no independent monitoring or enforcement. In principle, Canada has an independent body, the Secretariat for Internal Trade, but in practice (since the United Parcel Service case) it has played no role in disputes over incentives. In both Canada and Australia, consultations do occur between governments over subsidies that are of concern, as well as requests for information about bids, in order to overcome information asymmetries between states and investors. The National Governors Association in the United States has affirmed that state governments have the right to make such requests, but the extent to which they do is not known.

What we don't know

Overall incentive spending is not widely known for most areas, even the European Union, which could improve transparency in this area by having Member States indicate which individual state aids are being used to attract investment. This is an area sorely in need of further research. The United States and Canada both need research that aggregates total spending, but have a head start based on widespread press reporting of the costs of individual projects.

Furthermore, we especially do not have a good idea about overall spending, or even the cost of individual incentives, in developing countries. This is not likely to change soon, due to the numerous obstacles to transparency: some countries are non-democratic; some do not have sufficient administrative capability; their subsidy tools, particularly tax holidays, are not transparent; and there is little press coverage of any but the largest projects.

From a theoretical point of view, it is not proven that incentives affect the location of investment. While I believe they do, one useful approach to this question would be to replicate the Guisinger and Associates (1985) question: Would this investment have been made without incentives, if all other countries were still offering incentives? Surveying firms that had publicly said they would have made their investment without incentives would be especially illuminating.

Whether investment incentives are, in general, a good policy, or a good policy for developing countries, is by no means clear. Compared with what? This is a critical question, and it is not always clear from the many studies done what the other feasible alternatives are. Incentives vs. no incentives vs. no incentives + low taxes vs. low taxes vs. coordinated incentives? Any of these may be feasible in a particular situation. Perhaps the thing we can say with the most certainty is that countries that are not already good locations for investment ('weak fundamentals', in Aldaba's [2005] words) cannot become good locations just by offering investment incentives.

While Canada's Code of Conduct on Investment appears to have had only a small (at best) impact on relocation subsidies, Australia's no-raiding agreement (Interstate Investment Cooperation Agreement, IICA) appears to have had a measure of success, especially compared with decentralized cooperation attempts in the United States. Yet the reasons for its success are unclear. Small numbers cannot be the explanation; a three-state no raiding agreement in the US collapsed almost as soon as it went into effect. Australia has no independent monitoring body, as Sinnaeve (2007) recommends, yet poaching is almost absent and renewal of the IICA in 2011 seems like a foregone conclusion. The refusal of Queensland to join reduces its impact, but this is not due to partisan differences as all of Australia's states have Labor Party governments. What Australia does have is apparent agreement among its signatories that state investment incentives are a wasteful policy from a national viewpoint, a factor that was not present in the two US or one Canadian no-raiding agreement. As a no-raiding agreement would be more politically feasible than full-blown incentive regulation (Thomas, 2000, p. 268), the Australian example bears more study.

The rise of site location consultants has had a profound effect on bargaining between companies and governments, as theorists as varied as Thomas (2000), LeRoy (2005) and Markusen and Nesse (2007) have emphasized. From a theoretical point of view, they can be considered as analogous to credit-rating agencies in the world bond market (as analyzed in Sinclair 1994, 2005): they have specialized knowledge, they provide information to investors and help coordinate their behavior (Thomas, 2000, p. 211). Further comparative work of these two phenomena may prove illuminating in both economic development and international political economy.

The policy agenda

While differently situated countries have different incentive policy reform needs, the common denominator for all of them is transparency. Even in the European Union, which has the highest level of transparency in the world, state aid is not classified by whether it serves as an investment incentive. We know from experience that most though not all regional aid is used for incentives, but other types of aid are used for incentives as well (aid for energy saving has funded incentives for biofuel plants). In the United States, the press does a generally good job of reporting on incentives received by large projects, but reporters almost never calculate the present value as they should. Moreover, much goes under the radar, such as smaller projects and automatic incentives. Thus, my estimate in Chapter 6 again represents the state of the art in trying to calculate an aggregate value for state and local incentives. In Canada and Australia, in connection with their respective no-raiding agreements, provinces and states provide incentive reports to each other – but they are not public records. In Brazil and India, much of what is known about specific incentive agreements has been leaked to the press, which is to say that press reporting on incentives is more constrained than in North America or the EU. In countries such as China and Vietnam, there is no reporting at all.

1. European Union

Because incentive policy is well developed both substantively and in terms of enforcement (in particular, with the 2006 Commission v. France decision by the ECJ), the reform agenda is fairly short. Moreover, some of the shortcomings of EU policy I identified in *Competing for Capital* appear to be abating: R&D aid seems to be less of a threat to cohesion policy as Ireland, Spain and a number of new Member States have equaled or exceeded the EU-27 average for share of state aid devoted to R&D; while with the current crisis the attitude that state aid should be cut 'regardless of external circumstances' (Thomas, 2000, p. 271) has disappeared.

First, investment incentives should be explicitly identified and aggregated in state aid reporting. Second, the regional aid rules should definitively ban relocation subsidies. The controversy over Dell's investment in Poland and disinvestment in Ireland will certainly direct pressure on this issue. Third, the Dell Poland case also calls into question how the Commission deals with competing locations that are both eligible for regional aid. As I argued in Chapter 8, if the choice is between Lodz (with a 50 percent GGE aid limit) and Nitro (with a 40 percent GGE aid limit), it is hard to see how it is in the Community's interest for an investment in Lodz to receive more than a 10 percent GGE aid if it could have gone to Nitro with no aid at all. Thus I would suggest a rule that incentives should be restricted to the aid offered in the richer region plus the difference in applicable maxima for the two regions (or the amount dictated by the rules for large investment projects, if lower, of course). If the differential aid is less than the poorer region's cost disadvantage, the Community will benefit more if the project goes to the richer region. In the Dell case, since Slovakia would have given 0 at Nitro, Poland should have been limited to 10 percent for Lodz; if Slovakia were offering 20 percent, the limit at Lodz should be 30 percent and so on. Finally, though it can only be done by consensus, the EU should consider a minimum corporate income tax rate to limit the kind of unregulated competition for investment that Ireland's 12.5 percent rate represents (see Thomas, 2000, p. 270). However, I do not know what it would take to get Ireland to agree.

2. North America

In an ideal world, NAFTA would be moving toward EU state aid rules, but that is no more politically feasible today than it was ten years ago.

Nor is a Canada–US deal on subsidies in the offing, though calls for such an agreement go back at least to the 1990s (e.g., Morici, 1996). For Canada, then, I would recommend increasing transparency through the release of the annual provincial reports on incentives; beyond that, I would suggest reinforcing the ban on subsidized relocations in the Code of Conduct on Incentives, though that may not be critical as long as the subsidized relocations remain as small as they have in the last ten years.

In the United States, the battle for transparency is a hard state-by-state slog. While 27 states and the District of Columbia had no online disclosure of subsidies as late as November 2007, there is a clear, but slow, trend for more states and better disclosure (Mattera et al., 2007, pp. 3–5). As transparency improves, incentives will continue to be more politicized; likely directions for substantive reform are subsidies for retail outlets (recall the $2 billion in subsidies which generated 5400 jobs in the St. Louis area retail sector), anti-poaching rules, and stronger performance requirements and monitoring (see LeRoy, 2005, pp. 187–96 for further discussion and suggestions).

Investment incentives in Mexico are completely opaque; I have literally never seen an article in the English-language press, including *Site Selection* magazine, list the amount of incentives received for a project in Mexico. Achieving basic transparency is obviously the needed first step.

3. Developing countries

For the four countries discussed in Chapter 7, the twin recommendations are transparency and controlling subnational competition for investment. As the US example shows, this is easier said than done. In the case of Vietnam, however, it does appear the central government has regained control of provincial incentives beyond their permitted maxima. As UNCTAD (2008) suggested, it would make sense for Vietnam to focus its incentives so as to reduce the dilution of their regional policy effect. Still, this is not to detract from the country's achievement in carrying out an ambitious control agenda similar to the EU's.

For developing countries more generally, the most important issue may be performance requirements. Between high levels of capital mobility and the ubiquity of corporate rent-seeking, investment incentives are not going to be abolished any time soon. Certainly, developing countries should seek to negotiate regional controls on incentives if the opportunity presents itself, since most competition for investment remains regional. Moreover, given the high levels of incentives documented in several countries, it may well be possible that there is room for unilateral reduction of incentive use. As discussed in Chapter 8, the proliferation of bilateral investment treaties, especially those with TRIMS+ restrictions on performance requirements, threaten to limit a host's potential gains from foreign investment, Instead of signing one-sided agreements, developing countries should preserve as much policy space as possible by resisting restrictions on their performance requirements.

Conclusion

The consequences of competition for investment remain the same as they did ten years ago. Using investment incentives to promote an individual location has efficiency, equity and often environmental drawbacks, which must always be weighed against the possible gains of the individual jurisdiction. This weighing is best performed by an independent body, as governments do not take into account the effect of their incentives on other governments. For much of the world, however, this is not politically feasible, and will not become so until enough light has been shined on incentives that their consequences are broadly understood within the electorate. The need for transparency is as pressing as ever.

Notes

1 *Competing for Capital* Revisited

1. Alabama per capita income in 1999 was $18,189 (US Census Bureau, 2009). By contrast, the Czech Republic's gross national income per capita in 2000 was $4920 at current exchange rates and $13,610 at purchasing power parity (World Bank, 2002, p. 232). By 2006, when the Czech Republic landed the Hyundai plant, its gross national income per capita had grown to $12,680 at current exchange rates and $21,470 at purchasing power parity (World Bank, 2007, p. 334), while Alabama's had increased to $29,414 in chained 2000 dollars (Bureau of Economic Analysis, 2009).
2. As with many concepts, that of investment incentives is fuzzy around the edges. For example, the availability of a particular operating subsidy, such as research and development tax credits, may function as an incentive to invest. A low corporate tax rate can have the same effect.
3. At the time of this writing €1=$1.35 approximately.
4. Those which did not affect the location of the investment.
5. Lake Ozark, Missouri, 2007 population 1931, reported in a survey for Mason and Thomas (2010) that it had given approximately $1 billion in tax increment financing subsidies since the program was first adopted in Missouri in 1982.
6. Québec has targeted firms as small as ten employees to offer them relocation incentives to move from Ontario (Tuck, 1999).
7. In fact, oil wealth is a common denominator for the few countries that do not offer investment incentives. Neither Bahrain, Kuwait, Oman, Saudi Arabia or the United Arab Emirates provide grants or tax credits, but simply a low-tax regime for non-oil investment (Diamond and Diamond, 2006, chapters 38, 40–43).
8. One might ask, however, why firms would not simply go to the high-service jurisdictions without paying their fair share of taxes. A possible answer, for Scandinavian countries, at least, might be that the corporate share of taxation is very low, itself constituting a sort of incentive to invest (Oxelheim and Ghauri, 2008, p. 363.) Sweden, Finland and Denmark are all below the EU average for corporate income tax as a share of total tax revenue (OECD, 2007, p. 27).
9. See, for example, Charlton (2003).
10. At the same time, I argued previously (Thomas, 1997, p. 27) that Przeworski and Wallerstein's key result that governments could get out from under the dictates of structural dependence under certain circumstances was undermined by the fact that their equilibrium was threat-vulnerable, and that capital mobility provided the capacity for capital to threaten states. The same problem seems to exist with the international variant of their model (Wallerstein and Przeworski, 1995). Capitalists facing extraordinarily high tax rates on uninvested profits can threaten to reduce investment which,

while 'irrational' in the sense that it reduces their consumption, would inflict much higher losses on labor and government, making the threat credible and again undermining their equilibrium. Moreover, with mobile capital, the possibility of using transfer pricing to evade the high tax rates becomes important (Swank and Steinmo, 2002, p. 646).

11. For the details of all these calculations, see Chapter 6.
12. The McGuinty government followed up this initiative with a 5-year, $C650 million Next Generation of Jobs Fund originally announced in June 2007 (Artuso, 2007, p. 24) that grew to $1.15 billion by September (Leslie, 2007).
13. The one exception is Hong et al. (2009), discussed in Chapter 7 in the section on Vietnam, where this author suggested that the research team use Guisinger's wording.
14. In addition, De Mooij and Ederveen (2005, p. 25, table 4.2, full specification, pp. 26–7) conclude from a metaanalysis of 31 different studies with 427 estimated elasticities of the responsiveness of FDI to taxes, that more recent studies are slightly more likely to find a larger effect of taxes than older studies.

2 Models, Models and More Models

1. Ann Markusen raised this critique of Tiebout in 1974. See Markusen and Nesse (2007, pp. 16–17).
2. It would seem that the cut-off point is not necessarily zero. For instance, it is hard to imagine that an investor would proceed if she expected to make less than the risk-free return of Treasury bonds. However, whether the critical point is zero, the Treasury bond rate, or even some multiple of the Treasury bond rate, there would, under the spillover assumption, still be projects where the private rate of return is lower than the cut-off point, while the social rate of return is higher.
3. Moreover, Blomström and Kokko (2003, p. 19) point out that the existence of externalities does not automatically mean a particular host can absorb them: local firms must be capable of learning from foreign MNCs. Worse still, statistical meta-analyses are now casting doubt on the findings of positive spillovers at all (Havránek, 2009).
4. In addition, some critics argue that incentives are pure waste because they do not affect location decisions (see discussion at Thomas, 2000, p. 24).
5. LeRoy (2005, pp. 201–05) assesses problems with both of these for the US case.
6. It should be noted, however, that new investment may simply displace existing investment. For example, the North American automobile industry has long been plagued by overcapacity. Between 1979 and 1991, 20 new truck and auto assembly plants opened in the United States and Canada combined – and 20 closed (Rubenstein, 1992, p. 3, Table 1.1).
7. Van der Horst (2007, pp. 49–50) shows through simulation that tax cuts by EU countries have negative effects on other Member States, with cuts by bigger countries having bigger effects, though even the largest effect is only about 0.02 percent of EU GDP.

8. Cheshire and Gordon (1998, p. 325) consider the possibility that a policy could have negative payoffs at the 'very local' level and a positive one at a broader geographic scale. However, this does not equate to the 'winner's curse' box, because they argue that at the widest level the payoff would again be negative.
9. And not all of the new investment was in poorer states (Rodriguez-Pose and Arbix 2001, p. 142, figure 2).
10. Inexplicably, Barros and Cabral (2000, p. 365) see it as a goal of the EU to eliminate investment incentives entirely.
11. Haufler and Wooton (2008b, p. 4) point out that studies assuming a monopolist tended to find an equilibrium characterized by the host providing a subsidy, but studies assuming more than one firm tended to find that the host could impose a positive tax on the MNC.
12. However, in developing countries, it may be more plausible that the MNC will be a monopolist, as Albornoz and Corcos (2007, p. 20) note.
13. National statutory tax rate, state statutory tax rate (for US studies), marginal effective tax rate, average effective tax rate or average tax rates computed from micro or macro data (2005, pp. 21–2). All of these measures have their strengths and weaknesses; see especially OECD (2000).
14. See van den Berghe, 2001, pp. 3–4.
15. Recently, however, Piscitello and Rabbioso (2005) have suggested that it may sometimes make sense to offer subsidies to foreign MNCs for acquiring domestic firms. One key point is that the acquired firm is already linked to other domestic firms.
16. However, both Bartik (2007) and Fisher (2007) suggest that the elasticities (not the semi-elasticities) are small, in the range of –0.2 to –0.3. They conclude that cutting taxes or awarding incentives in the face of this inelastic demand means that total tax revenue will fall despite increased investment. It is unclear if these elasticities hold outside the United States.
17. 'Objective 2 of the Structural Funds aims to revitalise all areas facing structural difficulties, whether industrial, rural, urban, or dependent on fisheries' (European Union, 2010a).
18. That is, FDI for protected national markets did not promote, and may even have hindered, growth.

3 Policy Studies

1. A point emphasized by Blomström and Kokko (2003), who argue that tax holidays are not as 'innocuous' as they seem, because they create incentives for firms not only to engage in abusive transfer pricing, but also to repeatedly establish subsidiaries as existing tax holidays expire (2003, p. 17).
2. In the infamous case of a 1993 incentive for Intel Corp. in Rio Rancho, New Mexico, the state's department of economic development did not know how to do a present value calculation (Thomas, 2000, p. 194, n. 92)!
3. Clawbacks seem to be more routinely used in Europe than in the United States. However, LeRoy (2005, p. 189) finds that there are an increasing number of US jurisdictions where they are used.

4. This also creates the possibility of paying bribes in order to receive incentives.

4 Industry Case Studies: Steel, Biofuel Production, Semiconductors, Automobiles, Call Centers

1. However, the new Member States that joined in 2005 and 2007 were allowed to use state aid for restructuring of steel firms one time prior to accession (SeeNews, 2009).
2. Note that the EU has since adopted new guidelines for environmental and energy saving aid (see Chapter 8).
3. Slovak Economy Minister Maro S. Havran told *The Slovak Spectator,* 'We offered what we could. If Brussels says it must be less, we will have to lower it.... If Brussels says it will be 15 percent, it will be 15 percent' (Balogova, 2005a).
4. Note that the contact method need not be restricted to telephone. Contacts may be made by email, text message, web chat and so on. Moreover, some companies have moved to have more of their employees work from home (Fleischer, 2007, p. 22).
5. Kent McMullin of the Edmonton Economic Development Corporation stated he did not know the identity of the US cities. (Interview, Edmonton, 21 March 2007).
6. Interview with Dan Chugg, Alberta Film Commissioner, Edmonton, 19 March 2007.
7. Further, note that local governments are now banned from providing incentives by the Alberta-British Columbia Trade, Investment, and Labor Mobility Agreement (TILMA).
8. An economic development official in another province suggested that Nashville had also been in the running for this call center.
9. In the case of aid for Ford's Bridgend engine plant, the Commission rejected the UK government's attempt to make a comparison between costs in Wales and in Cleveland, Ohio, saying that it was doubtful it made sense to produce engines for the European market in the United States (European Union, 2002a). Shortly after the Commission announced its formal investigation, the UK withdrew the aid proposal in light of the Commission's opposition and no aid was granted (European Union, 2002b).

5 The Celtic Tiger: Incentives, Infrastructure, Tax Rates, Luck?

1. Note that there appear to be inconsistencies in the UNCTAD data. For example, an inflow of 10 percent of GDP may lead to a 30-percentage point increase in the stock of FDI as a share of GDP. Many such anomalies can be found in the data, but this dataset has the broadest global scope across a whole array of measures and countries.
2. O'Hearn (1995, p. 92) notes that several of the outward-oriented shifts had begun before the publication of Whitaker's *Economic Development.*

3. According to Kennedy (2001, p. 126), Ireland's GNP grew an average of 3.9 percent annually between 1960 and 1980, and at a 2.5 percent average annual rate from 1980 to 1993. GNP per capita grew by 2.9 percent and 2.1 percent in those periods, respectively. Kennedy notes that GDP per capita is not as good a measure of living standards for Ireland as GNP per capita, 'chiefly because of the large and increasing outflow of profits to multinational enterprises, which do not add to domestic living standards' (p. 124).
4. One official disputed whether the Telesis Report focused as much on overpaying for FDI as on the balance between attracting foreign investment and promoting indigenous industry. He also noted that Telesis raised the question of the extent to which firms fulfilled their job commitments, pushing IDA to measure actual jobs created rather than job commitments (Dublin interview #1, March 2009).
5. Especially relevant for the present work, the Report claims, 'Generally, a more effective limitation of State aids across Europe has the potential for achieving considerable savings all across the Community, at the expense of the multinationals' (Culliton et al., 1992, p. 28).
6. On 31 December 1992, the Irish pound was worth approximately $1.63 (Oanda.com, 2009).
7. This figure only represents grants, and does not include the benefits from Export Sales Relief or the 10 percent manufacturing tax rate, both of which disproportionately benefited foreign firms.
8. The report does note that non-aided plants lost jobs at an even higher rate (Culliton et al., 1992, p. 63).
9. In addition, there was a trend for a number of Cohesion and new Member States to have converged on the EU-27 average for the share of aid to R&D in total state aid (16 percent): Bulgaria, 15 percent; Czech Republic, 18 percent; Estonia, 22 percent; Spain, 19 percent; Romania, 26 percent and Slovenia, 12 percent. These totals exclude from the denominator crisis aid to the financial sector (European Union, 2010b).
10. As a result of the economic crisis, the Social Partnership collapsed in 2009 when the Irish Congress of Trade Unions withdrew over threats to cut public-sector salaries (Economist Intelligence Unit, 2009b).
11. The Guarantee Section of the EAGGF is the funding instrument of the Common Agricultural Policy (Rodriguez-Pose and Fratesi, 2004, p. 99). Of course, Ireland also received funding under the CAP.
12. In 1994, a new fund was added to the Structural Funds, the Financial Instrument for Fisheries Guidance (Rodriguez-Pose and Fratesi, 2002, p. 3).
13. For the 1989–94 programming period, Ireland received IR£793 per capita, compared with about I£600 for Spain, and IR£553 for Greece and Portugal (Flynn, 1993a, p. 5). In the 1994–99 period, Ireland received 'about 35 per cent more than poorer countries such as Greece and Portugal' (Flynn, 1993b, p. 10). In the 2000–06 programming period, Ireland's receipts fell due to its prosperity, and the country had to be divided into two regions in order to be eligible for any Objective 1 funding at all (Thomas, 2000, p. 100).

14. In fact, Sutherland was Commissioner for Competition in 1985–88 when DG-Competition began its more stringent enforcement of the state aid rules, a process that continued under his successor, Leon Brittan, in 1989–92 (Thomas, 2000, p. 111). Between them, they held the Competition portfolio for the entire period of the Single Market program.
15. Smith also credits the growth of the labor supply in the 1990s and fiscal adjustment as factors in Ireland's rapid growth (Smith, 2005, pp. 77–80, 82–5). However, I see the first as more a consequence of that growth (increased labor demand ended emigration and increased women's labor force participation), and the second as derivative from the Social Partnership. In addition, she assigns an independent role to the government's industrial policy while simultaneously disparaging the importance of low tax rates, as if they were not the centerpiece of the industrial policy.
16. That is, they no longer qualify for exemption from the general prohibition under Article 87 (3) (a), 'areas where the standard of living is abnormally low or there is severe underemployment' (Article 87 EEC). Generally speaking, regions which qualify for Objective 1 Structural Funds designation also receive Article 87 (3) (a) state aid designation. Thus, the Border, Midlands and West regions fall into these two categories.
17. Intel has in fact sharply reduced its net property, plant and equipment in Ireland from $2860 million in 2006 to $1536 million in 2008, while it has increased them in Israel (a major competitor for Ireland) from $1183 million to $2965 million in the same period (Intel Corporation, 2009, p. 111).
18. Hence the report limited itself to jurisdictions that were tax havens for financial transactions only.
19. Van der Horst shows that Ireland would be harmed by all versions of tax harmonization he simulates (30 percent minimum CIT rate, 33 percent harmonized CIT rate, and 20 percent harmonized CIT rate), while it would benefit from tax base harmonization without tax rate harmonization (van der Horst, 2007, Tables 2 and 3).
20. Though commentators such as Paul Krugman argue that Ireland would now be better off if it were free of the euro and able to devalue its currency.
21. As I argued in *Competing for Capital*, we can only determine if a tax provision functions as an incentive by comparing it with what competing jurisdictions do. Hence, I argued there that we should count the US use of generalized accelerated depreciation as 'functionally equivalent to state aid' because comparable tax provisions do not exist in the European Union on a scale similar to that of the US (Thomas, 2000, pp. 157–8).
22. Bulgaria, Cyprus, Latvia, Poland, Romania and Slovakia all have corporate income tax rates below 20 percent (European Union, 2009e, p. 11).
23. This has been obvious in multiple instances, most recently with the second referendum on the Lisbon Treaty approved in October 2009. Having originally rejected the Treaty in June 2008, the country sought and received guarantees from other EU Member States on tax sovereignty (as well as military neutrality and abortion laws; see Millard, 2009). This makes it less likely that Ireland's critics will be able to force an increase in its corporate income tax rate.

6 Who Provides the Most Investment Incentives: EU vs. US

1. The Council adopted its 'First Resolution on General Regional Aid Systems' 20 October 1971; OJ C111, 4 November 1971; cited in CEC 1972, point 145.
2. Note also that motor vehicles were exempt from the requirement for individual pre-notification under the MSF 2002 as well as having a different, flat-rate, reduction matrix; see Wishlade (2009, p. 44).
3. According to the Eurostat Regional Yearbook 2009, Dresden's GDP per capita was 87.38 percent of the EU-27 average, which I calculate to be $31,923 based on a 2006 GDP of €11,683.8 billion and a 2006 population of 494,094,000, converted at €1=$1.35.
4. Until 2007, all of Intel's chip fabrication plants had been located either in the United States, Israel or Ireland (Thomas, 2007c, p. 35).
5. While I have not calculated federal subsidies as I did in *Competing for Capital*, the corresponding amount of federal accelerated depreciation (rental housing, buildings and equipment) in the personal and corporate income tax totaled $45.3 billion in FY 2008 (Joint Committee on Taxation, 2008, p. 69).

7 The Spread of Investment Incentives to Developing Countries

1. Note that Dongguan does not have a national-level zone designation, either special enterprise zone or economic and technological development zone (Du et al., 2008, p. 427).
2. Chin (2010, pp. 37–8), notes that in the 1980s, Chinese cities had very little actual cash that could be used for incentives. Indeed, of the first three auto assembly joint ventures (American Motors Corporation, Peugeot SA and Volkswagen), 'only Guangzhou contributed cash directly to the project, which amounted to $4.3 million' (p. 38), with most of the subsidy coming in the form of free land and buildings.
3. This exposition draws primarily on Cavalcante and Uderman, 2004.
4. Rio de Janeiro state also offered incentives to Toyota (interview, Rio de Janeiro, July 2009).
5. Rodríguez-Pose and Arbix (2001, p. 138) report that inflation reached 80 percent per *month* in 1990.
6. Data from the Brazilian automobile manufacturers' association ANFAVEA (2009, pp. 40 and 56) bear out this prediction: Vehicle (car, light commercial, truck and bus) employment fell from 107,134 in 1994 (just before the fiscal war) to a low of 79,047 in 2003 despite a 15.6 percent increase in production, and the industry did not reach 1994 employment levels again until 2008, by which time vehicle production more than doubled. This supports their argument that the job creation justification of the incentives used by Rio Grande do Sul and other states was flawed.
7. They note (2001, p. 152) that two state governors who had been active in the bidding wars lost in the 1998 elections, in Rio Grande do Sul (see the discussion above regarding the new government's renegotiation of incentives with General Motors and Ford) and Minas Gerais.

8. Ferreira et al. (2005, pp. 303–4), for instance, see ICMS incentives as creating no new investment for Brazil and the subsidies as merely shifting the location among the various states.
9. Rodríguez-Pose and Arbix (2001, p. 148) note one such report stating that each auto assembly factory job in Rio Grande do Sul would create 150 indirect jobs.
10. Echoing some of the complaints against eminent domain raised in the United States, for example in the case Kelo v. City of New London (Connecticut), in which the US Supreme Court upheld the city's right to transfer property to a private developer for economic development purposes (Greenhouse, 2005).
11. 'Tax avoidance' refers to tax planning activities that reduce tax legally. 'Tax evasion' is the term for illegal activities to reduce tax.
12. 1 crore equals 10 million. At an exchange rate of approximately 50 rupees to the US dollar, 1 crore then equals $200,000. Hence 175,000 crore equals $35 billion.
13. Note that these figures exceed those given in the UNCTAD database.
14. Note that over the lifetime of an investment, as many as seven different corporate income tax rates could apply, depending on the incentive provisions (UNCTAD, 2008b, p. 55).
15. I am unaware of any estimates that have been made since the new investment regime went into effect in 2006.
16. Though it is not apparent from the text on page 25, note the wording of question 2.4 of the survey on page 58, which makes clear that the hypothetical situation was no incentives in Vietnam 'while other countries offer you investment incentives'. Disclosure: I served as a consultant on this project, and I suggested the wording to parallel that used in the Guisinger and Associates (1985) study for the International Finance Corporation.

8 Controlling Incentives and Maximizing the Value of Inward Investment

1. As Sinnaeve (2007, pp. 93–4) notes, the notification requirement has been relaxed by which it is possible to notify an aid *program*, after which individual applications of the program do not need to be notified in advance, but must still be reported on *ex post*, and through block exemptions (e.g., to small and medium-sized enterprises or SMEs) where notification is not required provided the aid fulfils all the requirements of the exemption regulation.
2. They may, however, give SME aid or R&D support.
3. With the influx of new Member States in 2005 and 2007, a number of areas, comprising about 3.6 percent of EU population, were no longer below 75 percent of the EU average, but are being given transitional status until 2010 (European Union, 2007b).
4. Regions that are disadvantaged in relation to national averages but not relative to EU averages are termed 'C'-level regions, and lower aid intensities are allowed than in 'A'-level regions.
5. For investments under €50 million, the normal aid maximum applies, and the case need not be individually notified in advance if it is given under the

terms of an approved aid scheme (whereas an ad hoc aid to a €45 million investment would need to be notified in advance).

6. However, the Commission did approve of Ireland granting €48.25 million in aid to Centocor several months after its denial of the Intel aid, a case that had the Irish worried again. In this case, however, the area where the investment was located was an area eligible for regional aid (Beesley, 2006, p. 20).
7. With the onset of the financial crisis in 2008, state aid skyrocketed to 2.2 percent of EU GDP. However, virtually all of the increase was crisis aid for the financial sector; excluding that, total aid was only 0.54 percent of GDP, up only slightly from 2007 (European Union, 2009h, p. 4).
8. With the dramatic improvement in repayment actions noted above, this may no longer be so pressing.
9. Although many DG Competition state aid documents are available in multiple languages, English is its main working language.
10. One newspaper article (*Irish Examiner*, 2009b) says that the Irish government was the source for the Commission's claim that the Limerick jobs were lost to China.
11. In other words, Dell and Poland could not have it both ways: Their public stance was that the closure of Limerick was unrelated to the opening of Lodz, so they could not claim them to be a single investment project in the same way Getrag Ford was; hence, Getrag Ford provided no precedent. At the same time, it is difficult to believe that the opening and closure were not part of the same decision process. Irish observers speculated as soon as Lodz was originally announced in 2006 that it would mean the end of manufacturing at Limerick (Brophy, 2006, p. B04; Carey, 2006, p. 16). Moreover, all the English-language press on this case sees it as a subsidized relocation, and a manager at Lodz said that employment will increase 'by several hundred people' at Lodz due to the shutdown at Limerick (PAP News Wire, 2009). A Polish official I spoke with in November 2009 stated that the Dell case was not a relocation, and if it had been it would have been ineligible for European Regional Development Fund support.
12. Italy and the European Communities raised the defense that these subsidies were '*de facto* green' – that is, they would have qualified for non-actionable status – as regional aid – had they been able to be notified in advance (they existed prior to the SCM agreement). While the US did not accept this position, both Canada and New Zealand did (Thomas, 2000, p. 262).
13. These examples are taken from the WTO website summary of the GATS, consulted 18 September 2007 at www.wto.org/english/docs_e/legal_e/ursum_e.htm#mAgreement
14. The Committee on Subsidies and Countervailing Measures Report (WTO, 2009b) erroneously states that no submission had been received from the United States by October 2009; however, the US notification was received by the WTO on 20 May 2009 (WTO, 2009c, p. 1).
15. According to Good Jobs First, Wal-Mart has received at least $1.2 billion in subsidies from US state and local governments since 1980, including $200 million from 2004 to 2007 alone (Mattera and Purinton, 2004; Good Jobs First, 2007a).

16. Nunavut, which did not exist when the agreement was signed in 1994, is not a party.
17. Saskatchewan is an exception, since municipalities are not prohibited from giving incentives. Even Wal-Mart has received support there (Klein, 2006).
18. Ironically, Victoria had resisted the original New South Wales proposal in 1996 (Millett, 1996, p. 7), but later Victorian Treasurer (now Premier) John Brumby came to champion the IICA.
19. Disclosure: This author was one of the signers of an *amicus curiae* brief in favor of plaintiffs when the case was before the US Supreme Court.

9 A Policy Agenda for the Twenty-first Century: Transparency and Beyond

1. Ronald Steenblik of the OECD suggests that photovoltaic cells should perhaps be added to this list now (personal communication, 28 April 2010).

Bibliography

Afonso, J. R. R., E. A. Araújo, and G. B. Júnior (2005) 'Fiscal space and public sector investments in infrastructure: a Brazilian case-study', IPEA Discussion Paper No. 1141, December.

Afonso, J. R. R. and R. Barroso (2007) 'Brazilian tax affairs', Berkeley Program in Law and Economics, Paper 0430078.

Agence France Presse (2004) 'Ford plans to build transmissions plant in Slovakia', 2 December.

—— (2009a) 'Dell closing Ireland plant with loss of 1,900 jobs', 8 January.

—— (2009b) 'Dell to sell Polish plant to Taiwan's Foxconn: Company spokesman', 2 December.

Aiyar, S. (2006) 'Good, bad, ugly', *India Today*, 9 October.

Albornoz, F. and G. Corcos (2007) 'Regional integration, subsidy competition, and the relocation choices of MNCs', *Berkeley Electronic Journal of Economic Analysis and Policy*, 7, 1–27.

Aldaba, R. M. (2005) 'FDI and corporate taxation: the Philippine experience', Philippine Institute for Development Studies, http://www.econ.hit-u.ac.jp/~ap3/apppfdi6/paper/PHILIPPINES.pdf, date accessed 15 July 2007.

Alden, E. (2005) 'US warns of tough stance on subsidies for airbus', *Financial Times*, 26 May, 10.

AMD (2007) *Annual Report 2006* (Sunnyvale, California: Advanced Micro Devices, Inc.).

—— (2010) *Annual Report 2009* (Sunnyvale, California: Advanced Micro Devices, Inc.).

Amy, J. (2008) 'SSAB adding $460M in Axis', *Mobile Register*, 22 October, 1.

ANFAVEA (2009) *Brazilian Automotive Industry Yearbook* (São Paulo: ANFAVEA).

Annan, G. (2008) 'Irish PM opens new round of talks on social-partnership agreement', *Global Insight*, February 19.

Arnold, K. (2009) 'Gerdau mill seeks state rescue funds', *Tulsa World*, 29 July, E1.

Arnold, S. (2004) 'Auto trade aid; $500m from province boosts Oakville's chances of attracting investor', *Hamilton Spectator*, 15 April, A01.

Artuso, A. (2007) 'New jobs fund for green tech; Grits hope to sell $650 million package to manufacturers', *Toronto Star*, 20 June, 24.

Axelrod, R. (1984) *The Evolution of Cooperation* (New York: Basic Books).

Aydin, U. (2007) 'From competition to cooperation: subsidies in the United States, Canada, and the European Union', Ph.D. dissertation, University of Washington.

Ayele, S. (2006) 'The industry and location impacts of investment incentives on SMEs start-up in Ethiopia', *Journal of International Development*, 18, 1–13.

Balogova, B. (2005a) 'Hankook tags Slovakia', *The Slovak Spectator*, 8 May.

—— (2005b) 'Hankook saga ends for Slovakia', *The Slovak Spectator*, 5 November.

Barnardos (2009) 'Statistics on child poverty', http://www.barnardos.ie/policies_and_campaigns/our-policy-priorities/child-poverty.html, date accessed 15 September 2009.

Barros, P. P. and L. Cabral (2000) 'Competing for foreign direct investment', *Review of International Economics*, 8, 360–71.

Barry, F., A. Hannan, and E. Strobl (1999) 'The real convergence of the Irish economy and the sectoral distribution of employment growth', in F. Barry, ed., *Understanding Ireland's Economic Growth* (Basingstoke: Palgrave).

Barry, F., J. Bradley, and A. Hannan (1999) 'The European dimension: the single market and the structural funds', in F. Barry, ed., *Understanding Ireland's Economic Growth* (Basingstoke: Palgrave).

Barry, F. (2007) 'Comments on Albert van der Horst, "Is EU coordination needed for corporate taxation?"' Unpublished paper, Trinity College Dublin.

Bartik, T. J. (1991) *Who Benefits from State and Local Economic Development Policies?* (Kalamazoo, Michigan: W.E. Upjohn Institute for Employment Research).

—— (2007) 'Solving the problems of economic development incentives', in A. Markusen, ed., *Reining in the Competition for Capital* (Kalamazoo: W.E. Upjohn Institute for Employment Research).

Basinger, S. and M. Hallerberg (2004) 'Remodeling the competition for capital: how domestic politics erases the race to the bottom', *American Political Science Review*, 98, 261–76.

Beesley, A. (2006) 'Competition commissioner signs off on EUR 48.25m Centocor grant', *Irish Times*, 26 January, 20.

Bilefsky, D. (2004) 'New entrants feel wage pinch', *Globe and Mail*, 28 April, B14.

Bishop, B. (2007) 'Why did China benefit from a joint venture policy? A case study of Shanghai', *China & World Economy*, 15, 89–103.

Bjorvaten, K. and C. Eckel (2006) 'Policy competition for foreign direct investment between asymmetric countries', *European Economic Review*, 50, 1891–1907.

Black, D. A. and W. H. Hoyt (1989) 'Bidding for firms', *American Economic Review*, 79, 1249–56.

Blakely, R. (2008) 'Serco gains a passage to India with Eur13m stake in Info Vision call centre operator', *The Times* (London), 12 December.

Blomström, M. and A. Kokko (2003) 'The economics of foreign direct investment incentives', Stockholm School of Economics Working Paper #168, January, www2.hhs.se/eijswp/168.pdf, date accessed 2 July 2007.

Blonigen, B. A. and M. G. Wang (2005) 'Inappropriate pooling of wealthy and poor countries in empirical FDI studies', in T. H. Moran, E. M. Graham, and M. Blomström, eds, *Does Foreign Direct Investment Promote Development?* (Washington: Institute for International Economics and Center for Global Development).

Blum, K. with R. Ginsberg (1995) *The Mercedes Benz Subsidy Package: Whose Benefits? Whose Losses* (Chicago: Midwest Center for Labor Research).

BNDES (2009a) 'Conditions for granting financial support', http://www.amazonfund.gov.br/, retrieval date 5 December 2009.

—— (2009b) 'BNDES breaks a new record, disbursing R$ 107.5 billion in 10 months', press release, 24 November, http://inter.bndes.gov.br/english/news/not127_09.asp, retrieval date 5 December 2009.

BNDES (2009c) *BNDES 2008 Annual Report* (Rio de Janeiro: BNDES).

Bondonio, D. and R. T. Greenbaum (2006) 'Do business investment incentives promote employment in declining areas? Evidence from EU Objective 2 Regions', *European Urban and Regional Studies*, 13, 225–44. consulted 7/10/07 at valutazione2003.stat.unipd.it/pdf/VeneziaMag2006/Paper/Bondonio_Greenbaum.pdf [page citations from this version]

Bornais, S. (2005) 'Snair's cash "bad for taxpayer"', *Halifax Daily News*, May 18, 12.

Botman, D., A. Klemm, and R. Baqir (2008) 'Investment incentives and effective tax Rates in the Philippines: a comparison with neighboring countries', IMF Working Paper WP 08/207, September.

British Columbia Ministry of Economic Development (2006) 'British Columbia, Canada: your gateway to opportunity', promotional packet.

Broadcast News (2006) 'BIZ-Sask-Canola-Plant', 8 September.

Brophy, C. (2006) '"Dell effect" in need of a quick reboot; the computer company needs a rethink after a dreadful year – but its rescue plan may be bad news for the Limerick plant', *Sunday Tribune*, 17 September, B04.

Brown, D. M. (2006) 'Still in the game: efforts to govern economic development competition in Canada', in Kathryn Harrison, ed., *Racing to the Bottom? Provincial Interdependence in the Canadian Federation* (Vancouver: UBC Press).

Bruns, A. (2005) 'By the time we get to Woodstock', *Site Selection* online, 4 July, http://www.siteselection.com/ssinsider/bbdeal/bd050704.htm, date accessed 20 July 2007.

Buchholz, D. (1998) 'Competition and corporate incentives: dilemmas in economic development', Ph.D. dissertation, Duke University.

Bureau of Economic Analysis (2009) 'Gross domestic product by state', http://www.bea.gov/scb/pdf/2009/06%20June/0609_gdp_state.pdf, retrieval date 6 January 2010.

Burridge, N. (2009) 'Britons face huge losses as holiday dreams turn sour', Press Association, 4 September.

Business and Finance (1998) 'Enterprise Ireland: a new state agency, which will incorporate the development, training and export activities of Forbairt, FAS, and the Irish Trade Board, will be in operation by July', 18 June.

Business Day (2006) 'Global operations in SA proliferate, but further expansion is Hamstrung by lack of state incentives that would attract major players', 3 November.

Business Line (2005) 'More TN Sops for ITES Sector', 9 September.

Cai, H. and D. Treisman (2006) 'Did government decentralization cause China's economic miracle?' *World Politics*, 58, 505–35.

Campos, M. (2009) 'The new state aid temporary framework', *Competition Policy Newsletter*, http://ec.europa.eu/competition/publications/cpn/2009_1_6.pdf, date accessed 24 February 2010.

Canadian Press (1996) 'New Brunswick Lures 62 T.O. Jobs', *Toronto Sun*, September 25, 69.

—— (2000) 'AM-Atlantic-today', February 7.

—— (2008) 'Impath networks to move head office to Halifax from Ottawa', May 27.

Carey, B. (2006) 'Not a good time for Dell', *The Sunday Times*, 17 September, Eire Business and Money, 16.

Carkovic, M. and R. Levine (2005) 'Does foreign direct investment accelerate economic growth?', in T. H. Moran, E. M. Graham, and M. Blomström, eds, *Does Foreign Direct Investment Promote Development?* (Washington: Institute for International Economics and Center for Global Development).

Cass, F. (2007) 'Attracting FDI to transition countries: the use of incentives and promotion agencies', *Transnational Corporations* 16, 2, 77–122.

Cavalcante, L. R. and S. Uderman (2004) 'The cost of structural change: a large automobile plant in a Brazilian less developed region', Regional Economics Applications Laboratory, Paper REAL 04-T-5.

Central Europe Energy Weekly (8 July 2006) 'Sweden's Sekab to launch Hungary's largest bio-ethanol project with EUR 343 mln investment'.

—— (18 August 2006) 'Czech firm PLP launches construction of CZK 1.26 bln plant for bioethanol and biomass production'.

Central Statistics Office Ireland (2000) *That was then, This is now: Change in Ireland 1949–1999*, http://www.cso.ie/releasespublications/documents/other_releases/thatwasthenthisisnow.pdf, date accessed 28 August 2009.

—— (2009a) 'Estimated population migration (thousand) by sex, year, country, and origin or destination', http://www.cso.ie/px/pxeirestat/Dialog/varval.asp?ma=PEA02&ti=Estimated+Population+Migration+(Thousand)+by+Sex,+Year,+Origin+or+Destination+and+Country&path=../Database/Eirestat/Population%20Estimates/&lang=1, date accessed 28 August 2009.

—— (2009b) 'Population 1901–2006', http://www.cso.ie/statistics/Population1901–2006.htm, date accessed 22 August 2009.

—— (2009c) 'Seasonally adjusted annual average standardised unemployment rates (SUR) (%) by Year', http://www.cso.ie/surveysandmethodologies/surveys_lab_force.htm, date accessed 31 August 2009.

—— (2009d) 'Seasonally adjusted annual average standardised unemployment rates (%) by Month', http://www.cso.ie/px/pxeirestat/database/eirestat/Live%20Register/Live%20Register.asp, date accessed 4 October 2009.

—— (2009e) 'Population and migration estimates, April 2009', 22 September, http://www.cso.ie/releasespublications/documents/population/current/popmig.pdf, date accessed 4 October 2009.

—— (2010) 'Seasonally adjusted standardised unemployment rates (SUR)', http://www.cso.ie/releasespublications/documents/labour_market/current/lreg.pdf, date accessed 7 June 2010.

Charlton, A. (2003) 'Incentive bidding for mobile investment: economic consequences and potential responses', OECD Development Centre Working Paper No. 203, January.

Chen, X. (2006) 'Regionalizing the global-local economic nexus: a tale of two regions in China', (Zurich: World Society Foundation Focus Series Papers), http://www.uic.edu/depts/soci/xmchen/WSF_Chen_5.pdf, date accessed 8 June 2009.

Cheshire, P. C. and I. R. Gordon (1998) 'Territorial competition: some lessons for policy', *The Annals of Regional Science*, 32, 321–46.

Chien, S.-S. and I. Gordon (2008) 'Territorial competition in China and the West', *Regional Studies*, 42, 31–49.

Chin, G. T. (2010) *China's Automotive Modernization: The Party-State and Multinational Corporations* (Basingstoke: Palgrave Macmillan).

Christiansen, H., C. Oman, and A. Charlton (2003) 'Incentives-based competition for foreign direct investment: the case of Brazil', OECD Directorate for

Financial, Fiscal, and Enterprise Affairs Working Papers on International Investment Number 2003/1, March.
CIA (2009) *The World Factbook*, https://www.cia.gov/library/publications/the-world-factbook/geos/vm.html, date accessed 10 August 2009.
Clark, D. (2007) 'Intel forges new strategy with Chinese fabrication plant; $2.5-billion project the result of lengthy planning, negotiations with state officials', *Globe and Mail*, 26 March, B6.
Coffin, B. (2008) 'Cheap cars, costly protests', *Risk Management*, December, 14.
Collins, J. (2008) 'Irish unit makes 10% of Microsoft's profits', *Irish Times*, 2 May, Finance p. 1.
—— (2009) 'Microsoft subsidiary has EUR 477m pretax profit', *Irish Times*, 29 April, Finance p. 21.
Commission of the European Communities (1972) *First Report on Competition Policy* (Luxembourg: Office for Official Publications of the European Communities).
—— (1990) *Industrial Policy in an Open and Competitive Environment: Guidelines for a Community Approach*, COM(90) 556 final, 16 November.
—— (1991) *The Regions in the 1990s – Fourth Periodic Report on the Social and Economic Situation and Development of the Regions of the Community*, COM(90) 609 final, 9 January.
Commission v. France (2006) Judgment of the Court in Case C-232/05, http://curia.europa.eu/jurisp/cgi-bin/form.pl?lang=en&jurcdj=jurcdj&numaff=&nomusuel=Commission%20v.%20France&ddatefs=01&mdatefs=10&ydatefs=2006&ddatefe=31&mdatefe=10&ydatefe=2006&docnodecision=docnodecision&allcommjo=allcommjo&affint=affint&affclose=affclose&alldocrec=alldocrec&docor=docor&docav=docav&docsom=docsom&docinf=docinf&alldocnorec=alldocnorec&docnoor=docnoor&radtypeord=on&newform=newform&docj=docj&docop=docop&docnoj=docnoj&typeord=ALL&domaine=&mots=&resmax=100&Submit=Rechercher, date accessed 30 January 2010.
Communist Party of India (Marxist) (2006) 'Note on special economic zones', press release, 19 October.
Cooper, R. N. (1972) 'Economic interdependence in the 1970s', *World Politics*, 24, 159–81.
Crafts, N. F. R. (1983) 'Gross national product in Europe 1870–1910; some new estimates', *Explorations in Economic History*, 20, 390.
Craver, R. (2005) 'N.C. learning how to deal: confidential documents show how state has played the incentives game to lure jobs, capital investment', *Winston-Salem Journal*, 14 August, 1.
Creaton, S. (1998) 'Business and finance: £ 1m fund targets US high-tech sector', *Irish Times*, 27 June.
Cullen, L. M. and Smout, T. C. (1977) 'Economic growth in Ireland and Scotland', in Cullen and Smout, eds, *Comparative Aspects of Scottish and Irish Economic and Social History, 1600–1900* (Edinburgh: John Donald).
Culliton, J. et al. (1992) *A Time for Change: Industrial Policy for the 1990s* (The Culliton Report) (Dublin: Stationery Office).
Czech News Agency (2005) 'Hankook to address other countries, Slovak exclusivity cancelled', 12 July.
—— (2006) 'Ministry says Hyundai confirmed Nosovice plant schedule', 16 May.
Daily Post (2010) 'Airbus fears over WTO rulings', 26 January, 22.

Damme, M. ed. (1997) *Perte Totale: La Fermeture de Renault-Vilvoorde* (Antwerp: Hadewijch).

David, P. A. (1984) 'High technology centers and the economics of locational tournaments', mimeo, Stanford University.

—— (1999) 'Comment on "The Role of Geography in Development," by Paul Krugman', in B. Pleskovic and J. E. Stiglitz, eds, *Annual World Bank Conference on Development Economics 1998* (Washington: World Bank).

Dembour, C. (2008) 'Competition for business location: a survey', *Journal of Industry, Competition, and Trade*, 8, 89–111.

DeMont, J. (1994) 'Fast Frank: how New Brunswick's premier turned his province into Canada's social laboratory', *Maclean's*, 11 April, 22–9.

de Mooij, R. A. and S. Ederveen (2005) 'Explaining the variation in empirical estimates of tax elasticities of foreign direct investment', Tinbergen Institute Discussion Paper TI 2005–108/3.

Denley, R. (2005) 'Let's not lose our heads over Dell: computer firm creates just 500 call centre jobs', *Ottawa Citizen*, 11 August, C1.

Department of Commerce (2007) Memorandum from Stephen J. Claeys to David M. Spooner, 30 January, 72 FR 5271, 5 February 2007, at ia.ita.doc.gov/frn/summary/italy/E7–1816–1.pdf, date accessed 19 June 2007.

Department of Foreign Affairs and Trade (2007) 'Australia-United States free trade agreement', www.dfat.gov.au/trade/negotiations/us_fta/final-text/chapter_11.htm, date accessed 20 October 2007.

Deslatte, M. (2007) 'Louisiana's final bid for steel plant didn't match German company request', Associated Press Worldstream, 3 April.

Devereux, M. P. and R. Griffith (2002) 'The impact of corporate taxation on the location of capital: a review', *Swedish Economic Policy Review*, 9, 79–102.

Devi, S. (2005) 'Intel to build dollars 3.5bn Israel plant', *Financial Times*, 2 December, 23.

Diamond, W. H. and D. B. Diamond, eds (2006) *Global Guide to Investment Incentives and Capital Formation* (The Hague: Kluwer Law International).

Dickie, M. (2007) 'Intel's China plant will test policy', *Financial Times*, 27 March, 27.

Dorgan, S. (2006) 'How Ireland became the Celtic Tiger', Heritage Foundation Backgrounder #1945, 23 June, http://www.heritage.org/research/worldwidefreedom/upload/bg_1945.pdf, date accessed 8 September 2009.

Dreyhaupt, S. J. (2006) *Locational Tournaments in the Context of the EU Competitive Environment* (Wiesbaden: Deutsche University Verlag).

Du, J., Y. Lu, and Z. Tao (2008) 'Economic institutions and FDI location choice: evidence from US multinationals in China', *Journal of Comparative Economics*, 36, 412–29.

East-West Gateway Council of Governments (2009) *An Assessment of the Effectiveness and Fiscal Impacts of the Use of Local Development Incentives in the St. Louis Region, Interim Report*, January.

Economist Intelligence Unit (2005) 'Slovakia industry: investment incentives sweeter than necessary?', EIU ViewsWire, 19 July.

—— (2008) 'Brazil: tax regulations', EIU ViewsWire, 23 September.

—— (2009a) 'Poland industry: Dell to relocate Europe production from Ireland to Lodz', EIU ViewsWire, 14 January.

—— (2009b) 'Ireland economy: fundamental change to tax system on the way', EIU ViewsWire, 9 September.

Economist Intelligence Unit (2009c) 'Brazil risk: tax policy risk', *Risk Briefing Select*, 21 October.
Elkins, Z., A. Guzman, and B. Simmons (2004) 'Competing for capital: the diffusion of bilateral investment treaties, 1960–2000', UC Berkeley Public Law Research Paper No. 578961, August.
Emirates News Agency (2008) 'Western region considers Ireland economic model', 2 March.
European Union (2001) 'Commission raises no objection to State aid in favour of Wacker Chemie GmbH', RAPID press release IP/01/657, 8 May.
—— (2002a) 'Commission opens enquiry into U.K. aid planned for Ford's Bridgend plant', RAPID press release, IP/02/239, 13 February, http://europa.eu/rapid/pressReleasesAction.do?reference=IP/02/239, date accessed 30 June 2007.
—— (2002b) 'State aid – United Kingdom', *Official Journal*, C324/11, 24 December.
—— (2004a) 'Commission approves aid in favour of AMD Fab 36 LLC & Co. KG in Saxony, Germany', RAPID press release, IP/04/147, 3 February.
—— (2004b) 'State aid for environmental protection', Europa Summaries of Legislation, updated 3 February 2004, date accessed 24 September 2007 at http://europa.eu/legislation_summaries/competition/state_aid/l26106_en.htm.
—— (2005a) 'State aid scoreboard. autumn 2005 update', date accessed 25 September 2007 at ec.europa.eu/comm/competition/state_aid/studies_reports/archive/2005_autumn_en.pdf.
—— (2005b) 'State aid action plan less and better targeted aid: a roadmap for state aid reform 2005–2009', ec.europa.eu/comm/competition/state_aid/reform/saap_en.pdf, date accessed 20 June 2007.
—— (2006a), 'State aid N 374/2006 – Ireland regional aid map 2007–2013', consulted online 6/30/07 at ec.europa.eu/comm/competition/state_aid/register/ii/doc/N-374-2006-WLWL-en-24.10.2006.pdf
—— (2006b) 'State aid scoreboard', statistical tables, 11 December 2006 update, ec.europa.eu/comm/competition/state_aid/studies_reports/stat_tables.html, date accessed 30 June 2007.
—— (2006c) 'State aid: commission endorses €53.5 million aid to GETRAG FORD for new transmission production plant in Slovakia', RAPID press release, IP/06/145, 9 February, http://europa.eu/rapid/pressReleasesAction.do?reference=IP/06/145, date accessed 30 June 2007.
—— (2006d) 'State aid N34/2006 – aid to Hankook – MSF 2002 Hungary', Commission document C(2006) 2328, 22 June, http://ec.europa.eu/competition/state_aid/register/ii/doc/N-34-2006-WLWL-en-22.06.2006.pdf, date accessed 30 June 2007.
—— (2006e) 'State aid N 158/2005 GETRAG FORD transmissions Slovakia (MSF 2002)', decisions letter, 8 February, http://ec.europa.eu/competition/state_aid/register/ii/doc/N-158-2005-WLWL-en-08.02.2006.pdf, date accessed 1 February 2010.
—— (2007a) 'State aid: commission endorses €111 million aid to Hyundai Motor Manufacturing Czech for a new car manufacturing plant in the Czech Republic', RAPID press release, IP/07/659, 7 May, http://europa.eu/rapid/pressReleasesAction.do?reference=IP/07/659, date accessed 30 June 2007.

European Union (2007b) 'State aid vademecum', ec.europa.eu/comm/competition/state_aid/studies_reports/vademecum_on_rules_2007_en.pdf, date accessed 30 June 2007.

—— (2007c) Decision letter on state aid case N 775/2006 – Germany, 13 June 2007, ec.europa.eu/comm/competition/state_aid/register/ii/doc/N%20775-2006-WLWL-EN-13.06.2007.pdf, date accessed 30 June 2007.

—— (2007d) 'State aid: commission endorses €262 million aid to AMD for large investment project in Dresden, Germany', RAPID press release, IP/07/1109, 18 July, http://europa.eu/rapid/pressReleasesAction.do?reference=IP/07/1109, date accessed 10 February 2010.

—— (2008a) 'State aid: commission closes inquiry into tax benefits for Hungarian steel producer Dunaferr', RAPID press release IP/08/1232, 1 August, http://europa.eu/rapid/pressReleasesAction.do?reference=IP/08/1232, date accessed 7 February 2010.

—— (2008b) 'Community guidelines on state aid for environmental protection', *Official Journal* C81/1, 1 April 2008, http://eur-lex.europa.eu/LexUriServ/LexUriServ.do?uri=OJ:C:2008:082:0001:0033:EN:PDF, date accessed 24 February 2010.

—— (2008c) 'Total state aid by Member State in million euro', Table ws2_1, downloaded from http://ec.europa.eu/competition/state_aid/studies_reports/expenditure.html, date accessed 4 April 2009.

—— (2009) DG-competition website, 'Regional Aid', http://ec.europa.eu/competition/state_aid/regional_aid/regional_aid.html, date accessed 10 August 2009.

—— (2009a) 'State aid by sector and objective, in million Euro (1992–2007)', http://ec.europa.eu/competition/state_aid/studies_reports/expenditure.html, date accessed 25 June 2009.

—— (2009b) 'State aid for horizontal objectives and sectoral aid as % of total aid (2007)', http://ec.europa.eu/competition/state_aid/studies_reports/expenditure.html, date accessed 19 July 2009.

—— (2009c) *VAT Rates Applied in the Member States of the European Community, Situation at 1 January 2009*, http://ec.europa.eu/taxation_customs/resources/documents/taxation/vat/how_vat_works/rates/vat_rates_en.pdf, date accessed 23 August 2009.

—— (2009d) 'Taxation trends in the European Union', press release STAT/09/92, 22 June, http://europa.eu/rapid/pressReleasesAction.do?reference=STAT/09/92&format=HTML&aged=0&language=en&guiLanguage=en, date accessed 23 August 2009.

—— (2009e) *Taxation Trends in the European Union – Main Results* (Luxembourg: Office for Official Publications of the European Communities).

—— (2009f) 'State aid: commission approves €54.5 million investment aid to Dell in Lodz, Poland', press release IP/09/1348, 23 September.

—— (2009g) 'Draft commission decision on the aid which Poland is planning to implement for Dell Products Sp. z.o.o., C46/2008 (ex N 775/2007)', n.d., http://ec.europa.eu/competition/state_aid/register/ii/doc/C-46-2008-WLWL-en-23.09.2009.pdf, date accessed 5 December 2009.

—— (2009h) 'State aid scoreboard, Autumn 2009 Update', 7 December, http://ec.europa.eu/competition/state_aid/studies_reports/2009_autumn_en.pdf, date accessed 31 January 2010.

European Union (2010a) 'Objective 2: revitalising areas facing structural difficulties', Regional Policy Inforegio, http://ec.europa.eu/regional_policy/objective2/index_en.htm, date accessed 27 January 2010.
—— (2010b) 'State aid for horizontal objectives and sectoral aid as % of total aid, 2008', http://ec.europa.eu/competition/state_aid/studies_reports/expenditure.html, Table ws3_1, date accessed 14 February 2010.
Eurostat (2002) *Eurostat Yearbook 2002* (Luxembourg: Office for Official Publications of the European Communities).
—— (2009) *Eurostat Regional Yearbook 2009* (Luxembourg: Office for Official Publications of the European Communities).
Evans, P. (1979) *Dependent Development: The Alliance of Multinational, State, and Local Capital in Brazil* (Princeton: Princeton University Press).
Farrell, D., J. K. Remes, and H. Schulz (2004) 'The truth about foreign direct investment in emerging markets', *The McKinsey Quarterly*, no. 1, www.mckinseyquarterly.com/article_page.aspx?ar=1386&l2=7&l3=10&srid=18&gp=1, date accessed 28 June 2007.
Fellman, M. W. (1999) 'Luck o' the Irish bestowed *on* U.S. call centers; U.K., Ireland, among booming markets', *Marketing News*, 7 June, p. 5.
Ferreira, S. G., R. Varsano, and J. R. Afonso (2005) 'Inter-jurisdictional fiscal competition: a review of the literature and policy recommendations', *Brazilian Journal of Political Economy*, 25, 295–313.
Field, N. (2001) 'Victoria trying to lure Castalloy', *The Australian Financial Review*, 21 August, 7.
Filho, W. G. and L. Silveira (2009) 'Estrela plans to build factory in Sergipe and reduce imports', *Gazeta Mercantil Online*, 6 February.
Financial Times (1996) 'Shaky truce on the social battlefield', 5 August, 13.
Finfacts (2006) 'Microsoft to hide Irish tax haven data of subsidiaries that have saved it billions of dollars in US taxes', 9 March, http://www.finfacts.com/irelandbusinessnews/publish/article_10005150.shtml, date accessed 18 July 2009.
Finlayson, D. (2004) 'Call centres employ over 7,000 in Edmonton', *Edmonton Journal*, 22 July, G1.
Fisher, P. (2002) 'Tax incentives and the disappearing state corporate income tax', *State Tax Notes*, 23, 767–74.
—— (2007) 'The fiscal consequences of competition for capital', in Ann Markusen, ed., *Reining in the Competition for Capital* (Kalamazoo: W.E. Upjohn Institute for Employment Research).
Fisher, P. S. and A. H. Peters (1998) *Industrial Incentives: Competition Among American States and Cities* (Kalamazoo: W.E. Upjohn Institute for Employment Research).
Fitzpatrick, M., B. Hill, and K. Seggewiss (2008) 'Dell closure may not signal death knell for call centres', Canwest News Service, 23 April.
Fleischer, J. (2007) 'Broader portfolios enhance your outsourcing options; Here are three key developments in call center outsourcing you should know about', *Call Center Magazine*, 1 May, 22.
Fletcher, K. (2002) 'Tax incentives in Cambodia, Lao PDR, and Vietnam', Paper prepared for the IMF Conference on Foreign Direct Investment, Hanoi, Vietnam (August).
Flynn, S. (1993a) 'Flynn enters fray over £8 bn', *Irish Times*, 29 June, p. 5.

Flynn, S. (1993b) 'Delors' guile and cunning come to the fore in EC funds deal; The dominant mood in the Irish camp after securing the Structural Funds agreement was of relief', *Irish Times*, 21 July, p. 10.

Flores, A. M. S. (2006) 'Dell to expand seat capacity', *Manila Standard*, 22 March.

Foreign Direct Investment (2009) 'Project profile – Dell looks east', 1 February.

Forfás (2009) *Forfás Annual Report 2008* (Dublin: Forfás).

Freeman, N. and C. Nestor (2004) 'Rethinking foreign investment in Vietnam: fuzzy figures and sentiment swings', in D. McCargo, ed., *Rethinking Vietnam* (London: RoutledgeCurzon).

Gabe, T. M. and D. S. Kraybill (2002) 'The effect of state economic development incentives on employment growth of establishments', *Journal of Regional Science*, 42, 703–30.

Gallagher, J. (2005) 'Tax breaks help firms expand in Detroit area', *Detroit Free Press*, 21 September.

Ganghof, S. and P. Genschel (2007) 'Taxation and democracy in the EU', Max Planck Institute Discussion Paper 07/02.

Global Subsidies Initiative (2010) Global subsidies research platform, 'Services', www.globalsubsidies.org/research-platform/rubrique.php3?id_rubrique=6, date accessed 2 February 2010.

Goff, K. (2005) 'Dell Inc. call center could bring 1,000 jobs: rumours fly that computer firm eyeing Kanata Research Park site', *Ottawa Citizen*, 14 July, D1.

Good, T. and J. McFarland (2004) 'Technology, gender and regulation: call centres in New Brunswick', in J. Stanford and L. F. Vosko, eds, *Challenging the Market: The Struggle to Regulate Work and Income* (Montreal & Kingston: McGill-Queen's University Press).

Good Jobs First (2007a) 'Wal-Mart continues to benefit from economic development subsidies; more than $200 Million Documented Over Last 3 Years', www.goodjobsfirst.org/news/article.cfm?id=142, date accessed 21 June 2007.

—— (2007b) 'Reform #1: require disclosure of subsidy spending and company compliance', www.goodjobsfirst.org/accountable_development/reform1.cfm, date accessed 5 July 2007.

—— (2007c) 'Reform #7: negotiate community benefits agreements with developers', www.goodjobsfirst.org/accountable_development/reform7.cfm, date accessed 5 July 2007.

—— (2009a) 'Case study of auto assembly plants', http://www.goodjobsfirst.org/corporate_subsidy/automobile_assembly_plants.cfm, date accessed 9 July 2009.

—— (2009b) 'Largest subsidy deals', http://www.goodjobsfirst.org/corporate_subsidy/reference_material.cfm, consulted 2 April 2009.

Good Jobs New York (2010) 'New York City's biggest retention deals sorted by size', http://www.goodjobsny.org/deals_size.htm, date accessed 1 April 2010.

Görg, H. and E. Strobl (2001) 'Multinational companies and productivity spillovers: a meta-analysis', *The Economic Journal*, 111, F723-F739.

Government Accountability Office (2005) *Government Performance and Accountability: Tax Expenditures Represent a Substantial Federal Commitment and Need to Be Reexamined* (Washington: GAO). www.gao.gov/new.items/d05690.pdf. date accessed 4 June 2007.

Government Accountability Office (2008) *International Taxation: Large U.S. Corporations and Federal Contractors with Subsidiaries in Jurisdiction Listed as Tax Havens or Financial Privacy Jurisdictions* (Washington: GAO). http://www.gao.gov/new.items/d09157.pdf. date accessed 18 July 2009.

Grayeff, Y. (2005) 'Finance committee approves $ 525m. grant for new Intel plant', *Jerusalem Post*, 29 November, 17.

Greenbaum, R. T. and D. Bondonio (2004) 'Losing focus? A comparative evaluation of spatially targeted revitalization programs in the US and the EU', *Regional Studies*, 38, 319–34.

Greenhouse, L. (2005) 'Justices uphold taking property for development', *New York Times*, 25 June, p. A1.

Green Scissors (2003) 'Issues overview', http://www.greenscissors.com/issues/overview.htm, date accessed 4 February 2010.

Groppe, M. (2006) 'State biodiesel plant will be world's largest', Knight-Ridder Tribune Business News, 9 March.

Guardian (2005) 'Two companies locating to P.E.I. will bring 65 new jobs: Currie', April 28, A3.

Guisinger, S. E. and Associates (1985) *Investment Incentives and Performance Requirements* (New York: Praeger).

Guisinger, S. E. (1985) 'A comparative study of country policies', in S. E. Guisinger and Associates, *Investment Incentives and Performance Requirements* (New York: Praeger).

Hájek, P. (2007) 'Keeping ahead in the auto sector', *Czech Business Weekly*, 19 March, www.pwc.com/cz/eng/ins-sol/issues/2007/KeepingAhead_PH.html, date accessed 28 June 2007.

Hall, P. A. and D. Soskice, eds (2001) *Varieties of Capitalism: The Institutional Foundations of Comparative Advantage* (Oxford: Oxford University Press).

Hall, P. A. and D. Soskice (2001) 'An introduction to varieties of capitalism', in P. A. Hall and D. Soskice, eds, *Varieties of Capitalism: The Institutional Foundations of Comparative Advantage* (Oxford: Oxford University Press).

Hallward-Driemeier, M. (2003) 'Do bilateral investment treaties attract FDI? Only a bit…and they could bite', World Bank.

Hardin, R. (1982) *Collective Action* (Baltimore: Johns Hopkins University Press for Resources for the Future).

Harding, A. (2010) 'Ameristeel comes with hands out', *Florida Times-Union*, 10 January, D-1.

Harding, T. and B. S. Javorcik (2007) 'Developing economies and international investors: do investment promotion agencies bring them together?' Unpublished paper, World Bank, 25 July.

Hartley, R. (2008) 'EU launches investigation into Dunaferr aid package', Metal Bulletin Daily Alerts, 21 April.

Haufler, A. and F. Mittermaier (2008) 'Unionisation triggers tax incentives to attract foreign direct investment', CESIFO Working Paper #2312, May.

Haufler, A. and I. Wooton (2006) 'The effects of regional tax and subsidy competition on foreign direct investment', *European Economic Review*, 50, 285–305.

—— (2008a) 'Competition for firms in an oligopolistic industry: do firms or countries have to pay?' Conference on Spatial Economics and Trade, University of Strathclyde, 26–7 June.

Haufler, A. and I. Wooton (2008b) 'Competition for firms in an oligopolistic industry: the impact of economic integration', Unpublished paper, October, available at www.cbs.dk, date accessed 26 January 2010.

Havránek, T. (2009) 'The supply of foreign direct investment incentives: subsidy competition in an oligopolistic framework', *Prague Economic Papers* 2, 131–55.

Head, C. K., J. C. Ries, and D. L. Swenson (1999) 'Attracting foreign manufacturing: investment promotion and agglomeration', *Regional Science and Urban Economics*, 29, 197–218.

Hemlock, D. (2005) 'Caribbean call centers booming', *Sun-Sentinel*, 6 March, 1E.

Hollingshead, N. (2009) 'Sand springs steel mill shutting down, for now', *Tulsa World*, 17 October, E6.

Hong, V. X. N., N. M. Tuan, and H. C. Hoa (2009) 'Sustainable development impacts of investment incentives: a case study of the mining industry in Vietnam' (Winnipeg: International Institute for Sustainable Development).

Houde, M.-F. and K. Yannaca-Small (2004) 'Relationships between international investment agreements', OECD Working Papers on International Investment 2004/1 (Paris: OECD).

Hymer, S. H. (1960) *The International Operations of National Firms, A Study of Foreign Direct Investment*, Ph.D. dissertation, Massachusetts Institute of Technology.

IBGE (Instituto Brasileiro de Geografia e Estatística) (2010), 'IBGE Releases Regional Accounts 2007', date accessed 6 January 2010.

IDA Ireland (2009) *Annual Report 2008* (Dublin: IDA Ireland).

India Business Insight (2004) 'Pharma firms ditch Gujarat over tax sops', 29 June.

Indian Embassy (1997) 'India and US sign investment incentive agreement', press release, 19 November, www.indianembassy.org/indusrel/iia111997.htm, date accessed 7 July 2007.

Indo-Asian News Service (2006) 'US businessmen keen to invest in Bihar: officials', 8 June.

Insight Economics (2006) *Inward Investment Attraction: Objectives and Best Practice Strategies*, report prepared for the National Manufacturing Forum, August (Melbourne and Perth: Insight Economics Pty Ltd), www.nationalmanufacturing.org/downloads/Strategic-actions-to-boost-Australian-Manufacturing.pdf, date accessed 19 September 2007.

Inter Press Service (2009) 'India: cheapest car rides on govt subsidies', 26 June, http://mwglobal.org/app_letters/?m=200906, date accessed 15 November 2009.

Internal Trade Secretariat (1994) *Agreement on Internal Trade: A Guide* (Ottawa: Internal Trade Secretariat).

Invest in Estonia (2009), 'Low cost of doing business', http://www.investinestonia.com/index.php/why-estonia?start=4, date accessed 4 July 2009.

Irish Examiner (2008) 'Battle of Limerick was lost to Poland last summer', 23 December.

—— (2009a) 'Revealed: Dell closure will lead to 9,500 job losses', 24 March.

—— (2009b) 'Dell workers to get 9k grants for training', 27 October.

Irish Independent (2009a) 'Intel R&D expansion to create 130 jobs for region', 28 February.

Irish Independent (2009b) 'Corporation tax rates drop as countries bid for foreign businesses', 7 August.

Irish Times (2005) 'Era of large scale State aid is nearing an end', 3 March, 18.

Jacobsen, J. K. (1994) *Chasing Progress in the Irish Republic: Ideology, Democracy and Dependent Development* (Cambridge: Cambridge University Press).

Jamaica Trade and Invest (2010) 'Background presentation on BPO/Call Centre', http://www.jamaicatradeandinvest.org/images/web/File/CCBPOINJAMAICA08.pdf?phpMyAdmin=b4964562dbfe5c2b0b0c09eb3eaed177, date accessed 10 February 2010.

Jauch, H. (2002) 'Export processing zones and the quest for sustainable development: a Southern African perspective', *Environment and Urbanization*, 14, 101–13.

Joint Committee on Taxation (2008) *Estimates of Federal Tax Expenditures for Fiscal Years 2008–2012* (Washington: U.S. Government Printing Office).

Jones, B. D. and L. W. Bachelor (1993) *The Sustaining Hand: Community Leadership and Corporate Power*, 2nd edition (Lawrence: University Press of Kansas).

Kansas City Business Journal (2006) 'Ethanex forms alliance with German governments', 20 September.

Kayne, J. and M. Shonka (1994) *Rethinking State Development Policies and Programs* (Washington: National Governors' Association).

Keenan, G. (2003) 'Ontario liberals urged to give Ford aid', *Globe and Mail*, 8 October, B1.

Kelly, D. (1991) 'Regina group grabs a chunk of Crown Life', *The Financial Post*, 10 September, 44.

Kennedy, K. A., T. Giblin, and D. McHugh (1988) *The Economic Development of Ireland in the Twentieth Century* (London: Routledge).

Kennedy, K. A. (2001) 'Reflections on the process of Irish economic growth', *Journal of the Statistical and Social Inquiry Society of Ireland*, XXX, 123–57.

Kerr, J. (2008) 'Brazilian government submits new tax reform proposal to Congress', *Global Insight*, 28 February.

Khanna, V. (2006) 'The Philippines; turning the corner', *The Business Times Singapore*, 10 November.

Kinetz, E. (2008) 'Tata Motors stops work indefinitely at Nano Plant', Associated Press Financial Wire, 3 September.

Kirby, P. (2002) *The Celtic Tiger in Distress: Growth with Inequality in Ireland* (Basingstoke, Palgrave).

—— (2007) 'Latin America's "new left" looks to Irish model', *Irish Times*, 29 December, p. 17.

—— (2010) *Celtic Tiger in Collapse: Explaining the Weaknesses of the Irish Model*, 2nd edition (Basingstoke: Palgrave).

Klein, G. (2006) 'Sod turned for civic election', *The Star-Phoenix* (Saskatoon), 15 March, A2.

Klemm, A. (2009) 'Causes, benefits, and risks of business tax incentives', IMF Working Paper WP/09/21.

Klemm, A. and S. Van Parys (2009) 'Empirical evidence on the effects of tax incentives', IMF Working Paper WP/09/136.

Koff, S. (2006) 'Court sides with Ohio on tax breaks; taxpayers lack standing to sue state, justices say', *Cleveland Plain Dealer*, 6 May, C1.

Koplow, D. (2006) *Biofuels – At What Cost? Government support for ethanol and biodiesel in the United States* (Geneva: Global Subsidies Initiative).

Krieger, M. (2007) 'Brosh and Eini look to bring out the luck of the Irish', *Jerusalem Post*, 24 October, p. 17.

Krishna, V. (2007) 'India beckons with tax breaks, other incentives: Canadian firms need to review the world map', *National Post*, 17 January, FP17.

Krugman, P. (1994) 'Introduction', in P. Krugman and A. Smith, eds, *Empirical Studies of Strategic Trade Policy* (Chicago: University of Chicago Press).

—— (1996) *Pop Internationalism* (Cambridge: MIT Press).

—— (2005) 'Toyota, moving northward', *New York Times*, 25 July.

Kutas, G., C. Lindberg, and R. Steenblik (2007) *Biofuels – At What Cost? Government Support for Ethanol and Biodiesel in the European Union* (Geneva: Global Subsidies Initiative).

Lam Toi Consulting (2009) Special search conducted for the author, August (Hanoi, Vietnam).

Landler, M. (2003) 'Eastern Germany is able to prevent industrial flight to third world', *New York Times*, 21 November, C1.

Larson, J. (2006) 'Software maker grows to Canada; Chandler Firm to perform R&D in Montreal', *The Arizona Republic*, 5 February, 5D.

Latin America News Digest (2009) 'Brazil biodiesel, ethanol news review (April 6–10, '09)', 14 April.

Lee, J. J. (1989) *Ireland 1912–1985: Politics and Society* (Cambridge: Cambridge University Press).

Leishemba, R. (2008) 'West Bengal's loss, Gujarat's gain: Tata to drive Nano from Sanand', Press Trust of India, 16 October.

Leonnig, C. D. (2009) 'Bailed-out firms have tax havens, GAO Finds', *Washington Post*, 17 January, p. D01.

LeRoy, G. (1994) *No More Candy Store* (Washington: Federation for Industrial Retention and Renewal and Grassroots Policy Project).

—— (1999) Personal communication with author, 10 May.

—— (2005) *The Great American Jobs Scam: Corporate Tax Dodging and the Myth of Job Creation* (San Francisco: Berrett-Koehler).

—— (2008) 'Foreign auto plants have received $3.6 billion in subsidies, mostly from Southern States', 'Clawback' blog, 15 December, http://clawback.org/2008/12/15/foreign-auto-plants-have-received-36-billion/, date accessed 1 April 2, 2010.

LeRoy, G. and T. Slocum (1999) *Economic Development in Minnesota: High Subsidies, Low Wages, Absent Standards* (Washington: Good Jobs First).

Leslie, K. (2007) 'Liberals job strategy created three jobs to replace each one lost: McGuinty', Canadian Press, 13 September.

Li, Q. (2006) 'Democracy, autocracy, and tax incentives to foreign direct investors: a cross-national analysis', *Journal of Politics*, 68, 62–74.

Lillie, N. (1999) 'Transnational labor mobilization in Europe: the case of Renault-Vilvoorde', Paper presented at the European Communities Studies Association meeting, Pittsburgh, 2 June.

Limerick Leader (2009) 'O'Donnell calls for more investment in Limerick', 25 September.

Lipson, C. (1984) 'Economic cooperation in economic and security affairs', *World Politics*, 37, 1–23.

Loewendahl, H. (2009) 'Foreign direct investment and incentives: the role of incentives in investment promotion', Workshop presentation, World Association of Investment Promotion Agencies, Ljubljana, Slovenia, November.

Lucey, C. (2009) 'EMU to blame for current economic woes', *Sunday Business Post*, 29 March.

Luger, M. I. and S. Bae (2005) 'The effectiveness of State business tax programs: the case of North Carolina', *Economic Development Quarterly*, 29, 327–45.

Lyman, B. (2007) 'Alabama power, AEA aid campaign', *Mobile Register*, 7 June, B01.

Lynch, R. G. (2004) *Rethinking Growth Strategies: How State and Local Taxes and Services Affect Economic Development* (Washington: Economic Policy Institute).

Lyons, M. (2000) 'Leixlip plant in running for major Intel investment', *Irish Times*, 3 May, 16.

—— (2006) 'Yorkton possible plant site: Regina other contender in Sask. for proposed canola crushing facility', *The Star Phoenix*, 15 August, C5.

Lyons, T. (2009) 'Intel mulls €1 bn plan for Kildare; massive boost for technology and construction jobs as chips giant eyes investment', *Sunday Times*, 8 March, Business p. 1.

M2 EquityBites (2009) 'Dell agrees sale of Polish manufacturing operations', 3 December.

Macdonald, I. (2009) 'First sod turned on $ 25 million pilot training academy at Wagga', ENP Newswire, 15 July.

Mackintosh, J. (2004) 'Car industry takes fast route to the east', *Financial Times*, 27 April, FT Report 4.

Maffini, G. and A. Marenzi (2007) 'Corporate tax systems and policies for attracting FDI in Latin America', Paper presented at the 19th conference of the Italian Society for Public Economics, 13–14 September.

Malesky, E. (2004) 'Leveled mountains and broken fences: measuring and analysing De Facto decentralisation in Vietnam', *European Journal of East Asian Studies*, 3, 307–36.

Malesky, E. J. (2008) 'Straight ahead on Red: how foreign direct investment empowers subnational leaders', *The Journal of Politics*, 70, 97–119.

Markusen, A. and K. Nesse (2007) 'Institutional and political determinants of incentive competition', in A. Markusen, ed., *Reining in the Competition for Capital* (Kalamazoo: W.E. Upjohn Institute for Employment Research).

Marsh, P. (2007) 'Hunt for ideal site leads from Cambridge to Dresden', *Financial Times*, 3 January, 3.

Martin, I. (2001) 'Dawn of the living wage: the diffusion of a redistributive municipal policy', *Urban Affairs Review*, 36, 470–96.

Mason, M. (2006) 'Intel to invest $1 billion in Vietnam as country strives to raise high-tech profile', Associated Press, 18 November.

Mason, S. and K. P. Thomas (2010) 'Tax increment financing in Missouri: an analysis of determinants, competitive dynamics, equity, and best practices', *Economic Development Quarterly*, 24, 169–79.

Mathew, V. (2004) 'Himachal woos pharma majors with tax sops', *Business Line*, 18 March.

Mattera, P. and A. Purinton (2004) *Shopping for Subsidies: How Wal-Mart Uses Taxpayer Money to Finance its Never-Ending Growth* (Washington: Good Jobs First).

Mattera, P., K. Walter, J. F. Blain, and M. Lee (2007) *The State of State Disclosure: An Evaluation of Online Public Information About Economic Development*

Subsidies, Procurement Contracts, and Lobbying Activities (Washington: Good Jobs First).
Mattera, P. (2009) *High Road or Low Road? Job Quality in the New Green Economy* (Washington: Good Jobs First).
Mayeda, A. (2005) 'Ottawa tech center's good news day: Dell to confirm 500 jobs for west-end call centre', *Ottawa Citizen*, 9 August, F1.
Mazerov, M. (2005) *The "Single Sales Factor" Formula for State Corporate Taxes: A Boon to Economic Development or a Costly Giveaway?* (Washington: Center on Budget and Policy Priorities).
Mazurek, J. (2002) 'How fabulous fablessness? Environmental challenges of economic restructuring in the semiconductor industry', in J. Park and N. Roome, eds, *The Ecology of the New Economy* (Sheffield: Greenleaf Publishing Ltd.).
Meade, G. (2009) 'MEPs demand answers over Dell move', Press Association, 25 November.
Mecoy, D. (2004) 'Dell chooses Oklahoma City', *The Oklahoman*, 29 October, A1.
Mejia, E., K. Nordstrom, and W. Schweke (2007) *Getting Our Money's Worth? An Evaluation of the Economic Model Used for Awarding State Business Subsidies* (Durham and Raleigh, North Carolina: Corporation for Enterprise Development and North Carolina Justice Center).
Microsoft Corporation (2007) *Annual Report* (Seattle: Microsoft).
The Middle East (2006) 'Business gives Sokhna the thumbs-up; Egyptian port', 1 October.
Milward, H. B. and H. H. Newman (1990) 'State incentive packages and the industrial location decision', in E. J. Yanarella and W. C. Green, eds, *The Politics of Industrial Recruitment* (Westport, Connecticut: Greenwood Press).
Millard, R. (2009) 'Relieved EU leaders to press last treaty holdouts', Agence France Presse, 4 October 2009.
Millett, M. (1996) 'Union cautions warring States', *Sydney Morning Herald*, 6 April, 7.
Mitra, K. (2008) 'Tata's options', *Business Today*, 19 October.
Mondaq Business Briefing (2004) 'Outsourcing in the Philippines', 17 May.
Mora, M. and R. Varsano (2001) 'Fiscal decentralization and subnational fiscal autonomy in Brazil: some facts of the nineties', IPEA Discussion Paper No. 854, December.
Moran, T. H. (1999) *Foreign Direct Investment and Development* (Washington: Institute for International Economics).
—— (2005) 'How does FDI affect host country development? Using industry case studies to make reliable generalizations', in T. H. Moran, E. M. Graham, and M. Blomström, eds, *Does Foreign Direct Investment Promote Development?* (Washington: Institute for International Economics and Center for Global Development).
Moran, T. H., E. M. Graham, and M. Blomström (2005) 'Conclusions and implications for FDI policy in developing countries, new methods of research, and a future research agenda', in T. H. Moran, E. M. Graham, and M. Blomström, eds, *Does Foreign Direct Investment Promote Development?* (Washington: Institute for International Economics and Center for Global Development).
Moreira, P. (2005) 'Halifax scores RIM technical support unit', *Globe and Mail*, 26 November, B6.
Morici, P. (1996) 'Resolving the North American subsidies war', *Canadian-American Journal of Public Policy*, 27, 1–34.

Muoi, N. P. (2006) 'Vietnam approves $605US million investment license for Intel to build microchip factory', Associated Press, 23 February.

Mutti, J. H. (2003) *Foreign Direct Investment and Tax Competition* (Washington: Institute for International Economics).

Mytelka, L. (1999) 'Locational tournaments for FDI: inward investments into Europe in a global world', in N. Hood and S. Young, eds, *The Globalization of Multinational Enterprise and Economic Development* (Basingstoke and New York: Palgrave Macmillan).

National Archives of Ireland (2009) 'History of Irish census records', http://www.census.nationalarchives.ie/help/history.html, date accessed 28 August 2009.

Neal, S. (1985) 'Thompson, other governors try TV in Saturn sweepstakes', *Chicago Tribune*, 27 February, Business p. 6.

Newton, P. (2007) 'Hyundai assembly Plant opens in Brazil', Global Insight, 23 April.

—— (2008) 'Toyota targeting Brazilian mass market with new plant plans', Global Insight, 18 August.

Ng, G. (2006a) 'Micron starts Nand flash memory production here; move by US giant raises hopes S'pore will be able to woo more big guns', *The Straits Times*, 14 June.

—— (2006b) 'Cutting-edge chips to be made in new $4.7b plant; Intel-Micron venture to produce wafers for advanced chips used in consumer gadgets', *The Straits Times*, 8 November.

Nguoi Lao Dong (20 July 2009) 'Long An: various faults in planning and land use' (in Vietnamese).

Nova Scotia Business, Inc. (2007) 'Case studies: Clarke Inc.', www.novascotiabusiness.com/en/home/casestudies/clarkeinc.aspx, date accessed 21 June 2007.

Nuckols, B. and M. Waggoner (2009) 'States give Hollywood a fortune in tax breaks', Associated Press State and Local Wire, 3 June.

Oanda.com (2009) 'FX History' lookup, http://www.oanda.com/convert/fxhistory, date accessed 26 July 2009.

Oates, W. A. (1972) *Fiscal Federalism* (New York: Harcourt Jovanovich).

O'Brien, C. (2008) 'Country following flawed economic model, says Cori', *Irish Times*, 19 June, p. 3.

O'Brien, K. J. (2006) 'Chip producer to expand Dresden Plant', *New York Times*, 30 May, C3.

O'Connor, O. (2000) 'Let's ensure Intel's faith in Irish economy is well founded; News of more jobs was especially welcome when we have been put on alert for the big bang', *Irish Times*, 23 June, 55.

O'Donnell, R. (2000) 'Europe: The Irish experience' (Dublin: National Economic and Social Council).

Ó Gráda, C. and K. O'Rourke (1996) 'Irish economic growth, 1945–88', in N. F. R. Crafts and G. Toniolo, eds, *Economic Growth in Europe since 1945* (Cambridge: Cambridge University Press).

O'Hearn, D. (1995) 'Global restructuring and the Irish political economy', in P. Clancy, S. Drudy, K. Lynch, and L. O'Dowd, eds, *Irish Society: Sociological Perspectives* (Dublin: Institute of Public Administration).

—— (2001) *The Atlantic Economy: Britain, the US and Ireland* (Manchester: Manchester University Press).

Olson, M. (1965) *The Logic of Collective Action* (Cambridge: Harvard University Press).

Oman, C. P. (2000) *Policy Competition for Foreign Direct Investment: A Study of Competition Among Governments to Attract FDI* (Paris: OECD).

Organization for Economic Cooperation and Development (1995) *Industrial Subsidies: A Reporting Manual* (Paris: OECD).

—— (1998) *Harmful Tax Competition: An Emerging Global Issue* (Paris: OECD).

—— (2000) *Tax Burdens: Alternative Measures* (Paris: OECD).

—— (2007) 'Taxation, 2004', *OECD in Figures 2007*, http://masetto.sourceoecd.org/vl=7592811/cl=12/nw=1/rpsv/figures_2007/en/c009/page27.htm, date accessed 9 July 2009.

Ó Riain, S. (2004) *The Politics of High-Tech Growth: Developmental Network States in the Global Economy* (Cambridge: Cambridge University Press)

—— (2008) 'Addicted to growth', Unpublished paper, November.

O'Sullivan, F. (2007) 'Economic policy harms exporters', *New Zealand Herald*, 28 April.

Othman, A. (2006) 'Brunei new investment deal', *Borneo Bulletin*, 10 February.

O'Toole, F. (2009) 'We ignored warnings about lax regulation', *Irish Times*, 17 February, p. 12.

Oxelheim, L. and P. Ghauri (2008) 'EU-China and the non-transparent race for FDI', *Journal of Asian Economics*, 19, 358–70.

Pearce, D. (2002) 'Environmentally harmful subsidies: barriers to sustainable development', keynote address in Section 1.1 at the OECD Workshop on Environmentally Harmful Subsidies, Paris, 7–8 November, http://www.oecd.org/dataoecd/42/24/35215571.pdf, date accessed 1 July 2009.

Perry, S. (1996) 'EU court rejects UK work-hours challenge', Reuters World Service, 12 November.

Peters, A. and P. Fisher (2004) 'The failures of economic development incentives', *Journal of the American Planning Association*, 70, 27–37.

Petry, C. (2008) 'The tougher the times, the sweeter the deal for employers', *American Metal Monthly*, 1 December.

Piscitello, L. and L. Rabbioso (2005) 'The impact of FDI on local companies' labour productivity: evidence from the Italian case', *International Journal of the Economics of Business*, 12, 35–51.

Pogatchnik, S. (2009) 'Irish unemployment hits 14-year high of 12.4 pct', Associated Press, 2 September.

Press Trust of India (2006) 'Finmin's concerns on revenue loss from SEZs still valid: FM', 20 September.

—— (2008) 'Chinese official offers sops to attract investments in Wuxi', 14 February.

—— (2009) 'DLF allowed to withdraws 4 SEZs, asked to refund tax sops', 2 June.

Productivity Commission (2004) *Annual Report 2002–03* (Canberra: Productivity Commission), http://www.pc.gov.au/__data/assets/pdf_file/0006/8835/annualreport0203.pdf, date accessed 21 September 2007.

Przeworski, A. and M. Wallerstein (1988) 'Structural dependence of the State on capital', *American Political Science Review*, 82, 11–29.

Qian, Y. and B. Weingast (1996) 'China's transition to markets: market-preserving federalism, Chinese Style', *Journal of Policy Reform* 1.

Quinn, J. (2009) 'Dell quits Ireland over staff costs', *The Daily Telegraph*, 9 January, p. 2.
Rawls, P. (2007a) 'Alabama begins special session to lure German steel mill for 2700 new jobs', Associated Press Financial Wire, 27 February.
—— (2007b) 'Competing with Louisiana, Alabama offers incentives to lure German steel', Associated Press Financial Wire, 2 March.
Reed, J. (2002) 'Poland in slow lane as Czechs win car plant: Toyota chose to invest in the Czech Republic rather than a slowing economy that bars the way of foreign business', *Financial Times*, 26 February, 13.
Reese, L. (1993) 'Local economic development practices across the northern border', *Urban Affairs Quarterly*, 28, 571–92.
Reuters (2009) 'Ford to invest $2.3 billion to boost output in Brazil', 20 November.
Richards, D., C. Harvie, H. Nguyen, and N. V. Lan (2002) 'The limping tiger: problems in transition for small and medium sized enterprises in Vietnam', in C. Harvie and B. C. Lee, eds, *The Role of SMEs in National Economies in East Asia* (Cheltenham: Edward Elgar).
Richer, S. (2005) 'N.S. incentive has Clarke East Coast Bound: wage rebates, promise of lower costs lure Ontario freight firm to Bluenose province', *Globe and Mail*, 1 April, B8.
Rives, K. (2005) 'Call center decides against outsourcing to India', *News and Observer*, 1 December.
Rodríguez-Pose, A. and G. Arbix (2001) 'Strategies of waste: bidding wars in the Brazilian automotive Sector', *International Journal of Urban and Regional Research*, 25, 134–54.
Rodríguez-Pose, A. and U. Fratesi (2002) 'Unbalanced development strategies and the lack of regional convergence in the EU', Unpublished paper, London School of Economics.
—— (2004) 'Between development and social policies: the impact of European Structural Funds in Objective 1 Regions', *Regional Studies* 38, 97–113.
Rogoway, M. (2006) 'Cutting-edge chips to be made in new $4.7b plant; Intel-Micron venture to produce wafers for advanced chips used in consumer gadgets', *The Oregonian*, 15 July, C01.
Rogowski, R. (2000) 'Globalization and governance: implications of Tiebout models for a world of mobile factors', Paper presented at the American Political Science Association, www.wcfia.harvard.edu/seminars/pegroup/rogowski.pdf, date accessed 8 July 2007.
Rolnick, A. J. and M. L. Burstein (1994), 'Congress should end the economic war among the states', Federal Reserve Bank of Minneapolis Annual Report, http://www.minneapolisfed.org/publications_papers/pub_display.cfm?id=672, date accessed 1 July 2009.
Rubenstein, J. M. (1992) *The Changing U.S. Automobile Industry: A Geographical Analysis* (London: Routledge).
Sarin, J. (2008) 'Late-starter Punjab now wants to ride IT bandwagon', Indo-Asian News Service, 13 November.
Sbragia, A. M. (1996) *Debt Wish* (Pittsburgh: University of Pittsburgh Press).
Schweke, W., C. Rist, and B. Dabson (1994) *Bidding for Business: Are Cities and States Selling Themselves Short?* (Washington: Corporation for Enterprise Development).

Science Foundation Ireland (2009) 'Introduction to SFI', http://www.sfi.ie/content/content.asp?section_id=207&language_id=1, date accessed 19 July 2009.

Seabra, M. (2008) 'Agreement coincides with tax reform in Brazil', *Gazeta Mercantil*, 24 November.

SeeNews (2009) 'Troubled Bulgarian Steel Mill Kremikovtzi's restructuring fails – European Commission', 16 December.

Seveanu, L. S. (2008) 'Nokia opens factory in Romania after employees in Germany express anger', *Associated Press Financial Wire*, 11 February.

Sheppard, B. H., Jr., E. V. Torrey, R. O'Sullivan, M. A. Garfinkel, G. Anderson, G. Fischer, G. H. Sampliner, and R. Teitelbaum (2005) 'International commercial dispute resolution', *The International Lawyer*, 39 Int'l Law. 235.

Sher, H. (1999) 'The 600 million question', *The Jerusalem Report*, 2 August, 40.

Shoesmith, C. (2006) 'Intel opens EUR 1.6 bn extension to Leixlip plant', *Irish Times*, 23 June, 1.

Sibley, L. (2008) 'California life science backers laud extension of tax deduction', *East Bay Business Times*, 23 September.

Sinclair, T. J. (1994) 'Passing judgment: credit rating processes as regulatory mechanisms of governance in the emerging world order', *Review of International Political Economy*, 1, 133–59.

—— (2005) *The New Masters of Capital: American Bond Rating Agencies and the Politics of Creditworthiness* (Ithaca: Cornell University Press).

Singh, H. (2009) 'Govt to chip in with India Microprocessor', *The Economic Times* (India), 14 July.

Sinnaeve, A. (2007) 'How the EU manages subsidy competition', in Ann Markusen, ed., *Reining in the Competition for Capital* (Kalamazoo: W.E. Upjohn Institute for Employment Research).

Site Selection online (2000) 'IBM's Cutting-Edge $2.5 Billion Fab Reaps $500 Million in NY Incentives', Site Selection Online Insider, November, www.siteselection.com/ssinsider/incentive/ti0011.htm, date accessed 20 July 2007.

—— (2004) 'Will China's domestic chip-making subsidies spark semiconductor downturn?', Site Selection Online Insider, December, www.siteselection.com/ssinsider/incentive/ti0412.htm, date accessed 20 July 2007.

—— (4 May 2006) 'Texas-size stakes: Austin lands Samsung's $4-billion Fab; Capital City finally rakes in Korean Giant's coveted chips', Site Selection Online Insider, www.siteselection.com/ssinsider/bbdeal/bd060504.htm, date accessed 20 July 2007.

—— (12 June 2006) 'Canadian Bakin': Linamar's 3,000-job expansion continues Ontario auto-sector sizzle', www.siteselection.com/ssinsider/bbdeal/bd060615.htm, date accessed 1 August 2007.

—— (10 July 2006) 'New York's big subsidies bolster upstate's winning bid for AMD's $3.2 Billion 30MM. Fab', Site Selection Online Insider, www.siteselection.com/ssinsider/bbdeal/bd060710.htm, date accessed 20 July 2007.

—— (2007) 'Compass points to magnetic south', July, http://www.siteselection.com/portal/, date accessed 7 February 2010.

SKRIN Market & Corporate News (2008) 'Tax break for OMK-Steel', 30 September.

Smith, N. J.-A. (2005) *Showcasing Globalisation? The Political Economy of the Irish Republic* (Manchester: Manchester University Press).

Smith, R. (2006) 'Bangor biodiesel plant could open by summer', *Kalamazoo Gazette*, 17 January, B2.

Smith, S. A. and J. Glenn (2006) 'Region lures biodiesel plant; world's largest facility to create 85 Kosciusko jobs', *Fort Wayne Journal-Gazette*, 9 March, B7.

Smyth, J. (2004) 'E1.6 billion investment by Intel will create 400 jobs; World's biggest semiconductor firm to build new factory at Leixlip site', *Irish Times*, 20 May, 1.

—— (2005a) 'Intel warns it will have to "reassess" future Irish investment', *Irish Times*, 3 March, 1.

—— (2005b) 'Intel plans two new chip plants at Leixlip site', *Irish Times*, 4 March, Finance 1.

SouthWest Organizing Project (1995) *Intel Inside New Mexico*, revised edition (Albuquerque: SouthWest Organizing Project).

State of Victoria (2003) 'States agree to end investment bidding wars', press release, Office of the Treasurer, 5 September, www.dpc.vic.gov.au/domino/Web_Notes/newmedia.nsf/b0222c68d27626e2ca256c8c001a3d2d/fb21eee7f27c4044ca256d9a0080fb0b!OpenDocument, date accessed 2 July 2007.

—— (2006) 'Historic anti-bidding war agreement renewed', press release, Office of the Treasurer, 30 March, www.dpc.vic.gov.au/domino/Web_Notes/newmedia.nsf/798c8b072d117a01ca256c8c0019bb01/5214506f6c9c5543ca257141007fee72!OpenDocument, date accessed 2 July 2007.

—— (2007) 'Investment agreement in the national interest', press release, Office of the Treasurer, 30 March, www.legislation.vic.gov.au/domino/Web_Notes/newmedia.nsf/798c8b072d117a01ca256c8c0019bb01/489d9d56455a3f37ca2572b10002a334!OpenDocument, date accessed 21 September 2007.

States News Service (2009) 'MEPs approve 14.8 million in aid to Ireland after Relocation of Dell Factory', 23 November.

Staunton, D. (2005) 'MEP accuses State of discarding Intel aid unnecessarily', *Irish Times*, 14 April, 18.

—— (2006) 'Ireland's competitive edge at risk, says Intel chairman', *Irish Times*, 27 January, 4.

Stewart, K. G. and M. C. Webb (2006) 'International competition in corporate taxation: evidence from the OECD Time Series', *Economic Policy* 21, 153–201.

Stiglitz, J. E. (2002) 'Employment, social justice, and societal well-being', *International Labour Review*, 141, 9–29.

Streuli, T. (2004) 'Dell chooses Okla. City for its new call center because of quality of workers', *The Journal Record*, 1 November.

Sutherland, P. (2008) 'So, how did we get here?', *Irish Times*, 11 February, Innovation section, p. 16.

Swank, D. and S. Steinmo (2002) 'The new political economy of taxation in advanced capitalist democracies', *American Journal of Political Science*, 46, 642–55.

Sweeney, P. (2004) 'Tax cuts did not create the Celtic Tiger' (Irish Congress of Trade Unions), Autumn, http://www.ictu.ie/download/pdf/tax_cuts_did_not_create_celtic_tiger.pdf, date accessed 29 July 2009.

Szladek, B. (2008) 'EU launches in-depth investigation into Hungarian state aid for steelworks Dunaferr', Hungary Business Newswire, 17 April.

Telesis Consulting Group (1982) *A Review of Industrial Policy* (Dublin: National Economic and Social Council).

Thai Press Reports (2008) 'Thailand Sahaviriya Iron and Steel may locate Iron Smelting Plant overseas', 13 November.

—— (2010) 'Thailand Sahaviriya Steel Industries Plc looks to acquire shares of Smelter in a neighbouring country', 9 February.

The Economist (2006) 'Cash cow; India's special economic zones', 12 October.

This Day (2009) 'Looking to Ireland as a model for development' 20 April.

Thomas, K. P. (1992) 'Capital beyond borders: how capital mobility affects bargaining between firms and states', Ph.D. dissertation, University of Chicago.

—— (1997) *Capital Beyond Borders: States and Firms in the Auto Industry, 1960–94* (Basingstoke: Macmillan).

—— (2000) *Competing for Capital: Europe and North America in a Global Era* (Washington: Georgetown University Press).

—— (2003) 'Geographic scales and the competition for economic growth: state, subnational governments, and cities', *American Behavioral Scientist*, 46, 987–1001.

—— (2007a) 'The sources and processes of tax and subsidy competition', in Ann Markusen, ed., *Reining in the Competition for Capital* (Kalamazoo: W.E. Upjohn Institute for Employment Research).

—— (2007b) 'Canada as exemplar: the code of conduct on incentives', Paper presented to the 19th Biennial Conference of the Association of Canadian Studies in the United States, Toronto, Ontario, 14–18 November.

—— (2007c) *Investment Incentives: Growing Use, Uncertain Benefits, Uneven Controls* (Geneva: Global Subsidies Initiative).

—— (2009) *Assessing Sustainable Development Impacts of Investment Incentives: A Checklist*, International Institute for Sustainable Development, available at http://www.tradeknowledgenetwork.net/research/pub.aspx?id=1069.

Thomson, A. (2008) 'Jamaica's E-services leads Caribbean's outsourcing challenge', *The Miami Herald*, 28 August.

Thornton, P. (2006) 'South African break convinces budget to expand call centres', *The Independent*, 3 November, 46.

Tiebout, C. M. (1956) 'A pure theory of local expenditures', *Journal of Political Economy*, 64, 416–24.

Toronto Star (2000) 'Intel gives Israel ultimatum', 5 September.

Tuck, S. (1999) 'Quebec Lobs Salvo in high-tech tax war; rich subsidies entice technology firms, as other provinces roll out their own artillery in the "new battleground"', *Globe and Mail*, 7 January, C1.

Tucker, E. (1998) 'Boost for Brussels over illegal state aid', *Financial Times*, 16 November, 4.

Tully, K. (1997) 'Smooth operators', *Corporate Location*, November/December, pp. 37–8.

Tutton, M. (2005) 'RIM picks Halifax for tech-support centre', *Ottawa Citizen*, 26 November, D1.

UNCTAD (2003) *World Investment Report 2003: FDI Policies for Development: National and International Perspectives* (Geneva: United Nations Conference on Trade and Development).

—— (2008a), FDI-Stat Interactive Database, http://stats.unctad.org/fdi/ReportFolders/reportFolders.aspx?sCS_referer=&sCS_ChosenLang=en (based on WIR 2008 data).

UNCTAD (2008b) *Investment Policy Review: Vietnam* (New York and Geneva: United Nations).

UNDP (1998) *Human Development Report 1998* (Oxford: Oxford University Press).

UNDP (2007) *Human Development Report 2007/2008* (Basingstoke: Palgrave Macmillan).

United News of India (2007) 'Nandigram "disturbances" not to impact investments to WB: Minister', 28 November.

US Census Bureau (2009) 'Alabama quick facts from the U.S. Census Bureau', http://quickfacts.census.gov/qfd/states/01000.html, date accessed 20 June 2009.

US Fed News (2008) 'Rep. Boucher to host former Irish Prime Minister for Ninth District Conference', 21 August.

US Department of State (2009) 'Background note: Vietnam', http://www.state.gov/r/pa/ei/bgn/4130.htm, date accessed 12 February 2010.

van den Berghe, D. (2001) 'The geography of international strategy: a multi-level framework', Erasmus Rotterdam Institute of Management paper ERS-2001–51-ORG, September.

van der Horst, A. (2007) 'Is EU coordination needed for corporate taxation?', in T. Callan (ed.), *Budget Perspectives 2008* (Dublin: Economic and Social Research Institute), pp. 47–70.

Velloor, R. (2007) 'India going all out to woo wafer fab plants', *The Straits Times*, 26 February.

Venkatesan, R. and S. Varma (1998) *Policy Competition Among States in India for Attracting Foreign Direct Investment* (New Delhi: National Council of Applied Economic Research).

Vernon, R. (1971) *Sovereignty at Bay* (New York: Basic Books).

VietNamNet (6 November 2004) 'Fiscal incentives can't foster investment: experts', http://english.vietnamnet.vn/news/2004/11/343390/, date accessed 12 August 2009.

—— (4 January 2006) 'Government moves on illegal incentives', http://english.vietnamnet.vn/biz/2006/01/529126/, date accessed 11 August 2009.

—— (10 January 2006) 'Govt goes after rogue officials in investment', http://english.vietnamnet.vn/biz/2006/01/531059/, date accessed 12 August 2009.

—— (12 July 2006) 'Da Nang scraps unlawful investment incentives', http://english.vietnamnet.vn/biz/2006/07/590397/, date accessed 9 August 2009.

—— (5 October 2006) 'Gia Lai offering incentives for investment', http://english.vietnamnet.vn/biz/2006/10/619148/, date accessed 9 August 2009.

—— (21 November 2006) 'News highlights November 21', http://english.vietnamnet.vn/reports/2006/11/636089/, date accessed 9 August 2009.

—— (3 April 2007) 'Decentralisation raises worries about breaking investment master plan', http://english.vietnamnet.vn/biz/2007/04/680594/, date accessed 9 August 2009.

—— (13 October 2008) 'Vietnam will filter FDI: MPI', http://english.vietnamnet.vn/biz/2008/10/808262/, date accessed 9 August 2009.

—— (14 October 2008) 'Investment promotion activities in chaos', http://english.vietnamnet.vn/biz/2008/10/808443/, date accessed 9 August 2009.

Vietnam News Briefs (25 August 2008) 'Foreign investment: Canon opens largest laser printer factory in northern Vietnam'.

—— (23 December 2008) 'Foreign investment: Canon starts work on 4th factory in Vietnam'.

Vietnam News Briefs (24 December 2008) 'Trade: Vietnam gives preferential tax to $7.9 bln steel-seaport project'.

—— (13 February 2009) 'Thousands of farmers file complaints against Vedan'.

—— (19 March 2009) 'Foreign investment: MPI to keep close watch on FDI projects'.

—— (29 January 2010). 'Business: Intel partners with Viettel to produce 3G Computers'.

Villadiego, R. (2006) 'American outsourcing firms bullish about the Philippines', *The Filipino Express*, Magazine, 9–15 October, 15.

Vitug, M. (2006) 'Lost in translation; poor english skills threaten the Philippines' dreams of becoming a new call center magnet in Asia', *Newsweek International*, 29 May.

Vnexpress.net (22 June 2005) 'Considering investment incentives "fence-breaking"' (in Vietnamese).

Vu, T. T. A., V. T. Le, and T. T. Vo (2007) 'Provincial extralegal investment incentives in the context of decentralisation in Vietnam: mutually beneficial or race to the bottom?' UNDP Policy Dialogue Paper, November.

Wallace, R. and S. O'Brien (2000) 'Car job bounty used as lure to firms in Victoria', *The Advertiser*, 23 June, 5.

Wallerstein, M. and A. Przeworski (1995) 'Capital taxation with open borders', *Review of International Political Economy*, 2, 425–45.

Ward, A. (2004) 'Slovakia to win Hyundai plant', *Financial Times*, 1 March, 15.

Weber, R. and D. Santacroce (2007) *The Ideal Deal: How Local Governments Can Get More for Their Economic Development Dollar* (Washington and Chicago: Good Jobs First/University of Illinois at Chicago Center for Urban Economic Development).

Werneck, R. L. F. (2006) 'An evaluation of the 2003 tax reform effort in Brazil', *Brazilian Journal of Political Economy*, 26, 75–94.

Willemot, B. and A. Fort (2007) 'ECJ Judgment of 5 October 2006 Commission v. France: a major step forward for the recovery policy', *Competition Policy Newsletter*, Spring, pp. 101–03, ec.europa.eu/comm/competition/publications/cpn/cpn2007_1.pdf, date accessed 20 June 2007.

Williams, C. (2009) 'Columbus secures 872 NCR jobs', *Columbus Ledger-Enquirer*, 3 June.

Wishlade, F. (1997) 'EC competition policy and regional aid: an agenda for the year 2000?', European Policies Research Centre, Regional and Industrial Research Paper Series Number 25, December.

—— (2008a) 'All's well that ends well? Recent developments in EU competition policy and regional aid control', European Policy Research Papers, European Policies Research Centre, University of Strathclyde, Glasgow.

—— (2008b) 'The control of regional aid to large investment projects: workable compromise or arbitrary restraint', *European State Aid Law Quarterly*, 3, 495–506.

—— (2009) 'Measure for measure: recent developments in EU competition policy and regional aid control', European Policies Research Centre, University of Strathclyde, Glasgow.

Woodcock, G. (2006) 'Engine plant headed our way', *Toronto Sun*, 20 May, D3.

World Bank (2002) *World Development Report 2002: Building Institutions for Markets* (Oxford: Oxford University Press).
—— (2007) *World Development Report 2008: Agriculture for Development* (Washington: The World Bank).
World Trade Organization (1994) *Agreement on Subsidies and Countervailing Measures*, www.wto.org/english/res_e/booksp_e/analytic_index_e/subsidies_02_e.htm#article6B1, date accessed 20 June 2007.
—— (2009a) 'United States – measures affecting trade in large civil aircraft', www.wto.org/english/tratop_e/dispu_e/cases_e/ds317_e.htm, summary as of 21 January 2009, date accessed 2 February 2010.
—— (2009b) 'Report (2009) of the committee on subsidies and countervailing measures', document G/L/906, 26 October, docsonline.wto.org, date accessed 2 February 2010.
—— (2009c) 'New and full notification pursuant to Article XVI:1 of the
GATT 1994 and Article 25 of the agreement on subsidies and countervailing measures: United States', document G/SCM/N/155/USA, 20 May, docsonline.wto.org, date accessed 2 February 2010.
Wrynn, J. (1998) 'Embracing EU social market could make us look less hypocritical when seeking funds', *Irish Times*, 24 November, 16.
Yuill, D., K. Allen, J. Bachtler, K. Clement, and F. Wishlade (1994) *European Regional Incentives 1994–95* (London: Bowker-Saur).
Zahariadis, N. (2008) *State Subsidies in the Global Economy* (Basingstoke and New York: Palgrave Macmillan).
Zhou, C., A. Delios, and J. Y. Yang (2002) 'Locational determinants of Japanese foreign direct investment in China', *Asia Pacific Journal of Management*, 19, 63–86.

Interviews

Dublin interview #1, March 2009.
Dublin interview #2, March 2009.
Dublin interview #3, March 2009.
Dublin interview #4, March 2009.
Dublin interview #5, March 2009.
Dublin interview #6, March 2009.
Dublin interview #7, March 2009.
OECD official, Paris, 1998.
Chinese academic, Beijing, June 2009.
State government officials, Rio de Janeiro, 23 July 2009.
Tax specialist #1, São Paulo, 28 July 2009.
Tax specialist #2, São Paulo, 29 July 2009.
Liam MacGabhann, Irish Permanent Representation to the EU, Brussels, 24 July 2000.
Official at the French Permanent Representation to the EU, Brussels, July 2000.
Gaston Reinesch, Director-General, Luxembourg Ministry of Finance, Brussels, 25 July 2000.

Provincial internal trade and investment officials of all 10 Canadian provinces, March–May, 2007 (in-person interviews in Victoria, Vancouver, Edmonton, Regina, Winnipeg, Toronto, Ottawa, Montréal, Québec City, Fredericton and Halifax, telephone interviews for Prince Edward Island and Newfoundland and Labrador).
State of Victoria Treasury official, telephone interview, November 2009.
Polish investment official, Ljubljana, Slovenia, November 2009.

Index